THE OFFICIAL
TT REVIEW 2007
ISLE OF MAN

HONDA
The Power of Dreams

A Vintage TT year

ISLE OF MAN 1907-2007

Honda machines and riders have totally dominated the Centenary TT races.

On the most demanding road circuit in the world, Honda's CBR1000RR Fireblade and CBR600RR once again proved to be the ultimate machines, with cutting-edge technology, supreme quality and ultimate reliability.

Bennetts Superbike race
First six bikes home - CBR1000RR

PokerStars Supersport race
First three bikes home - CBR600RR

PokerStars Senior race
First four bikes home - CBR1000RR

Manufacturers Award
Honda wins Manufacturers Award in all solo classes

John McGuinness
Has now won 13 TTs and is the fastest man round the circuit - 130.354 mph average lap speed

Ian Hutchinson
Wins first TT - Supersport race

Dave Molyneux
Wins both Baveria Beer sidecar races bringing total race wins to 13

Most successful manufacturer
Honda is the most successful manufacturer in the TT's 100-year history with 135 victories

www.honda.co.uk

THE OFFICIAL

REVIEW 2007

TT

ISLE OF MAN

Published in August 2007

A catalogue record for this book is available from the British Library

ISBN 978 1 84425 466 8

Library of Congress catalog card no. 2007927394

Haynes Publishing, Sparkford,
Yeovil, Somerset BA22 7JJ, UK
Tel: +44 (0) 1963 442030
Fax: +44 (0) 1963 440001
E-mail: sales@haynes.co.uk
Website: www.haynes.co.uk

Haynes North America, Inc.,
861 Lawrence Drive, Newbury Park,
California 91320, USA

Printed and bound by J.H.Haynes & Co Ltd,
Sparkford, Yeovil, Somerset BA22 7JJ, UK

This product is officially licensed by the
Department of Tourism and Leisure
(a Department of the Isle of Man Government)

Editor Gary Pinchin
Designer Lee Parsons
Design Assistant Carole Bohanan
Editorial Director Mark Hughes

Contributing writers Gary Pinchin, Dave Fern, Mac McDiarmid, Steve Burns, John Watterson

Contributing photographers Double Red, Stephen Davison, Mac McDiarmid, Jon Stroud, Dave Purves, John Watterson, Ian Allen

Special Sales & Advertising Manager
David Dew (david@motocom.co.uk)

CONTENTS

PREFACE   6
BY ADRIAN EARNSHAW MHK, MINISTER OF
TOURISM AND LEISURE, ISLE OF MAN

FOREWORD   8
JOHN McGUINNESS REVEALS WHY
THE TT MEANS SO MUCH TO HIM

INTRODUCTION   10
MAC McDIARMID PUTS 100 YEARS OF
GLORIOUS TT HISTORY INTO PERSPECTIVE

THE 130MPH LAP   12
McGUINNESS REVEALS WHAT IT REALLY TAKES
FOR A FAST LAP AROUND THE MOUNTAIN COURSE

TOP 10 RIDERS   24
THE UPS AND DOWNS OF TEN STANDOUT RIDERS
FROM THIS YEAR'S TT – PLUS FOUR OF THE TOP ROOKIES

Bennetts
PRACTICE WEEK   34
SO MANY RIDERS, SO MANY LAPS, SO MANY TALES.
THE TOP STORIES FROM A WEEK OF PRACTICE

Bennetts
SUPERBIKE TT   **70**
McGUINNESS KICKS OFF RACE WEEK WITH A
STUNNING VICTORY ON HIS HM PLANT HONDA

PokerStars
SUPERSTOCK TT   **92**
BRUCE ANSTEY IS RELENTLESS IN PURSUIT OF
ANOTHER RACE WIN IN THE BIG PRODUCTION BIKE RACE

PokerStars
SUPERSPORT TT   **108**
IAN HUTCHINSON WINS HIS FIRST TT BUT
ANSTEY SETS THE EARLY PACE UNTIL AN ILL-FATED PITSTOP

Bavaria Beer
SIDECAR TT   **126**
DOUBLE-TOPS FOR DAVE MOLYNEUX AFTER
NICK CROWE HITS PROBLEMS IN BOTH RACES

PokerStars
SENIOR TT   **142**
A RACE OF RECORDS FROM KING OF THE
MOUNTAIN JOHN McGUINNESS

1907 TT RE-ENACTMENT   **162**
100 YEARS ON, REM FOWLER'S NORTON STILL
HAS THE ADVANTAGE ON THE ORIGINAL ST JOHN'S COURSE

Dunlop
LAP OF HONOUR   **170**
THE LAP OF HONOUR WAS FIRST RUN IN 1979
BUT THIS YEAR WAS THE BIGGEST AND BEST EVER

MCN
PARADE OF CHAMPIONS   **180**
NEVER BEFORE HAS THERE BEEN SUCH A
GLITTERING GATHERING OF TT LEGENDS AND THEIR BIKES

PRE-TT CLASSIC, BILLOWN   **194**
NOT CONTENT WITH MODERN RACING, GUY
MARTIN STARS IN THE CLASSIC RACES ON A '70S TRIUMPH

POST-TT RACES, BILLOWN   **198**
MANX HERO CONOR CUMMINS WRAPS UP HIS
TT IN STYLE ON THE ROADS NEAR CASTLETOWN

GALLERY   **200**
THE TT IS ALL RACING AND IT'S THE ULTIMATE
BIKING HOLIDAY, HERE'S THE SNAPS TO PROVE IT

Minister of Tourism and Leisure
PREFACE

© Stephen Davison

A s a dyed-in-the-wool TT fan, it gives me sincere pleasure to provide the preface for this official review of the 2007 centenary races.

In the history of motorcycle sport, no event has played a greater role than the TT. Quite simply, it is unique and unparalleled, and this year it was as thrilling as ever.

Good weather underpinned a week of brilliant racing, particularly the 600cc Supersport class, the race of the meeting. Added to this, the record-breaking form, which continued throughout, was capped in fine style by the undoubted present-day TT champion, John McGuinness, topping 130mph in Friday's Senior.

Without doubt John is a very fine rider, as is our sidecar champion Dave Molyneux, winner of the two sidecar events. Both know, however, that waiting in the wings are younger men eager to wear the laurels.

In the sidecars, Manxman Nicky Crowe, although denied his chance of victory by mechanical problems, emerged as the new lap record holder. Similarly, in the solos, Ian Hutchinson, team-mate of John, chalked up his first of what I am sure will be many wins on the HM Plant 600cc CBR Honda, again at record speed.

This review will be a real treasure for race fans to read and have on their book-shelf – a true reminder of this year's special TT and its rich and wonderful past which has provided so many magical memories for us.

To have endured in the way it has is a remarkable achievement and, looking ahead, the TT is in good shape and in good hands. Long live the TT!

Adrian Earnshaw MHK
Minister of Tourism and Leisure
Isle of Man

© Stephen Davison

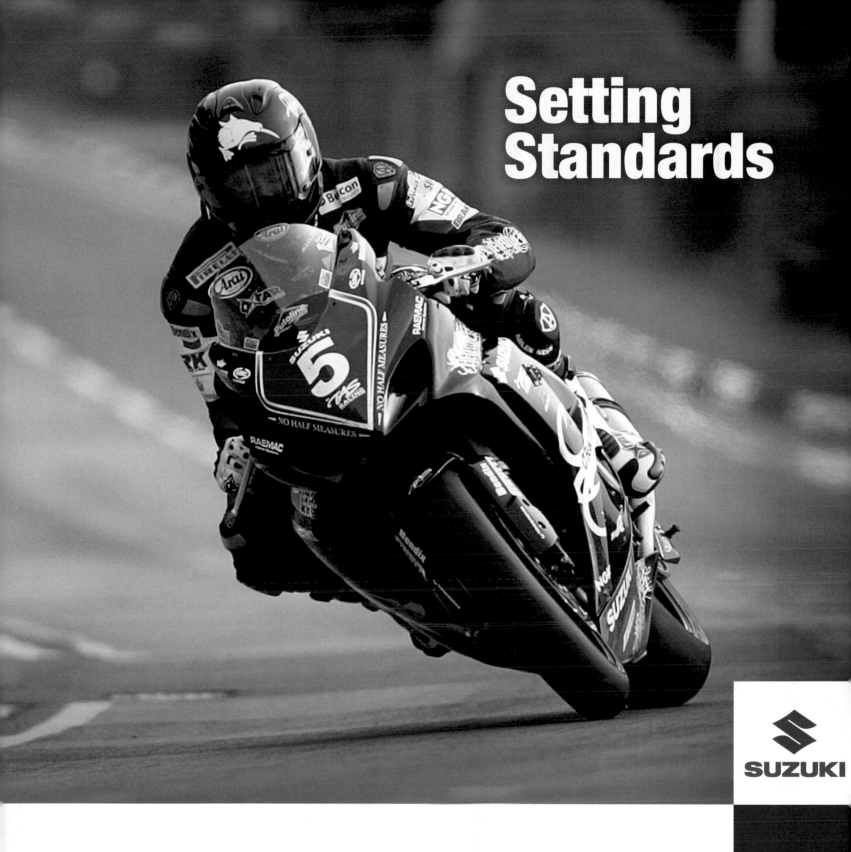

Setting Standards

Racing around 37.73 miles of the Isle of Man TT course requires total commitment and unwavering focus. Relentless, you might say.

Bruce Anstey and the Relentless Suzuki by TAS Racing squad have those qualities in spades - just what was needed to win the 2007 Superstock TT during June's Centenary TT Festival. Luckily, they also had a near-standard Suzuki GSX-R1000K7.

The machine that sets such unbelievably high standards on the roads is, of course, available in your local Suzuki dealer showroom now.

For more information on the GSX-R1000, visit www.suzuki.co.uk or call 0845 850 8800

$\color{gray}\text{S}$ **SUZUKI**

Way of Life!

John McGuinness
FOREWORD

The centenary TT was a fantastic occasion. We had lap records and 60,000 people. It was unbelievable.

And, of course, I had an incredible TT, with my wins in the Superbike and the Senior, as well as second places in the Superstock and Supersport.

There were so many people that I felt like a proper rock star. It was massively overwhelming. From early in the morning there were people waiting outside the motorhome door for an autograph. I couldn't believe the attention.

I'm just a brickie from Morecambe and first came here in 1982 when I was 10. My dad took part in the races at Jurby Roads and while we were over we caught a couple of days of TT practice. I remember sitting at the bottom of Bray Hill with my parents and being frightened to death. I also remember crying on the ferry going home because we couldn't stay to watch the races.

I went to the TT every year after that, first with my parents, then on my own – and that time I missed a chemistry exam. We lived in Heysham, not far from the ferry terminal, so I rode my BMX bike there and sneaked on, riding up the blind side of the ferry staff when the trucks were going on.

That shows you how long I've had the TT in my blood and what it means to me. The TT has been so memorable for me. Since I first raced here in 1996 I've had some fantastic bikes and ridden for some great teams, and of course I've achieved more than I could ever have imagined as a kid.

I love racing – but especially I love the TT. Not just the racing, but the massive sense of history as well – the tales, the exploits. After winning the Senior this year, I received a fantastic text from a mate, referring to Bob McIntyre, and it said, 'Bob Mac 1957, John Mac 2007'. How cool is that?

I'm delighted to have been asked to write the foreword for this superb publication, the official book of record of the 2007 Isle of Man TT sponsored by Bennetts, and I hope you will enjoy reliving all the centenary events through its pages.

John McGuinness
June 2007

DUNLOP
DOMINATION

» Three victories and eight other podium places at the Centenary Isle of Man TT

» Record-breaking race times and blistering average lap speeds

» Introducing the NEW Triple Tread Compound for ultimate performance

» Race-bred technology now available for the street

» True technology transfer

"DUNLOP'S TRIPLE TREAD COMPOUND TECHNOLOGY JUST KEEPS GETTING BETTER.
THE MANUFACTURER'S RUBBER HELPED ME TO WIN THE 2007 SUPERBIKE AND SENIOR
TT RACES AND SET A NEW LAP RECORD AT 130.354MPH" John McGuinness

THE SPORTMAX FAMILY

» GP Racer Slick » GP Racer » Qualifier RR » Qualifier D209 » **www.dunloptyres.co.uk**

INTRODUCTION

THE CENTENARY TT. SO MANY MEMORIES. SO MUCH TO CELEBRATE.

By Mac McDiarmid

They came to celebrate. Sixty-odd thousand eager souls arrived to mark the centenary of the TT races, this year sponsored by Bennetts. They came for the greatest road races in the world, for the Party on the Prom, for parades of past champions, for Ramsey – or was that Yamsey? – Sprint, Honda Day in Peel, stunt shows, trials, classic races, the TT Re-enactment, to meet their mates at Glen Maye and Port Erin and a hundred other places...and 60,000 other mates they never knew they had. And a quick lap at dawn and big-name bands and wet T-shirt competitions. And beach racing and good Manx beer and kippers and blow me if that isn't the tastiest special I've ever seen. They came in their thousands to enjoy Bikers' Island. They came to be there for the Big One.

And big, it was, in every sense. Big events, big names, big atmosphere. And big in the global sense, too, for 2007 didn't simply mark a century of motorcycle TT racing. It marked, to most intents and purposes, the entire history of motorcycle sport. For this is where bikes evolved from primitive boneshakers. This is the place, more than any other, where for decades every manufacturer aspired to prove his products. This is the focus of two-and three-wheeled ambitions and dreams beyond number, where the brothers Collier plotted to win in a

Plumstead shed, where Mr Honda himself vowed to hit the big time. If anywhere encapsulates that vibrant century, it's the Isle of Man. If bike racing has a home, this is it.

It's the home, too, of simpler racing pleasures, as Manx as the TT itself. Cakes and tea at Braddan church, a tempting whiff of bacon butties in the air. The wooden stands across the road rich with the smell of wild garlic crushed underfoot under the dappled shade of trees that were already old when it all began.

It used to be the whiff of Castrol 'R', left in a heady aromatic wake by the passing machines. Now it's the wail of fours, their brutal power threatening to tear the tarmac off the Island, punctuated here and there by a thundering Aprilia or Ducati twin. Or by the calm, clear tones of Charlie Lambert commentating from the grandstand and quick words grabbed from nervy riders by Chris Kinsey's roving microphone. This year Radio TT alone was celebrating its 42nd birthday, as old as Honda's immortal 250cc six.

"Roads close in 15 minutes."

"No flash photography, please."

"And away goes Michael Rutter, making a welcome return..."

"And now to Maurice Mawdsley at Glen Helen...."

If Charlie sets the racing scene, Maurice Mawdsley's Manx brogue it is which begins to unfold the day's action. For his commentary position is the first with race positions as the leading riders tip their bikes around the stone wall at Glen Helen and fire them up the hill to Sarah's Cottage. That hill

© Jon Stroud

alone is paved with history, for it's the same one on which Agostini and Hailwood both came to grief in a soaking Senior precisely 42 years before, Mike the Bike picking up his battered MV to take the win.

And 58 years before that, in 1907, Charlie Collier peddling furiously to urge his Norton-Peugeot up that same hill, then just a ribbon of rutted gravel. And Jack Marshall exchanging pleasantries with a helper, jogging alongside his Triumph.

These days, they're doing over 100mph before nailing the front wheel to the tarmac to slow for Sarah's right-hander. In 1907 they didn't even have front brakes. Geoff Duke, Stanley Woods, Joey Dunlop, Steve Hislop – they've all stamped their mark on this same ground, made records and reputations, fired the imaginations of fans and riders to come.

And Charlie Lambert's most esteemed predecessor, of course – Peter Kneale, the voice of the TT. We remembered him with fondness, too, along with others who couldn't make the trip.

And over most of it smiled Mannanan, who's ruled the weather hereabouts since before anyone so much as thought of motorcycles, let alone hurling them down Bray Hill. As complexions turned ever pinker under the Manx sun, the riders also turned up the heat, blistering to new lap records.

First John McGuinness, modestly, in the opening Bennetts Superbike race. Then Bruce Anstey, remarkably, taking a near-stock Suzuki around at 128.4mph – faster than the absolute lap record set a mere two years before. And Nick Crowe, emerging from Dave Molyneux's shadow with a scintillating 116.667mph, only for luck to twice abandon him, allowing 'Moly' a double sidecar win.

The most memorable solo race for many a year saw young Ian Hutchinson take a hard-fought maiden TT win in the Junior, as behind him fellow tyro Guy Martin set the fastest of a succession of new lap records, a staggering 125.161mph.

Then the big one, the Senior, and the answer to the question posed all week: would anyone lap at 130mph? The answer, of course, was a resounding 'yes', but first McGuinness tantalised us all with an opening lap at 129.883mph, less than one second short of 130mph. Second time around there was no mistake: 130.354mph.

It was a year...no, a century...to remember.

John McGuinness
130MPH LAP

John McGuinness confirmed his place as the fastest rider in TT history with a lap at 130.354mph during the Senior TT sponsored by PokerStars

By Mac McDiarmid

© Stephen Davison

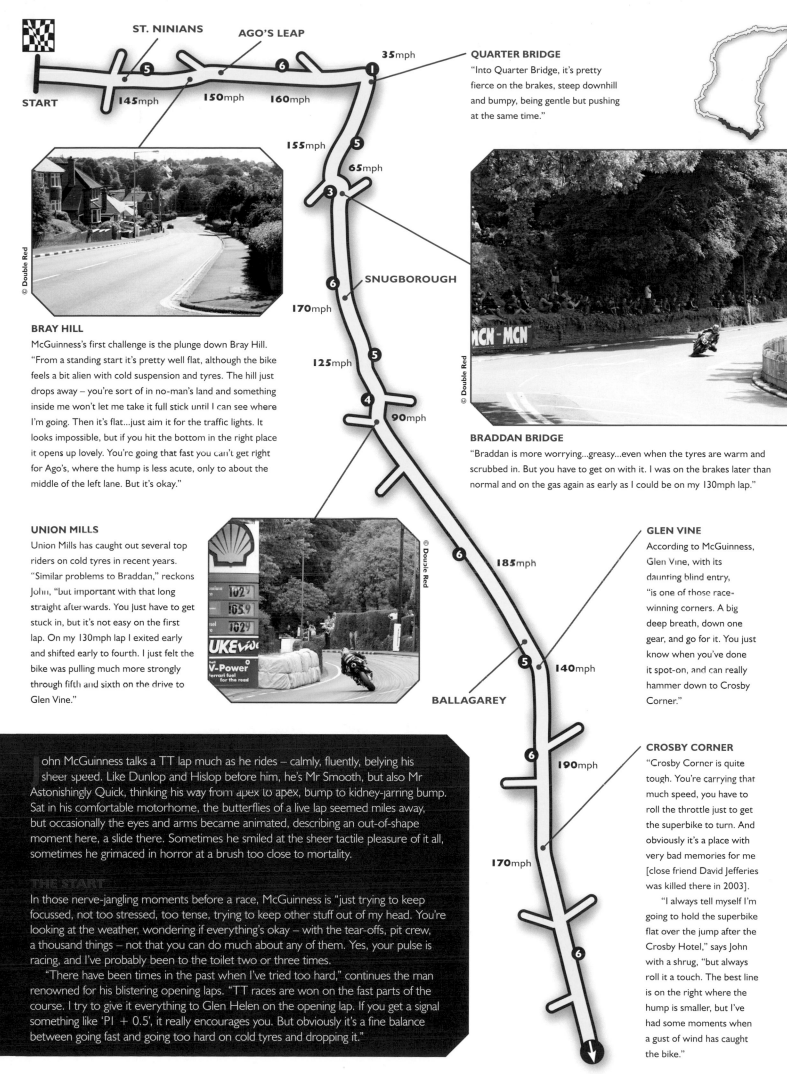

ST. NINIANS

AGO'S LEAP

5

6

35mph

1

START

145mph   150mph   160mph

155mph

5

65mph

3

6

SNUGBOROUGH

170mph

125mph

5

4

90mph

6

185mph

5

140mph

BALLAGAREY

6

190mph

170mph

6

QUARTER BRIDGE

"Into Quarter Bridge, it's pretty fierce on the brakes, steep downhill and bumpy, being gentle but pushing at the same time."

© Double Red

BRAY HILL

McGuinness's first challenge is the plunge down Bray Hill. "From a standing start it's pretty well flat, although the bike feels a bit alien with cold suspension and tyres. The hill just drops away – you're sort of in no-man's land and something inside me won't let me take it full stick until I can see where I'm going. Then it's flat...just aim it for the traffic lights. It looks impossible, but if you hit the bottom in the right place it opens up lovely. You're going that fast you can't get right for Ago's, where the hump is less acute, only to about the middle of the left lane. But it's okay."

UNION MILLS

Union Mills has caught out several top riders on cold tyres in recent years. "Similar problems to Braddan," reckons John, "but important with that long straight afterwards. You just have to get stuck in, but it's not easy on the first lap. On my 130mph lap I exited early and shifted early to fourth. I just felt the bike was pulling much more strongly through fifth and sixth on the drive to Glen Vine."

BRADDAN BRIDGE

"Braddan is more worrying...greasy...even when the tyres are warm and scrubbed in. But you have to get on with it. I was on the brakes later than normal and on the gas again as early as I could be on my 130mph lap."

GLEN VINE

According to McGuinness, Glen Vine, with its daunting blind entry, "is one of those race-winning corners. A big deep breath, down one gear, and go for it. You just know when you've done it spot-on, and can really hammer down to Crosby Corner."

CROSBY CORNER

"Crosby Corner is quite tough. You're carrying that much speed, you have to roll the throttle just to get the superbike to turn. And obviously it's a place with very bad memories for me [close friend David Jefferies was killed there in 2003].

"I always tell myself I'm going to hold the superbike flat over the jump after the Crosby Hotel," says John with a shrug, "but always roll it a touch. The best line is on the right where the hump is smaller, but I've had some moments when a gust of wind has caught the bike."

ohn McGuinness talks a TT lap much as he rides – calmly, fluently, belying his sheer speed. Like Dunlop and Hislop before him, he's Mr Smooth, but also Mr Astonishingly Quick, thinking his way from apex to apex, bump to kidney-jarring bump. Sat in his comfortable motorhome, the butterflies of a live lap seemed miles away, but occasionally the eyes and arms became animated, describing an out-of-shape moment here, a slide there. Sometimes he smiled at the sheer tactile pleasure of it all, sometimes he grimaced in horror at a brush too close to mortality.

THE START

In those nerve-jangling moments before a race, McGuinness is "just trying to keep focussed, not too stressed, too tense, trying to keep other stuff out of my head. You're looking at the weather, wondering if everything's okay – with the tear-offs, pit crew, a thousand things – not that you can do much about any of them. Yes, your pulse is racing, and I've probably been to the toilet two or three times.

"There have been times in the past when I've tried too hard," continues the man renowned for his blistering opening laps. "TT races are won on the fast parts of the course. I try to give it everything to Glen Helen on the opening lap. If you get a signal something like 'P1 + 0.5', it really encourages you. But obviously it's a fine balance between going fast and going too hard on cold tyres and dropping it."

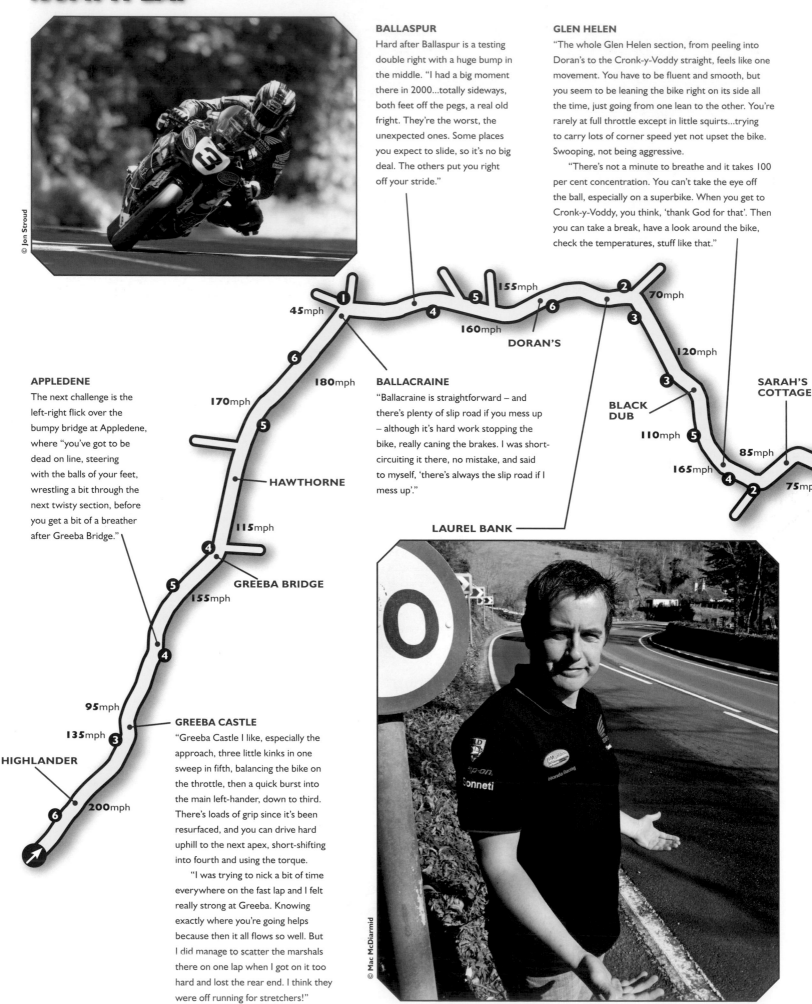

© Jon Stroud

BALLASPUR

Hard after Ballaspur is a testing double right with a huge bump in the middle. "I had a big moment there in 2000...totally sideways, both feet off the pegs, a real old fright. They're the worst, the unexpected ones. Some places you expect to slide, so it's no big deal. The others put you right off your stride."

GLEN HELEN

"The whole Glen Helen section, from peeling into Doran's to the Cronk-y-Voddy straight, feels like one movement. You have to be fluent and smooth, but you seem to be leaning the bike right on its side all the time, just going from one lean to the other. You're rarely at full throttle except in little squirts...trying to carry lots of corner speed yet not upset the bike. Swooping, not being aggressive.

"There's not a minute to breathe and it takes 100 per cent concentration. You can't take the eye off the ball, especially on a superbike. When you get to Cronk-y-Voddy, you think, 'thank God for that'. Then you can take a break, have a look around the bike, check the temperatures, stuff like that."

APPLEDENE

The next challenge is the left-right flick over the bumpy bridge at Appledene, where "you've got to be dead on line, steering with the balls of your feet, wrestling a bit through the next twisty section, before you get a bit of a breather after Greeba Bridge."

BALLACRAINE

"Ballacraine is straightforward – and there's plenty of slip road if you mess up – although it's hard work stopping the bike, really caning the brakes. I was short-circuiting it there, no mistake, and said to myself, 'there's always the slip road if I mess up'."

GREEBA CASTLE

"Greeba Castle I like, especially the approach, three little kinks in one sweep in fifth, balancing the bike on the throttle, then a quick burst into the main left-hander, down to third. There's loads of grip since it's been resurfaced, and you can drive hard uphill to the next apex, short-shifting into fourth and using the torque.

"I was trying to nick a bit of time everywhere on the fast lap and I felt really strong at Greeba. Knowing exactly where you're going helps because then it all flows so well. But I did manage to scatter the marshals there on one lap when I got on it too hard and lost the rear end. I think they were off running for stretchers!"

45mph
155mph
70mph
160mph
180mph
120mph
170mph
110mph
165mph
85mph
75mph
115mph
155mph
95mph
135mph
200mph

DORAN'S
BLACK DUB
SARAH'S COTTAGE
HAWTHORNE
LAUREL BANK
GREEBA BRIDGE
HIGHLANDER

© Mac McDiarmid

© Mac McDiarmid

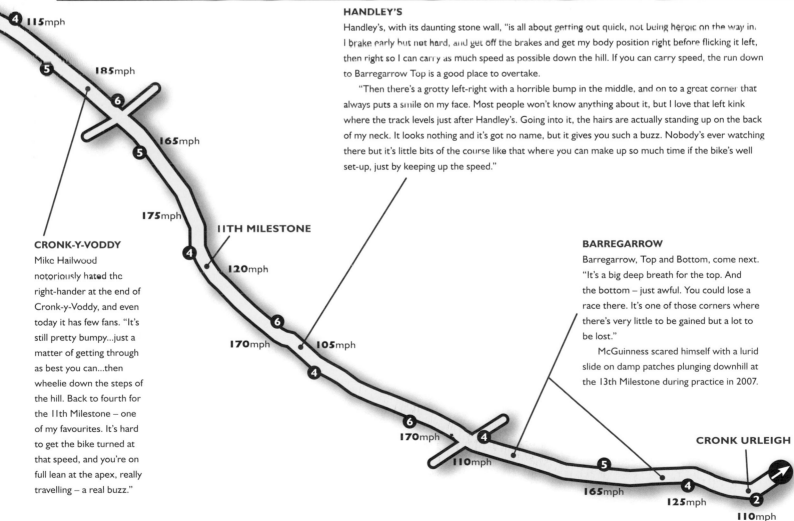

HANDLEY'S

Handley's, with its daunting stone wall, "is all about getting out quick, not being heroic on the way in. I brake early but not hard, and get off the brakes and get my body position right before flicking it left, then right so I can carry as much speed as possible down the hill. If you can carry speed, the run down to Barregarrow Top is a good place to overtake.

"Then there's a grotty left-right with a horrible bump in the middle, and on to a great corner that always puts a smile on my face. Most people won't know anything about it, but I love that left kink where the track levels just after Handley's. Going into it, the hairs are actually standing up on the back of my neck. It looks nothing and it's got no name, but it gives you such a buzz. Nobody's ever watching there but it's little bits of the course like that where you can make up so much time if the bike's well set-up, just by keeping up the speed."

4 115mph

5 185mph

6

165mph

5

175mph

CRONK-Y-VODDY

Mike Hailwood notoriously hated the right-hander at the end of Cronk-y-Voddy, and even today it has few fans. "It's still pretty bumpy...just a matter of getting through as best you can...then wheelie down the steps of the hill. Back to fourth for the 11th Milestone – one of my favourites. It's hard to get the bike turned at that speed, and you're on full lean at the apex, really travelling – a real buzz."

11TH MILESTONE

4

120mph

6

170mph **105mph**

4

6

170mph

4

110mph

BARREGARROW

Barregarrow, Top and Bottom, come next. "It's a big deep breath for the top. And the bottom – just awful. You could lose a race there. It's one of those corners where there's very little to be gained but a lot to be lost."

McGuinness scared himself with a lurid slide on damp patches plunging downhill at the 13th Milestone during practice in 2007.

CRONK URLEIGH

5

165mph

4

125mph

2

110mph

John McGuinness
130MPH LAP

© Stephen Davison

© Stephen Davison

RHENCULLEN

John rarely uses markers for his peel-in and braking points. "Mainly, I just pick them by eye, although I do aim for the telegraph pole at Rhencullen before that wheelie onto the tabletop. It's fourth gear and mega-bumpy, but there's nothing you can do about that except let the bike take it, if it can."

This was Steve Hislop's favourite section and McGuinness also relishes the second "big, fast wheelie out of the dip at the exit and on past Bishopscourt. Get into top, then it goes left, then right. On the superbike you're in a two-wheel drift... a complete passenger...sat on a moving torpedo that's doing its own thing, and you just have to let it do it at about 180mph."

ALPINE

135mph

155mph

185mph

BISHOPSCOURT

155mph

45mph

165mph

115mph

DOUGLAS CORNER

175mph

140mph

90mph

175mph

© Double Red

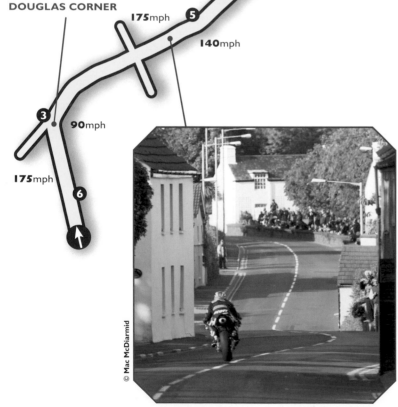

© Mac McDiarmid

KIRK MICHAEL

Kirk Michael holds few horrors. "Third gear for Douglas Road Corner...it's bumpy going in. Into fourth, fifth, quite quickly, holding a tight line...watch for the kerb jumping out...wheelie off the crest of the hill... It's a real blast going through here with the exhaust rattling back off the buildings. Then back a gear but no brakes for the left-right-left out of the village."

BALLAUGH

"The trick for the run down to Ballaugh," he explains, after pausing for breath, "is to do as little as possible. Straight-line everything, really kissing the kerbs, rather than taking racing lines which only scrub off speed. Well, apart from Alpine which is back one gear. If you go in too fast the back wheel jumps in the air over that ridge and the bike won't turn. Then there's another bit of a breather down to Ballaugh itself, where you really jump hard on the brakes, like it's a short circuit.

"Quick shift...bang, bang...through the left-hander out of the village. It used to be really rough and chattery. The resurfacing is good, but if you're in too low a gear it spins up and hurts the tyre."

Charging out of Ballaugh, riders still think of the late Gwen Crellin, who for so many decades waved and checked them off from the marshals' post opposite her cottage. Then back into action, "down to fifth for Ballacrye, take the jump in the middle of the right lane if you can. Trouble is, the left-hander's quite ripply, which sometimes throws you off-line."

© Stephen Davison

SULBY STRAIGHT

Until the mid-1980s Sulby Straight was ferociously bumpy, with riders simply hoping to keep the bike on a grey blur between two green ones. Even now, explains McGuinness, "it still feels like 300mph, like your head's being ripped off by the wind. At Sulby Bridge I just hit the brakes when I'm scared, although just up the road at Ginger Hall I use the telegraph pole at the apex as a bit of a guide, because it's so obvious."

BALLACRYE

75mph

185mph

5

6

145mph

125mph

5

140mph

6

205mph

50mph

SULBY BRIDGE

1

120mph

3

95mph

2

2 85mph

3

120mph

© Mac McDiarmid

GINGER HALL

QUARRY BENDS

"You get another rest before the Quarries, which are straightforward now. The hardest part is the right-hander going in, because it's really bumpy and you're carrying a lot of speed, still in fifth gear after only a bit of braking. Then give it a squirt to the first left-hander, down to fourth, up to fifth for the second pair of bends. I put the superbike into top before the kink on to Sulby Straight, because the kink puts you on the smaller part of the tyre and top gear helps the drive."

© Double Red

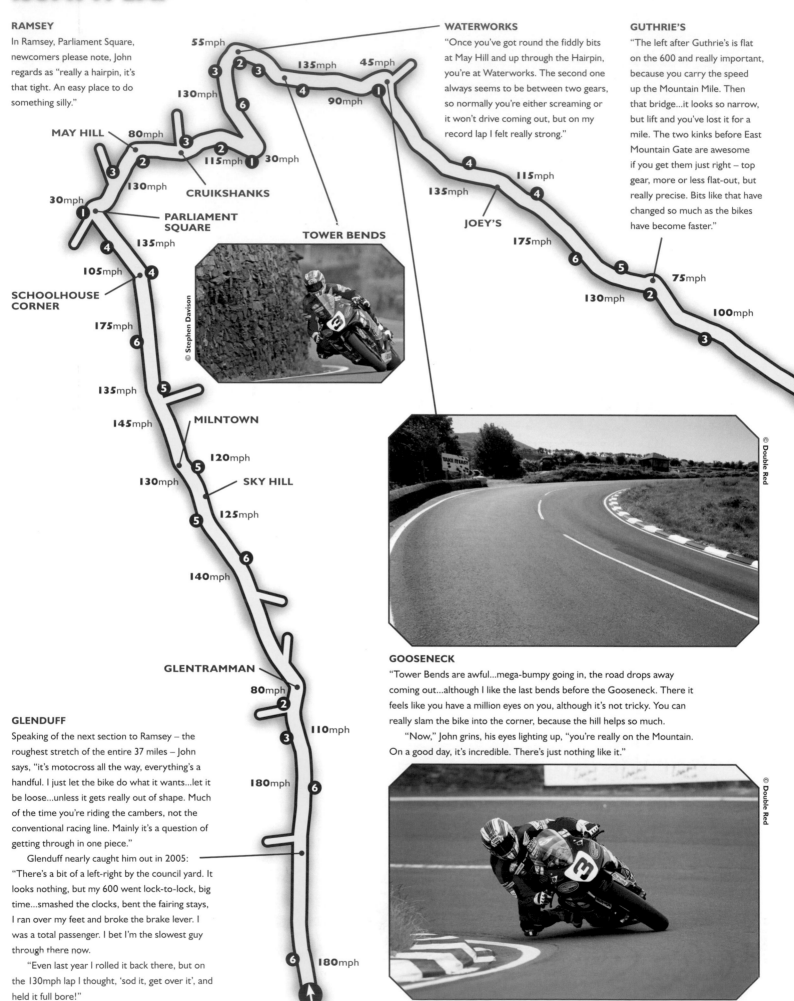

John McGuinness
130MPH LAP

RAMSEY
In Ramsey, Parliament Square, newcomers please note, John regards as "really a hairpin, it's that tight. An easy place to do something silly."

55mph
135mph
45mph

3
2
3
4
1
90mph

130mph
6

MAY HILL   **80**mph
3
2
115mph   **1**   **30**mph
3
130mph
CRUIKSHANKS

30mph
1
PARLIAMENT SQUARE

4   **135**mph

105mph   **4**

SCHOOLHOUSE CORNER

175mph   **6**

TOWER BENDS

© Stephen Davison

135mph   **5**

145mph   **MILNTOWN**

5   **120**mph

130mph   **SKY HILL**

5   **125**mph

6

140mph

WATERWORKS
"Once you've got round the fiddly bits at May Hill and up through the Hairpin, you're at Waterworks. The second one always seems to be between two gears, so normally you're either screaming or it won't drive coming out, but on my record lap I felt really strong."

4

135mph   **115**mph

4

JOEY'S

175mph
6
5

GUTHRIE'S
"The left after Guthrie's is flat on the 600 and really important, because you carry the speed up the Mountain Mile. Then that bridge...it looks so narrow, but lift and you've lost it for a mile. The two kinks before East Mountain Gate are awesome if you get them just right – top gear, more or less flat-out, but really precise. Bits like that have changed so much as the bikes have become faster."

75mph
2
130mph
100mph

3

6

© Double Red

GOOSENECK
"Tower Bends are awful...mega-bumpy going in, the road drops away coming out...although I like the last bends before the Gooseneck. There it feels like you have a million eyes on you, although it's not tricky. You can really slam the bike into the corner, because the hill helps so much.

"Now," John grins, his eyes lighting up, "you're really on the Mountain. On a good day, it's incredible. There's just nothing like it."

GLENTRAMMAN
80mph
2

GLENDUFF
Speaking of the next section to Ramsey – the roughest stretch of the entire 37 miles – John says, "it's motocross all the way, everything's a handful. I just let the bike do what it wants...let it be loose...unless it gets really out of shape. Much of the time you're riding the cambers, not the conventional racing line. Mainly it's a question of getting through in one piece."

Glenduff nearly caught him out in 2005: "There's a bit of a left-right by the council yard. It looks nothing, but my 600 went lock-to-lock, big time...smashed the clocks, bent the fairing stays, I ran over my feet and broke the brake lever. I was a total passenger. I bet I'm the slowest guy through there now.

"Even last year I rolled it back there, but on the 130mph lap I thought, 'sod it, get over it', and held it full bore!"

3   **110**mph

180mph
6

© Double Red

6   **180**mph

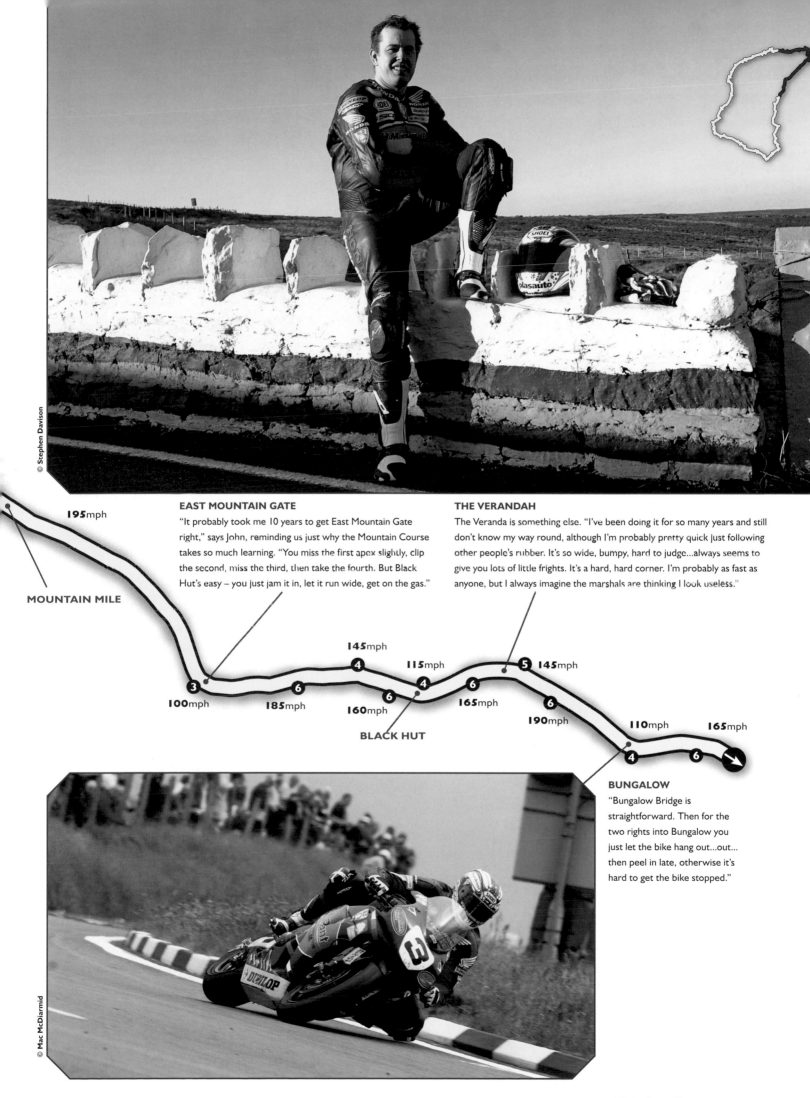

EAST MOUNTAIN GATE

"It probably took me 10 years to get East Mountain Gate right," says John, reminding us just why the Mountain Course takes so much learning. "You miss the first apex slightly, clip the second, miss the third, then take the fourth. But Black Hut's easy – you just jam it in, let it run wide, get on the gas."

THE VERANDAH

The Veranda is something else. "I've been doing it for so many years and still don't know my way round, although I'm probably pretty quick just following other people's rubber. It's so wide, bumpy, hard to judge...always seems to give you lots of little frights. It's a hard, hard corner. I'm probably as fast as anyone, but I always imagine the marshals are thinking I look useless."

195mph

MOUNTAIN MILE

145mph

115mph

145mph

3

100mph

6

185mph

4

6

160mph

4

6

165mph

5

6

190mph

4

110mph

6

165mph

BLACK HUT

BUNGALOW

"Bungalow Bridge is straightforward. Then for the two rights into Bungalow you just let the bike hang out...out... then peel in late, otherwise it's hard to get the bike stopped."

© Stephen Davison

© Mac McDiarmid

John McGuinness
130MPH LAP

© Stephen Davison

© Double Red

BRANDYWELL

"At Brandywell I tend to go in quite slow, run parallel with the fence, then turn in late and get on the gas hard and early."

From here it's downhill all the way to Hillberry, about five miles, the engine eager for revs.

WINDY CORNER

"The 32nd and 33rd, you can really nail them, and Windy's straightforward since they changed it last year – a bit like Charlie's at Cadwell. It's a real rush into the 33rd – I think I make time there. Again I just judge the line, although I have a peripheral sense of the fence posts turning yellow around where you peel in."

KEPPEL GATE

"Keppel's another awkward one, with the bend before trying to chuck you in the wrong place. But there's plenty of grip so you can really attack it."

190mph

HAILWOOD RISE

DUKE'S 32ND

155mph

90mph

180mph

120mph

100mph

185mph

33RD MILESTONE

110mph

170mph

85mph

KATE'S COTTAGE

"Kate's is always a bit of a moment as there's usually a damp patch which makes you freeze and pray the thing grips."

© Double Red

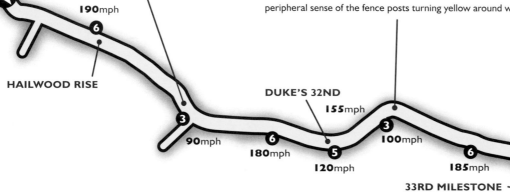

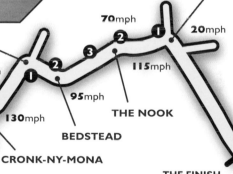

CREG-NY-BAA

John gives the superbike a dab of back brake to stop it getting too high over the jump on the drop to the Creg, "where you just guess it, get round safe and steady, get it upright as quick as you can and gas it. On my 130mph lap I spun it up on the exit when I got on the gas far too hard, so hard I couldn't possibly have been riding any harder."

GOVERNOR'S BRIDGE

"After a horrible right-hander [The Nook], it's a quick blast to Governor's...steep and deceptively hard to stop. If it's been dry you can have a bit of a go over the bridge, but it can be nasty where the surface changes. Obviously you want to get on to the straight as quick as possible, but it bites if you get too greedy with the throttle."

SIGNPOST

70mph

20mph

150mph

2

3

115mph

6 205mph

1

2 180mph

95mph

THE NOOK

180mph

185mph 125mph

85mph

6

5

130mph

BEDSTEAD

3

4

165mph

CRONK-NY-MONA

BRANDISH

Brandish was altered after the 2006 TT. "It's miles quicker than before – two gears faster – although the new layout seems to suck you in early."

HILLBERRY

Hillberry, at around 125mph, is back two gears and on the gas as quick as you can. "I felt strong there on my record lap and also at Cronk-ny-Mona, which I really like anyway," John grins. "You can really throw it in, although the road falls away on the exit so you don't want to run wide. Signpost comes up at you blind and fast."

THE FINISH

By the time John's passing the scoreboard on a flying lap he's just snicking into top gear and ready for it all over again – faster than any man before him.

REFLECTING ON THE 130MPH LAP

"On my second lap of the Senior I thought, 'if I'm going to do the 130mph lap, then this is the time to do it.' I had half a tank of juice and I was leading on the road, so I had no-one under my feet. Going into the lap, I'd got good drive out of Governor's and I just said to myself, 'really concentrate on the lap now'.

"But it wasn't so much a case of concentrating to do 130mph – I was concentrating to win the race. Yeah, 130mph is a landmark, but it will be beaten. No-one can ever take a race win from me.

"I'd love to know what a perfect lap would be. Even on my record lap I was a bit tense, holding on to the bars too tight. At Sulby I consciously had to relax a bit.

"Even if you resurfaced the entire course, I'm not sure you would go any faster. I'd love to be able to piece together my best section time from every corner and see what the lap time would be."

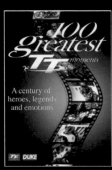
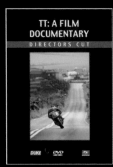
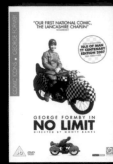
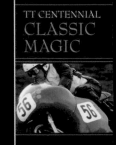

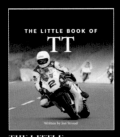

earth, captured forever.

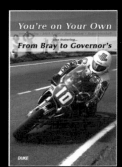

HE HISTORY OF
HE TT 1907-2006
he definitive history of the
orld-famous road races,
cked with great stories,
onderful archive footage,
scinating interviews and
detailed narrative charting
e story of the TT from
beginnings in 1907,
pdated to include TT 2006.
9.99 240mins No.2143N

YOU'RE ON YOUR OWN
AND FROM BRAY TO
GOVERNOR'S
Two classic TT films from
1982, featuring legends
including Mick Grant, Ron
Haslam, and Joey Dunlop.
You're On Your Own takes
you closer to iconic riders than
ever before. From Bray to
Governor's puts you on-board
with Grant for a phenomenal
lap of the TT circuit.
£14.99 55mins No.1656

ISLE OF SPEED
- THE 1952 SENIOR TT
A rare and recent find, this
excellent colour film from
the Esso archives features
Duke, Armstrong, Amm,
Graham, Coleman and other
great names on Norton,
AJS, Velocette, MV Agusta
et al. Pure nostalgia including
early on-bike camera and
'slo-mo' filming!
£12.99 30mins No.1657

Tourist Trophy Recreation Captured in Crystal

This is a unique opportunity to own a faithful recreation
of a stunning piece of TT history. Duke has specially
commissioned this amazingly detailed, official 3D replica
of the Senior Trophy, laser-etched in crystal, to mark the
Centenary.

The Senior Trophy has been an icon of the Isle of Man
TT for 100 years and the ultimate accolade in motorcycle
racing.

Since it was first handed to Charlie Collier in 1907, the
Senior Trophy has been the goal of the greatest racers in
history, and the original bears the names of the legends
who have tamed the unforgiving TT circuit in the
quest for glory.

Each piece comes in a specially commissioned,
velvet-effect lined presentation case.

200mm (8 inches) version £49.99 No.9698
80mm (3 inches) version £14.99 No.9697

T HIGHLIGHTS
OLUME 2 1965-1968
urray Walker and Peter
rnold commentate on four
bulous years of TT racing,
cluding one of the greatest
ces of all time - the 1965
nior TT.
0.99 43mins No.9902

1,000 Limited Edition Signed Centenary TT Celebration Set

This limited edition collection of exclusive memorabilia has been created to ensure the memories of the Centenary TT celebrations
live on. It contains an extraordinary array of unique, must-have collectables capturing the action and atmosphere of the 100th TT.

The Celebration Set includes a numbered 2-disc limited edition DVD from Duke, featuring the official review of the racing, St John's classic re-enactment and the Parade of Champions.
You also receive a very special edition of TT 2007, the Centenary celebration book from Lily Publications. Each volume of the 160-page, full-colour, leather-effect bound book is presented
with a certificate of authenticity numbered and signed by celebrated author Mick Duckworth.

The Isle of Man Post Office has recreated the 1907 TT race programme, together with time keeper's notes, presented here with a very special cover featuring the Stanley Woods TT stamp
with a unique one-day-only Post Mark denoting 10.00 am, 28th May, 2007 - exactly 100 years after the start of the first race around the original TT course. The first 1,000 of the covers are
signed by none other than ex-World Champion John Surtees MBE and absolutely exclusive to this review collection!

Each set also contains a special edition hardback copy of the official TT 2007 programme, including all the TT 2007 race results, and specially commissioned Isle of Man Treasury coins
marking the TT Centenary.

Each Celebration Set is accompanied
by a certificate of authenticity,
individually hand-signed
by a TT legend
£175.00 No.LA20

HE MAGIC OF THE TT
ENTENARY EDITION
elebrating the TT's 100th
rthday, respected writer Mac
cDiarmid's evocative book
esents a lavishly
ustrated collection of themed
apters commemorating the
eatest motorcycle road
cing event.
.99 320pp No.H4431

TOP TEN RIDERS

By Gary Pinchin

Hibernia 1½

A18 Snaefell 5
Douglas 13½

A18 Ramsey 1¾

© Stephen Davison

JOHN McGUINNESS

HM PLANT HONDA
PADGETTS HONDA

Bennetts **SUPERBIKE**	**1st**
PokerStars **SUPERSPORT**	**2nd**
PokerStars **SUPERSTOCK**	**2nd**
PokerStars **SENIOR**	**1st**

Unbelievable! McGuinness said it. We all said it. But his 130mph lap was just the icing on a celebratory cake for the acknowledged King of the Mountain.

His two Superbike race wins took his tally in the class to eight victories and 12 podiums in the 14 races in which he has taken part since 2000 – and he achieved this year's double with virtually the same HM Plant Honda that he'd used in 2006. No wonder he made a big play with his team bosses for keeping the bike.

McGuinness said he received a text message after the Senior from Mark Davies, formerly the boss of Honda UK, and now head of Honda Europe, saying 'words fail me mate'. McGuinness sent one back saying 'thanks, but can I keep the superbike please?' He genuinely wants to keep that bike.

Yet last winter McGuinness had been dismayed not to be offered the factory-kitted bike that Leon Camier races in BSB. Instead it went to Ian Hutchinson, leaving McGuinness to rely on old faithful – the 2006 TT-winning bike.

"I was annoyed that I didn't get offered Camier's bike," said McGuinness. "But I've been in that position before. Factory bikes can be a handful around here. If I'd stamped my feet I'm sure I could have got a factory bike, but I was happy with mine.

"The bike was the same as last year apart from stiffer yokes – the others were a bit too flexy – and the engine had more power. I've had that much good luck here. My bikes never missed a beat this fortnight. And I kept thinking, my luck had to run out."

Behind the public gaze, McGuinness wasn't too happy with the way he was treated by Honda during the winter. He rode a Superstock on short circuits last year as part of his deal but when the team pulled the plug on that and switched their focus to Supersport, McGuinness was amazed that Hutchinson got the job and he was left out in the cold. And then there was the factory bike issue. But rather than depress him, it actually relit a fire inside McGuinness.

"I sat back with my TT wins last year thinking 'I'll get a Honda job', and then I heard Hutchy was going to get it. That kickstarted my season. I trained really hard and was more focussed than ever. I wasn't James Toseland fit, but I was in a lot better shape than I'd been for years. I lost weight and I felt great on and off the bike."

McGuinness got a ride with Padgetts in British Supersport to become one of Hutchinson's rivals, and was devastated not to beat him in the TT race.

"Clive Padgett is the nicest bloke you'll ever meet in the world. It's a magic little team. Clive has enough stuff in their truck to win a world championship.

"He worked and worked to find me more power at the TT. He asked the Japanese people sharing the Padgetts awning which pipe was the best to use on the CBR600RR. When they said Moriwaki, he had one couriered in two days later.

"I felt like I let Clive down. It's a passion for him. At 5.00am he was there with the boys working on my bike. I rode my heart out to try and win it. But you know in yourself if you've done everything you can. I lost by only two and a half seconds over 150 miles. We were lapping at 125mph on knackered tyres on the fourth lap. I was ten seconds inside the lap record last year. We were another ten seconds inside this year. That's 20 seconds in two years. Incredible. I mean, that's raised the bar like you wouldn't believe.

"I couldn't get my words out after the Supersport. It was an unreal race. I wanted so much to beat the HM Plant Honda team. I've nothing against any of them but they let me go. In all fairness, looking back and having lost my job – it was one of the best things that could have happened to me.

"But what about Bruce [Anstey on the Relentless Suzuki] in the Superstock race? 128mph with a bike that's got a key in the ignition. You could ride it down to the shops for a paper. That's unbelievable. The Superstock was an amazing race."

In finishing runner-up in both of those races and taking his two Superbike wins, McGuinness paid tribute to the team members around him who made it all possible.

"My boys were brilliant. I insisted at the start of the year who would be with me.

"Julian Boland has done my wheel changes for the past two years and he's so meticulous. I watch him undo the rear wheel, carefully place the wheel spindle so it doesn't roll away, start to tighten the spindle by hand so

> ## "I'D HATE TO WATCH MYSELF OUT ON THE COURSE. PEOPLE COME BACK TO ME AND TELL ME HOW OUT OF SHAPE I AM IN CERTAIN PLACES…"

there's no chance of cross-threading it with the wrench – I'm almost wanting to scream at him to hurry. But there's no need, he's just very precise and you know he's going to get the job done with no problems.

"Ian Whitlow has been with me a long time. He did my visor, my drink, screen and fuel cap, and updated me with the race information. Mark Beaton did my fuel – he was doing it for the first time but what a guy.

"Mark and Julian normally work for Hutchy in the British Supersport series so there were some split allegiances, but I'd like to think we all worked as a team during the TT. But I demanded that Julian worked for me. Last year he was with me at the North West, TT and Ulster, and this year at the North West. I didn't want to break the tie he had with the bike. He loves it. So do I. That's how I wanted my side of things because those were the tools for the job."

Prior to the Isle of Man TT Races sponsored by Bennetts, McGuinness talked about not coming home. He'd never spoken like that before and it was almost as if he'd had a scary premonition that something serious might happen to him. So did he go to the 2007 TT fearing the worst?

"I'M NOT HERE TO PROVE ANYTHING. I RACE FOR MYSELF. BUT EVERY SINGLE PERSON ASKED ME IF 130MPH WAS POSSIBLE AND IT FELT LIKE I ALMOST HAD TO DO IT TO MAKE EVERYONE HAPPY…"

"I'd feel a lot better if I tipped off at Quarter Bridge or something silly like that," he said. "I've raced here for years and never had a problem. And all the time I've lost mates like Mick [Lofthouse], DJ [David Jefferies], Gus [Scott]. It's like some of them knew. When Gus died, he made a point of giving his house keys and van keys to Becky before the race…

"I think it's in the back of my mind that sometime my luck is going to run out – although 'run out' is the wrong way to say it because I feel like I've been riding within myself. But it's just that the speeds have gone way up and we keep pushing harder and harder.

"I'd hate to watch myself out on the course. People come back to me and tell me how out of shape I am in certain places. You've got people, racers, who come here to see what the TT is all about and walk away from Bray Hill because they can't bear to watch. But the place has got a hold on me. It draws me back."

McGuinness survived intact but the centenary event came to a close in such a horrible way. While he was celebrating his Senior victory and the 130mph lap record, there was tragedy up on the Mountain, with one rider and two spectators killed, and two marshals seriously hurt. The terrible news clearly affected McGuinness and he became very subdued.

"It sounds weird but I was worrying about something bad happening while in bed on the morning of the Senior. I'm a massive TT fan but of course I don't want to see things like this happen. It's so tragic when anyone dies, let alone spectators who've just gone out to enjoy watching the racing.

"It was such a shame for the event. The marshalling was brilliant and they've done a particularly great job in the last couple of years. They were really cautious this year in adopting a policy of 'if in doubt get the flags out', but you're better off being safe than sorry."

The fatal accident, however, had nothing to do with swaying McGuinness into suggesting he may quit the TT. He'd already made his feelings known in the post-Senior press conference but had slightly altered his position when he gave an interview much later that evening.

"I said 'I don't feel the need to prove myself any more', but even that's not quite what I meant," he tried to explain. "I'm not here to prove anything. I race for myself. But every single person asked me if 130mph was possible and it felt like I almost had to do it to make everyone happy, so they could go home having seen someone do it!

"I don't know whether or not I'm finished here at the TT. I started here in 1996 and have done 11 TTs. I've had such a lot of luck and sometimes I think it's going to run out at some stage.

"Hizzy did it though, didn't he? He won 11 TTs and then walked away. I'd like to do that in the same style – but I'd also like to stay as some sort of ambassador for the event and help bring on new names."

© Double Red

2

© Double Red

IAN HUTCHINSON

HM PLANT HONDA
BIKE ANIMAL HONDA

Bennetts **SUPERBIKE**	**3rd**
PokerStars **SUPERSPORT**	**1st**
PokerStars **SUPERSTOCK**	**3rd**
PokerStars **SENIOR**	**3rd**

Hutchinson clinched the first TT victory of his career with a brilliant ride in the Supersport race and picked up three other podium finishes with his third places in the Superbike, Superstock and Senior races to underline his position as one of the brightest TT stars of the future.

But at one stage it looked as if he might have become an also-ran at this year's TT after damaging his shoulder in a crash at Oulton Park three weeks earlier. Hutchinson didn't make a big deal about it at the time but the truth is he was struggling throughout the TT just to hang on to the handlebars, especially on the superbike. He arguably had the most advanced motorcycle in the Bennetts Superbike and PokerStars Senior TT races but couldn't quite fulfil its, or his, full potential, finishing third in both events.

Before the TT Hutchinson said that the Centenary meant nothing to him, that winning was everything – but he changed his mind after the races and said: "It felt really special to win the Supersport race. I realised the Centenary meant so much to so many people once I got here and saw everyone and experienced the atmosphere. I'm so pleased for the team I got the Supersport win, as my boys worked so hard throughout the TT."

But Hutchinson is a canny rider, especially on the roads. "The pressure was on in that race because one mistake on a 600 and you lose so much time. I didn't want to push any harder than I was doing because that's when you make mistakes, so I tried to make sure all my lines, my braking, everything, was perfect."

But to finish on the podium in every race on his fourth visit to the Isle of Man TT was an outstanding achievement. "I'm pleased I was up there each race but the big bike rides were not for me this year. I was too worried about the damp early on in the Superbike race and that cost me. I got a couple of yellows in the Senior and once Guy [Martin] caught me on the road that was it."

3

GUY MARTIN

HYDREX HONDA

Bennetts **SUPERBIKE**	**2nd**
PokerStars **SUPERSPORT**	**3rd**
PokerStars **SUPERSTOCK**	**DNF**
PokerStars **SENIOR**	**2nd**

All race week Guy Martin was threatening to win his first TT but he went home without achieving his life-long ambition. But the 25-year-old Lincolnshire loon kept smiling and netted runner-up finishes in the Superbike and Senior races plus a third in the PokerStars Supersport.

Before the TT Martin had tried to psyche out John McGuinness. The two of them had clashed at the North West 200 and Martin claimed to have "fried his rival's brain", but after the event paid homage to him.

"Massive respect to John," he humbly said after the Senior. "Two big-bike TT wins! I can do this and that, but this TT has proved I'm not ready to win a TT yet. But I'll be back."

Martin's outspoken motor-mouthing marks him out as the TT's biggest character and long may he continue to speak his mind. But this year he backed it up with some outstanding riding, even if he didn't win a TT.

What he did do, though, was push McGuinness harder than anyone has before. It was only down to a little bit of inexperience in the pit stops that his crew lost out to the HM Plant team. That's not a criticism of the Hydrex team, just that McGuinness is a smart operator with 11 years of TT races behind him!

Martin also had his fair share of problems in practice and in the races. In the Senior the chain was jumping the sprockets, but he coaxed the bike home. Running out of fuel in the Superstock event, however, was the biggest disappointment, especially after practice had shown the bike to have more than enough capacity to go the distance. But, as ever, Martin shrugged the disappointment aside, saying in the press conferences that he wasn't going to sit there and moan about what might have been.

A gifted engineer and race tuner in his own right, Martin is such a massive bike fan that he also rode – and won – in the Billown Pre-TT Classic races, took part in the 1907 Re-enactment and even went to Peel for a steam rally to look at some old classics on one of his days off, only to come back raving about the fully operational threshing machine he'd seen!

STILL PUSHING THE BOUNDARIES

ISLE OF MAN TT
1907 - 2007
ISLE OF MAN CENTENARY

Micron riders celebrated the Isle of Man Centenary TT in style last week with another series of impressive results in the Superbike and Supersport races. Not to mention Dave Molyneux's two victories in the Sidecar TT events.

After nearly 30 years of continuous involvement in the TT, we're still using our hands-on experience of hundreds of laps of the world's most demanding race circuit to continually improve the style and engineering of all our products.

Micron is at the forefront of technology and performance, remaining the top choice for many road racers and road riders alike. Benefit from our success and award-winning Hydroform manufacturing process to take your riding experience to the next level.

Micron – performance through technology

SUPERBIKE

2	Guy Martin	Honda CBR1000RR Fireblade
6	Ryan Farquhar	Honda CBR1000RR Fireblade
8	Conor Cummins	Yamaha YZF-R1
10	Steve Plater	Yamaha YZF-R1

SUPERSPORT

2	John McGuinness	Honda CBR600RR
5	Nigel Beattie	Yamaha YZF-R6
6	Conor Cummins	Yamaha YZF-R6
7	Ryan Farquhar	Kawasaki ZX6-R
8	Steve Plater	Yamaha YZF-R6

SENIOR

2	Guy Martin	Honda CBR1000RR Fireblade
6	Conor Cummings	Yamaha YZF-R1

SIDECAR

1	Dave Molyneux / Rick Long	
	Honda CBR600RR	
3	Steve Norbury / Scott Parnell	
	Honda CBR600RR	

2006 MCN award

micron
PERFORMANCE THROUGH TECHNOLOGY

FOR MORE INFORMATION VISIT OUR WEBSITE OR CALL US ON :
TEL: 01773 876333 www.micronexhausts.com

4

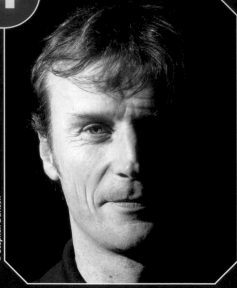

© Stephen Davison

BRUCE ANSTEY
RELENTLESS SUZUKI
by TAS

Bennetts SUPERBIKE	DNF
PokerStars SUPERSPORT	4th
PokerStars SUPERSTOCK	1st
PokerStars SENIOR	DNF

When John McGuinness said that Bruce Anstey had raised the bar with his 128mph lap time on his way to victory in the PokerStars Superstock race, he wasn't kidding. Anstey's performance on what's meant to be a road-going GSX-R1000 with a fork kit and shock was simply stunning – so stunning it made everyone wonder why teams bother building fully tuned race engines for the so-called big-bike classes.

But how is it that a rider can take a TT victory and yet still have his week viewed as something of a disappointment? So much was expected of Anstey this year but his two retirements in the big-bike races and fourth place in the Supersport took the gloss off his brilliant Superstock victory.

Anstey is one of those riders who likes his bike to feel perfect – then it seems he can do exactly as he wishes. But if the bike isn't right, no amount of effort will turn a result.

That was the case with his Superbike. All week the team struggled to get the Suzuki to handle, and it was only when the WP shock was swapped for an Ohlins unit that the problem was cured. Sadly, Anstey never got the chance to prove it. In the Superbike race a two-bit electronics amplifier broke up and killed the ignition – but Anstey reported that he knew the handling was cured just from the run down Bray Hill. Then in the Senior he pulled in, claiming he had handling problems again.

But it was in the Supersport race that he was robbed. His fourth place doesn't reflect how close he was to winning. He smashed the lap record on the first lap and did it again on lap two, going into the pits with a 4.5secs lead over McGuinness. But then the bike simply refused to fire up after re-fuelling and he lost some 23secs, dropping to fourth place. And once Hutchinson got by him on the road he knew that victory was impossible.

5

© Stephen Davison

Bennetts SUPERBIKE	8th
PokerStars SUPERSPORT	6th
PokerStars SUPERSTOCK	5th
PokerStars SENIOR	6th

CONOR CUMMINS
MJF MILLSPORT YAMAHA

Fifth in the Superstock, sixth in the Supersport and sixth in the Senior, to go with his eighth in the Superbike, hoisted Conor Cummins right up in the ranks of top TT runners at this year's Centenary races in only his second year of racing on the Mountain course.

He also became the fastest Manxman, but said: "Being the fastest Manxman doesn't really bother me. What matters is the results, and everything went according to plan. We struggled in the pits with the wheel spindle in both Superbike races but other than that the entire fortnight was spot-on, and that's thanks to the team – they did a great job.

"I learned a lot from the Superbike race and in the Senior I got my head down from the start and went at it. It felt like I made the next step and next year I'm going to be going at it full tilt."

6

© Stephen Davison

Bennetts SUPERBIKE	5th
PokerStars SUPERSPORT	10th
PokerStars SUPERSTOCK	14th
PokerStars SENIOR	4th

IAN LOUGHER
STOBART HONDA
BLACK HORSE FINANCE HONDA

Fifth in the Superbike and fourth in the Senior were the best results for Ian Lougher in what can only be described as a disappointing TT. He was only 14th in Superstock – predictable since his bike was down on power all week – and 10th in Supersport, where everyone expected him to feature strongly.

He was one of only three riders to lap at 128mph in practice, along with McGuinness and Martin, yet he was baffled why he couldn't do it in the two Superbike races. "One lap the bike felt great, the next my feet were off the pegs. The bike was so quick, I just wish I could have done more with it.

"My Supersport bike felt a little over-geared. I did 121mph in practice from a standing start so I expected more in the race. The engine showed good power on the dyno and felt strong at the North West, and had good top speed here but seemed sluggish getting there."

7

Bennetts **SUPERBIKE**	4th
PokerStars **SUPERSPORT**	13th
PokerStars **SUPERSTOCK**	4th
PokerStars **SENIOR**	DNF

MARTIN FINNEGAN
ALPHA BOILERS KLAFFI HONDA
ALPHA BOILERS MV AGUSTA

After a disappointing 2006, this was a big year for Martin Finnegan to re-establish himself as one of the TT's star men. He arrived with a much more TT-based Klaffi Honda, rather than the full-on WSB bike of last year, and opened his account with fourth in the Superbike race, but the bike blew up in the Senior.

The big man finished a distant 13th in Supersport and took fourth place in Superstock, although he had massive expectations in that race. His rivals feared him too, but Finnegan got a big shock when his supposedly superfast MV Agusta was blown away by the Hondas.

He said: "I had a couple of moments with the MV, tucking the front in fast corners, but otherwise the bike was good. But it was a tough race. The Hondas couldn't get into the top positions last year so it's a bit funny how they're so fast this year."

8

Bennetts **SUPERBIKE**	7th
PokerStars **SUPERSPORT**	DNF
PokerStars **SUPERSTOCK**	DNF
PokerStars **SENIOR**	5th

ADRIAN ARCHIBALD
RELENTLESS SUZUKI BY TAS

As with Finnegan, this was Adrian Archibald's big chance to put the record straight and rebuild lost confidence after a difficult 2006 season when he signed for a private Yamaha team, left after a disastrous North West, and rejoined the TAS team for the rest of the year.

But it was another tough TT for the 37-year-old from Ballymoney. He finished seventh in the first Superbike race, plagued by handling problems that also affected team-mate Anstey's GSX-R1000, so we only got a glimpse of Archibald at his best in the final race of the week when he, like his team-mate, opted for an Ohlins shock and finished a more competitive fifth in the Senior.

In the Supersport his GSX-R600 blew a head gasket, while his superstocker simply didn't handle from the moment it tankslapped its way down Bray Hill first time round, and Archibald wisely pulled in at the end of the first lap.

9

Bennetts **SUPERBIKE**	6th
PokerStars **SUPERSPORT**	7th
PokerStars **SUPERSTOCK**	DNF
PokerStars **SENIOR**	DNF

RYAN FARQUHAR
MARK JOHNS MOTORS HONDA
HARKER KAWASAKI

Ryan Farquhar's 2006 season was wrecked almost before it started by a wrist injury sustained in one of the Irish road races, so there were question marks about how he would shape up on his return.

But running a Mark Johns Honda in Superbike and Kenny Harker Kawasakis in Supersport and Superstock put him back in the underdog privateer role in which he has thrived in the past.

He didn't get near his previous fastest lap of 125.74mph in practice, achieving 124.3mph on the final Friday. Although he kicked off his race week with a promising sixth place in the Bennetts Superbike race, he broke down on the first lap of the Senior and so we never saw his true potential on the Honda.

He finished seventh in the Supersport race on the ZX-6RR but ran out of fuel in the Superstock race at Bedstead towards the end of the second lap when lying sixth.

10

Bennetts **SUPERBIKE**	DNF
PokerStars **SUPERSPORT**	DNF
PokerStars **SUPERSTOCK**	DNF
PokerStars **SENIOR**	8th

MICHAEL RUTTER
ISILON MSS DISCOVERY
KAWASAKI

This was not the TT return he had hoped for after being away for seven years. Michael Rutter injured his wrist in the Snetterton BSB round the week before TT practice started and he knew then he had damaged his scaphoid.

Not only was he struggling on the bikes at the TT, his team were plagued with engine failures – five of them in all – and he ended up borrowing a spare engine from Ryan Farquhar in Supersport (but went out with an oil leak) and a road engine for the Senior to salvage an eighth place from an otherwise disastrous fortnight.

Rutter remained philosophical and said: "That's the TT for you. I'm so disappointed with the way things have gone but it was great to finish the week with all six laps of the Senior. The TT is fantastic – it's just been a bit unkind to us this year but I want to come back next year and give it a real good go."

NEWCOMERS

Top newcomers breathe fresh life into TT

© Dave Purves

© Double Red

Bennetts **SUPERBIKE**		**10th**
PokerStars **SUPERSPORT**		**8th**
PokerStars **SUPERSTOCK**		**15th**
PokerStars **SENIOR**		**7th**

STEVE PLATER
AIM YAMAHA

© Stephen Davison

Bennetts **SUPERBIKE**		**14th**
PokerStars **SUPERSPORT**		**12th**
PokerStars **SUPERSTOCK**		**18th**
PokerStars **SENIOR**		**DNF**

KEITH AMOR
UEL DUNCAN HONDA

THE WORLD'S TOUGHEST ROAD RACE HAS A BRIGHT FUTURE WITH RIDERS LIKE STEVE PLATER, KEITH AMOR, GARY JOHNSON AND JIMMY MOORE WILLING TO EXPERIENCE ITS CHALLENGES

By Gary Pinchin

This year's crop of top TT newcomers established some bright prospects for the future wellbeing of the event, with Steve Plater, Keith Amor, Gary Johnson and American Jimmy Moore being among the stand-out performers.

Plater, although an experienced Superbike racer, achieved a life-long goal of racing at the TT, and although he would have been satisfied with a top-15 finish, he ended up with seventh in the Senior on the AIM Yamaha after kicking off his week with 10th in the Superbike race.

Plater, already a North West and Macau GP winner, came in for flak for his aggressive riding on the roads, but he adopted a meticulous attitude to learning the TT course, helped by having the vastly experienced Steve Mellor heading up the AIM team and by enlisting the help of former TT winner Mick Grant.

Plater said: "It was a nerve-wracking experience learning the course but I like to be nervous. I was under a lot of criticism coming here but I had Grantie with me. He's been the most influential person in my career, always there for me no matter what. Steve Mellor took the pressure off me too – he's been coming here since 1976 and knows the score."

Plater did 125.80mph on his final lap of the Senior and said: "I took a while to settle. I struggled to get my head around four hours of doing nothing then jumping on the bike and trying to break the lap record. Well not the record, but you know what I mean. But I was really pleased to set my fastest lap of the TT on the final lap of the last race."

Plater enjoyed his TT but, unlike other newcomers, he rarely talked about the adrenalin rush of riding the course. To him it was a job, something to which he had to give 100% commitment in order to learn the course section by section, being analytical in his approach, and get the job done.

But he said: "It was a great experience and I loved the challenge of the course. Whether I'll be back next year depends on what else I'm doing but I definitely want to return and win a TT in the future."

Keith Amor became the only Uel Duncan Honda rider after team-mate Cameron Donald was injured at the North West. Amor had shown his potential on the roads at the 2006 North West and Ulster GPs and acquitted himself well at the TT, with 12th place in the Supersport race his best result of race week.

But he lapped at 124.85mph in the Senior before breaking down: "I was devastated. The clutch went at the start of the third lap and I had no drive. We had made some changes to the bike after the Superbike race and it felt so much better – like a different bike. My out lap was quicker than I'd done all fortnight.

"You'll not be able to keep me away from this. I'll never miss the TT again for all the tea in China. It has been an incredible experience."

Gary Johnson opened his race week with 20th in the Superbike and then placed 16th in the Senior, but his best result came in the Superstock race when he finished 12th after a blistering 122.89mph first lap from a standing start.

Hard-up Johnson couldn't even afford to compete in the Snetterton BSB round just before the TT and used the same Speedfreak Yamaha R1 for all three TT races in which he took part. After his impressive practice times, Johnson was moved from number 82 to 28 in the starting order and went on to finish an impressive 20th in the Superbike race, followed by 12th in the Superstock and 16th in the Senior.

Johnson said: I was well pleased with my result in the Superbike race as I only had the superstocker and to be 12th in the Superstock race was good, especially as I got a silver replica, much more than I expected when I arrived on the Island."

American Jimmy Moore overcame a scare in practice week to post a best result of 15th place in the Supersport race as well as two solid finishes in the Superbike and Superstock races. It would have been three but he was robbed in the Senior when he ran out of fuel.

Moore rode Black Horse Finance Hondas out of the same awning as Ian Lougher and was bowled over by his TT experience.

He said: "The Supersport race was the most fun. My bike was shaking, dancing, jumping around and that was really good fun. I did 121mph on my last lap – that felt really fast. The bike was flawless and I experienced that happy place you need to be to ride here and live to tell about it!

"This place is amazing. I found the place that everyone told me about. I was right there on my own having a great street ride.

"It's like a privilege that someone allows you to use 37.73 miles of these incredible roads to ride. It's so peaceful and so enjoyable. I'll come back if I can, if someone will have me."

© Double Red

Bennetts SUPERBIKE	20th
PokerStars SUPERSPORT	DNS
PokerStars SUPERSTOCK	12th
PokerStars SENIOR	16th

GARY JOHNSON
SPEEDFREAK YAMAHA

© Stephen Davison

Bennetts SUPERBIKE	33rd
PokerStars SUPERSPORT	15th
PokerStars SUPERSTOCK	25th
PokerStars SENIOR	DNF

JIMMY MOORE
BLACK HORSE FINANCE HONDA

Bennetts
PRACTICE WEEK
All the details, and inside stories from the top riders

By Gary Pinchin

© Stephen Davison

SATURDAY MAY 26

The honour of opening Saturday's first, untimed, Bennetts TT practice session fell to Scotland's Keith Amor and Woodhall Spa's Steve Plater, who were followed by the other 12 newcomers in a controlled lap behind the travelling marshal. Sweden's Christer Miinin immediately stopped in the pits before eventually getting in a controlled lap later in the session.

Gary Carswell (Bolliger Kawasaki) and Ian Lougher (Stobart Honda) led out the main practice with spectators also treated to their first sight of the returning Michael Rutter (MSS Discovery Kawasaki). Ian Hutchinson was fastest through the Sulby Straight at an unofficial 186mph.

Later in the session Roy Hanks and Dave Wells led out the sidecars with Klaus Klaffenbock registering the fastest time through Sulby at 145mph.

Conditions were described as fine and dry, although there were reports of light rain on the Mountain between the Ramsey Hairpin and Gooseneck.

A total of 189 machines went through scrutineering: 58 Superbikes, 29 Supersports, 4 Seniors, 34 Superstocks and 64 Sidecars.

MONDAY MAY 28

The riders were hit with an evening of inconsistent weather conditions for the first timed practice session. After a delayed start, the session got underway at 6.30pm. Ryan Farquhar and Ian Lougher were first out with Lougher immediately taking advantage of the dry conditions.

John McGuinness posted the fastest time of the evening on his HM Plant Honda Superbike, with 124.983mph on his second lap out. There were other notable performances from Ian Hutchinson (123.558mph) and Martin Finnegan (122.118mph). Ian Hutchinson also scored the fastest time through the Unisys speed trap at Sulby, recording 192mph.

In the Supersport class, Manxman Conor Cummins recorded the fastest time of the night with a blistering 120.053mph, followed by Chris Palmer and Ian Lougher, while New Zealander Bruce Anstey on the Relentless TAS Suzuki was fastest in the Superstock class at 121.350mph.

In the sidecars, the three remaining newcomers who hadn't completed a lap in Saturday's first practice went out behind Roy Hanks on a controlled lap. After a 10-minute gap, Dave Molyneux/Rick Long and

Klaus Klaffenbock/Christian Parzer set off. In improving conditions, Nick Crowe and Dan Sayle lapped at 113.988mph. There were also notable performances from John Holden/ Andrew Winkle (110.509mph) and Klaffenbock/Parzer (109.483mph).

Marc Ramsbotham was taken to hospital for an X-ray after a spill at Waterworks and Ian Armstrong was reported as having an elbow injury following an incident at Laurel Bank. In the sidecars Andy King/Steve Pooley came off at the 32nd and had arm and hand injuries respectively.

Despite the slightly overcast conditions, spectators flocked to the grandstand and were treated to some stunning laps in this session, most notably from John McGuinness on the HM Plant Honda.

McGuinness posted an unofficial Superbike lap record of 128.492mph, although his time was slower than his outright record in last year's Senior race. Nick Crowe and Dan Sayle continued to set the pace in the sidecars while Bruce Anstey recorded the night's fastest times in the Supersport and Superstock classes.

The session got underway on time at 6.15pm. A new system saw the top 30 riders lined up on Glencrutchery Road on the signal, thereby avoiding a scramble with the rest of the riders. Conditions were described as ideal as McGuinness passed lead-off pair Adrian Archibald and Ryan Farquhar to be first home on the first practice lap and followed this with his unofficial Superbike record time on his second lap.

There were other notable performances from Guy Martin (126.931mph), Ian Lougher (126.346mph) and Ian Hutchinson

(126.269mph). Michael Weynand was able to get four laps on his Bolliger Kawasaki Superbike and posted a time of 121.839mph on the fourth, which left him eighth fastest on the night.

In the sidecars, Dave Molyneux and Rick Long's difficulties continued as they only got as far as Bray Hill before pulling in with mechanical problems. They were forced to watch as their rivals Nick Crowe and Dan Sayle again set the fastest practice time with a 114.208mph lap. Meanwhile Klaus Klaffenbock stopped at Sulby with reported suspension problems.

William Dunlop came off at Waterworks and was described as having minor abrasions.

Alan Chamley and Conor Cummins collided at Laurel Bank. Chamley was initially knocked out while Cummins – who didn't fall – was described as shaken but unhurt. There were also incidents for Roger Maher and Karsten Schmidt at Waterworks and Quarterbridge respectively, but both reported only minor injuries.

A total of 243 machines went through scrutineering: 70 Superbikes, 67 Supersports, 5 Seniors, 33 Superstocks and 68 Sidecars.

Opposite top: Michael Rutter, seen at Creg-ny-Baa, had a turbulent week with the MSS Kawasakis.
© Double Red

Opposite bottom: Marshalling received nothing but praise from riders during the incident-packed practice sessions.
© Double Red

Above: Normally used to working for BSB's rising star Tom Sykes, the Stobbie boys prepare the bike for Ian Lougher.
© Jon Stroud

Left: Ryan Farquhar leaps Rhencullen on his Harker Kawasaki.
© Double Red

PRACTICE WEEK DIARY

Above: Paul Hunt stops to check out the damaged muffler on his Yamaha.
© Double Red

Below: During practice week there was much more work done in the MSS Kawasaki pit than just fitting wheels.
© Double Red

Opposite: John McGuinness flying through Union Mills during practice.
© Double Red

THURSDAY MAY 31

The leading contenders for Saturday's Superbike race continued to make their mark in the Bennetts TT practice sessions as records tumbled in near-perfect conditions. A packed grandstand was bathed in sunshine as blistering times were posted on the track.

John McGuinness dominated the session and confirmed that he would again be the man to beat in the Superbike race. His second lap of 129.084mph was confirmed as a record practice lap time and he was only fractionally outside his outright lap record of 129.45mph set in last year's Senior TT.

After a 15-minute hold-up at the beginning of the session, caused by road traffic accidents outside the course, Adrian Archibald and Michael Rutter were first off, but it was Ian Hutchinson who served notice that he was coming into form with a 127.48mph lap, the fastest first lap. However, McGuinness then replied with his sensational practice lap record.

Guy Martin indicated that McGuinness wouldn't have things all his own way with a fastest lap of 128.166mph while Ian Lougher and Martin Finnegan also featured in the top five times of the night.

Michael Rutter on the MSS Discovery Kawasaki had clutch problems on his first lap but his team rallied round and he was able to finish the session in a creditable seventh with a time of 125.003mph.

Bruce Anstey continued to dominate the Superstock and Supersport classes with the fastest time in both classes on the night. His 125.120mph in Superstock saw him finish ahead of McGuinness (124.295mph), and he also finished top of the pile in the Supersport class with a 122.619mph, which put him ahead of the impressive Guy Martin (122.229mph).

In the sidecars Dave Molyneux was finally able to put his problems behind him and he got valuable track time with a couple of quick laps, including 111.874mph on his second lap, but he was again forced to play second fiddle to the week's leading pairing of Nick Crowe/Dan Sayle, who clocked the night's fastest time – 114.125mph.

James Coward was reported to have lower leg fractures after an accident at Cruickshank's.

A total of 250 machines went through scrutineering: 75 Superbikes, 74 Supersports, 1 Senior, 33 Superstocks and 67 Sidecars.

Final practice for the Isle of Man TT Races sponsored by Bennetts was seriously affected by an incident in the Black Dub section of the course when three riders crashed, resulting in a roadside hedge catching fire.

The session, held in glorious conditions, had only been underway for a matter of minutes when the red flag was brought out at the Grandstand after Michael Weynand crashed heavily, also bringing down Victor Gilmore and Jim Hodson, fortunately without serious injury to the three riders. The Belgian rider, who had been in scintillating form during the week, suffered heavy bruising to his ankles and feet, while Gilmore suffered shoulder injuries; Hodson escaped unscathed.

With the fire brigade called out to deal with the fire and a road sweeper summoned to sweep the track, the session was halted for almost an hour. When it did resume, solo riders were only able to complete one lap, seriously affecting the plans of some who would have been hoping to use the session to make some final, pre-race adjustments.

Riders in the numbers 1–30 bracket were able to complete their lap at a reasonable speed but one man who didn't was Guy Martin, who only managed to get as far as the Hawthorn before coasting to a halt.

When the session re-started, the first pairing away were Martin Finnegan and Michael Rutter, but it was Ian Hutchinson who set the pace with a fine lap of 127.049mph, followed by Bruce Anstey at 126.017mph and Ryan Farquhar at 124.317mph. Martin Finnegan (124.206mph), Adrian Archibald (124.201mph) and Michael Rutter (124.114mph) completed the top six.

Practice pace-setter John McGuinness opted to take out his Supersport machine and the move paid dividends as he posted the best 600cc lap of the night at 122.423mph. He was followed by Shaun Harris, who recorded his first 120mph lap of the week at 120.560mph, and Conor Cummins, who posted a lap of 118.500mph.

In the Superstock Hutchinson again set the pace with a speed of 125.570mph. Finnegan, who looked to be a serious contender for honours on his MV Agusta, was again high on the leaderboard at 124.325mph, closely followed by

Archibald at 123.963mph. James McBride, who had been posting some impressive times throughout the week, lapped at 121.904mph ahead of Paul Hunt (121.158mph) and Nigel Beattie (121.094mph). Meanwhile, Gary Johnson almost joined his fellow Lincolnshire newcomer Steve Plater in lapping at more than 120mph with an excellent speed of 119.810mph.

The sidecars managed to get in two laps in their shortened session but Dave Molyneux and Rick Long finally showed something like their usual form and a lap of 112.778mph not only placed them top of the night's session but also restored some pre-race confidence.

John Holden and Andrew Winkle continued their fine form with a lap of 111.235mph, their best ever, while Steve Norbury and Scott Parnell also got themselves back into contention with a lap of 110.191mph. Allan Schofield and Peter Founds, who had been in the top five all week, recorded their first ever 110mph lap with a speed of 110.167mph. Greg Lambert and Gary Partridge, another pairing to suffer reliability problems during the course of the week, put in a fine performance with a lap of 108.506mph.

Diary source: Simon Crellin, TT Press Officer

JOHN McGUINNESS
HM PLANT HONDA
PADGETTS HONDA

Best laps

Bennetts
SUPERBIKE 1st, 129.084mph, Thursday
PokerStars
SUPERSTOCK 2nd, 122.423mph, Thursday
PokerStars
SUPERSPORT 4th, 124.295mph, Thursday

Above: On only the Tuesday of practice week John McGuinness said his Superbike – updated from 2006 with new yokes and slightly uprated engine and ECU – was ready to race.
© Double Red

Opposite: McGuinness should have felt comfortable on the Padgetts Honda, having had half a season racing the same bike in British Supersport prior to the TT.
© Double Red

John McGuinness predictably set the pace during practice week. He stunned everyone with a 128.49mph lap on Tuesday, when most other riders were still setting up their bikes, and clocked a stunning 129.08mph on Thursday, a fraction off his own 129.45mph lap record set in last year's Senior race.

Incredibly, though, McGuinness said that Thursday's track conditions were far from ideal and that he could barely see where he was going on the second lap!

"The first lap on Thursday was horrendous," he said. "I was leading on the road by the time I got on to the Cronk-y-Voddy and I was the fly sweeper. I didn't touch my tear-offs all the way to the Mountain because I figured there would be no flies up there. But when I finally got there and pulled, both tear-offs came off in one go – so by the time I got to the Mountain the second time around, there wasn't a right lot I could see."

Rain on Wednesday had washed dirt from the earth banks on to the road and that meant that track conditions were far from ideal. "The lap times were good considering the road conditions," continued McGuinness. "All the shit from the side of the road had dried out and turned to dust on Thursday so there were places where there was no grip. I couldn't get on the gas early in places; considering that, it was a good lap and not at all scrappy."

McGuinness has been the man to beat at the TT since 2003 but even he admits he has struggled in one particular area on the 37.73-mile course.

"I've always struggled over the Mountain but I felt really good over there on Thursday. Martin Finnegan was with me all the way to Ramsey but I dropped him over the Mountain. I couldn't see him at all when I looked back and that made me feel good."

McGuinness, though, denied that he had been deliberately forcing the pace through practice week to demoralise his rivals.

"I've not been thinking like that at all," he said. "It's important for your self-confidence to have a good go and maybe that's how I've always worked in the past – wanting a confidence-boosting lap early in practice week."

Part of the equation had to be running virtually the same superbike as 2006 – while team-mate Ian Hutchinson was given the tricked-out HRC factory-supported machine that Leon Camier races in BSB in Bike Animal colours.

McGuinness's Fireblade chassis was identical to the bike he raced in last year's North West 200, TT and Ulster GP apart from new HRC kit yokes to stiffen up the front end ("last year's yokes were too flexy") while the engine had been upgraded for more power with a new ECU to suit.

"The thing that pissed me off most," said McGuinness, "was not even being offered Camier's factory bike. I could probably have got a factory bike if I'd stamped my feet but I know what they can be like to set up. But I've been in that position before of having a super-trick bike and they can be a handful around here.

"Sometimes it's better to go with something more simple. Last year, with this same bike, I got pole in the North West 200. I won superbike TTs and set a new lap record. I qualified pole at last year's Ulster and set the first 130mph lap there. At the North West this year I got my first superbike race win there.

"My superbike was ready to race on Tuesday, if I'm honest. It feels part of me, like a big armchair. I can settle back and hustle it around."

And McGuinness didn't even have a tyre advantage this year with all the leading Dunlop runners on the same rubber. "Last year I had specially built stuff," he said, "but now nearly everyone has made the switch to Dunlops and they've made a batch of TT-spec tyres which are similar to the ones Lavilla used at Thruxton – we tested them at Castle Combe. They have good grip and stability, which is so important at the Isle of Man."

McGuinness was second quickest on his Supersport bike, the same Padgetts Honda CBR600 that he had been racing all year in British Supersport. Not surprisingly, he wasn't forced to make any major alterations and team boss Clive Padgett remarked: "When I asked John if he needed any changes to the bike he said, 'could you scuff up the seat a little for me?'. If that's all he wanted, I knew there couldn't be too much wrong with the bike!"

In Superstock, too, McGuinness was on the pace, setting fourth quickest time on a bike that everyone thought wouldn't be competitive at the TT in the more standard format demanded by the regulations.

On the Friday night McGuinness was the toast of a special Honda barbeque at the HM Plant team hospitality near the paddock. He told the assembled guests and media: "Isn't it wonderful to be here with the Island so packed? It proves there's still worth in the TT. Look at the TT now: we've got big articulated trucks, huge teams, top-class hospitality. Ten years ago we were all in transit vans and smelly tents. How times have changed."

Privately, McGuinness spoke of experiencing strange things during practice week that actually spooked him. He said: "Saturday and Monday were some of the weirdest light I've experienced at the TT. I can't even begin to describe it except that I was riding along thinking how surreal it was out there.

"Then we had drizzle. At 180mph you'd think the water would fly off the screen but it was like the water globules had been greased and they just stuck to the screen in blobs.

"It was like they were teasing me. Another little weird aspect of the TT put there to throw me...

"Then Thursday we had flies. We had no flies all week but suddenly it was fly-tastic. You never know what the TT is going to throw at you but you can guarantee it will always be something to make you stop and think..."

"I'VE ALWAYS STRUGGLED OVER THE MOUNTAIN BUT I FELT REALLY GOOD OVER THERE ON THURSDAY. MARTIN FINNEGAN WAS WITH ME ALL THE WAY TO RAMSEY BUT I DROPPED HIM OVER THE MOUNTAIN. I COULDN'T SEE HIM AT ALL WHEN I LOOKED BACK AND THAT MADE ME FEEL GOOD."

NEW RANGE OF
FIREPLACES
NOW ON SHOW AT
CLASSIC MOULDINGS
Tel: 853020

IAN HUTCHINSON
HM PLANT HONDA

Best laps

Bennetts
SUPERBIKE 4th, 127.547, Thursday
PokerStars
SUPERSTOCK 12th, 119.975mph, Thursday
PokerStars
SUPERSPORT 1st, 125.570mph, Friday

Ian Hutchinson's HM Plant Honda headed the Superstock leaderboard with his 125.57mph lap on Friday evening to topple the acknowledged king of the class Bruce Anstey.

Anstey had done 125mph laps on Tuesday and Thursday on his Relentless Suzuki GSX-R1000 and everyone expected the Suzukis and even the Yamahas to have the upper hand over the Honda Fireblades. The Blades historically lack engine performance both on the short circuits and on the roads, but at least on the roads their sweet-handling chassis come into their own.

Though he wasn't about to admit it, Hutchinson went to the TT still struggling with the shoulder injury he sustained at Oulton Park in the fourth round of the British Supersport series three weeks earlier. It badly affected him at the North West 200 and he wasn't in perfect shape when he arrived on the Island.

So Hutchinson shocked everyone with his fast time, especially as it was only his third lap all week on the Fireblade. He said: "I only rode it for the first time on Thursday and did 122mph, but it was way too soft so all we've done is fit some stiffer springs – and it's mega." He also lapped at over 127mph on Leon Camier's British Superbike Bike Animal Honda (rebranded in HM Plant livery for the TT) and said it had gone really well for him.

Below: Ian Hutchinson was fast on the Superbike even though he was still suffering from a shoulder injury sustained in a British Supersport round.
© Stephen Davison

"After the way things went at the North West, with my shoulder not being right and me taking a lot of time to get comfortable on the bike, I'd expected it would take all week to get the superbike right. But here my shoulder's OK and we've just been chipping away, biding our time.

"My first lap on Thursday was superb but on the second lap I caught [Martin] Finnegan's Klaffi Honda and he kept outbraking me so I screwed up the lap. I don't see the point in that last-minute stuff in practice. I'd pulled ten seconds on him and he outbrakes me, to – what? – find one-tenth in Ramsey? What's that all about?

"My lap on Thursday [when Hutchinson topped the time sheets] was a mega-steady lap so I was surprised to do 127mph. There was lots of traffic, I got a rain flag at Greeba and two other yellows. The track was dusty too so there wasn't a lot of grip."

Crew chief was Tom Larsen (Leon Camier's right-hand man in BSB), who has only two TTs under his belt – with Ian Lougher in 2005 and Iain Duffus in 1998. Larsen said that Hutchinson started the week with a really soft suspension set-up but had come all the way round to virtually the same stiff settings as in BSB. He also revealed that Hutchinson was using the same anti-spin system as Camier.

"We've changed the suspension valving from what we learned from the Castle Combe test earlier in the year and at the North West races," said Larsen, "and now it's just about pre-load and damping clickers. We've calmed any wheelie problems as much as we can around here with engine and chassis changes but you can only go so far with chassis changes without compromising something else."

Hutchinson's Supersport best was 119.9mph on Tuesday and Thursday – 2.7mph down on Anstey's pace-setting time. It was perhaps surprising that the bike with which he's most familiar, running it every week in British Supersport, was his least competitive, but Hutchy explained: "I'm happy with the 600. I had a good lap on it on Thursday. It was a short lap so they add time to give you a lap speed. They had me down for 119.9mph but it was worth more than that."

"MY FIRST LAP ON THURSDAY WAS SUPERB BUT ON THE SECOND LAP I CAUGHT [MARTIN] FINNEGAN'S KLAFFI HONDA AND HE KEPT OUTBRAKING ME SO I SCREWED UP THE LAP..."

KEITH AMOR

UEL DUNCAN HONDA

Best laps

Bennetts
SUPERBIKE 40th, 117.647mph, Thursday
PokerStars
SUPERSTOCK 23rd, 117.508mph, Thursday
PokerStars
SUPERSPORT 33rd, 117.458mph, Friday

"I RECKON I'VE GOT THREE CORNERS RIGHT, SO THAT'S 250 TO GO."

Keith Amor, a newcomer to the Island, quickly fell under the spell of the TT course. The Scottish rider came to the fore in last year's North West 200 when he qualified his private Suzuki on the front row, and finished sixth in the Superstock race. Later in the season he won a race at the Ulster Grand Prix and he was also the fastest-ever newcomer on the Dundrod course.

This year was Amor's TT debut with the experienced Uel Duncan team, and he became the team's sole rider on the Island after lead rider Cameron Donald smashed his collarbone at the North West.

"It's been a hectic week," Amor said. "On Monday I did four laps on the superstocker but it wasn't handling. Tuesday, I did two laps on the superstocker and one lap on the 600. Second lap on the 600 the rear brake seized up at Ballacraine, and the clutch went on the superbike – it was slipping the entire lap. Then my 600 blew up and sent a con-rod through the front of the motor. But I reckon I'm about 80 per cent there, knowing my way round – and I've been round with Uel and Cameron.

"I'm enjoying it so much. It's phenomenal. It's far more than I expected. I was speechless on Saturday night after my first lap. The guys asked me what I thought and I just shook my head and smiled. It's breathtaking, man!

"It can't be legal – it just doesn't seem right! I've never experienced anything like it. It's just so intense. It's like skydiving without the fear. At Bray Hill I hold my breath – all the way. I love it. There's nothing I'd rather do – it's that exhilarating.

"I reckon I've got three corners right, so that's 250 to go. John [McGuinness] said it's best to stay in the middle of the road and when it starts to flow I'll be fine. I concentrated on the bottom here to Ramsey today [Thursday of practice week]. From Ginger Hall to Ramsey it's important to get my road position right. Up to now I've been too much power, too much brakes – but now I'm smoothing it out!"

Amor saw the other side of the TT when he was the first on the scene of the three-rider crash at the Black Dub early in Friday evening practice, involving Belgian rider Michael Weynand, Ballymoney's Victor Gilmore and Jim Hodson from Wigan.

According to eye-witness reports, Weynand's Bolliger Kawasaki hit the wall and the tank became detached from the bike, slid along the road and then split open on impact with a wall, igniting the fuel which in turn set fire to vegetation. Practice was halted at 18.50 while a local fire tender was despatched to deal with the blaze and a road sweeper to clear all the debris, and didn't resume for an hour.

"I'd followed the Kawasaki guy but backed off a bit just before the Glen Helen section," said Amor, who arrived at the crash site as the incident happened. "Then I saw marshals running and the yellows out just as I arrived on the corner. I braked as hard as I could and there was debris everywhere. I saw two guys on the track on the right and the Kawasaki guy on the left, and the ivy and trees were already burning. I stopped the other side of the accident because it was obvious they'd red-flag it."

Left: Newcomer's orange bib or not, Keith Amor settled in quickly to the demands of the TT and seemed to thoroughly enjoy himself.
© **Double Red**

GUY MARTIN
HYDREX HONDA

Best laps

Bennetts
SUPERBIKE 2nd, 128.166, Thursday
PokerStars
SUPERSTOCK 7th, 122.380mph, Thursday
PokerStars
SUPERSPORT 3rd, 122.228mph, Thursday

Guy Martin's practice week was eventful. He crashed in Saturday's untimed practice session at Governor's Bridge when he discovered there was too little turning circle with the superbike-spec lockstops on his Hydrex Honda superbike. "There wasn't enough lock," he said, "so I took a dab, but the camber there falls away and I just toppled over."

On Monday night his superstock stopped near Ramsey so he settled down to catch forty winks.

"We ran a different ECU and a quickshifter on the superstocker for the first time on Monday because the FIM rules allow us and the original TT rules didn't. The bike stopped so I kept my ear plugs in, went as far away from the track as possible and caught up on some kip."

On Tuesday his 600 pressurised so much, due to a kinked breather, that it blew the pipe off and sprayed oil over Steve Plater, who was following, before Martin pulled off the course at the Black Dub.

TT newcomer Plater explained: "I was following Martin and could smell oil. I looked down to check my boots and they were okay. Then I thought, 'it's getting misty'. Then I realised, 'shit, it's Martin's bike'. I backed right off and next moment there was a trail of oil on the road, but luckily he pulled up."

Then on Friday Martin's superbike holed a radiator. He said: "We'd changed the shim stacks in the forks because we were struggling over a couple of sections such as the end of the Cronk-y-Voddy and the 13th Milestone. It was lock-to-lock there. But I never got a chance to try it fully in the final practice. But even going down Bray Hill the first time it felt loads better – and it still turns well which is a bonus. The session was stopped by that crash at Glen Helen but even though I raced back, I missed the single lap by five minutes, which was a bit annoying. Still, better that it happens now than in the race."

Martin's superbike had been built with a fresh approach for the TT. For BSB the team's engines, at number one rider Karl Harris's request, have been built with kit pistons and rods by private tuner Chris Mehew to give a smooth spread of power, but for the TT the spec was very different.

The team ditched the complicated traction control system for the Mountain course, claiming that the rear wheel is off the ground so much over the bumps that's it's simply a waste of time trying to use such electronic controls.

Hydrex were leaving nothing to chance, flying in suspension specialist Javier Muñoz from Spain. Formerly with Showa, he now runs a company called Pro-Shock and worked with the team for the Albacete pre-season test, Brands and Oulton BSB races, plus the North West.

Team boss Shaun Muir explained: "Guy's superbike engines – we have one for practice and one for the race – have been built really safe, but we've gone for a bigger hit of power. It's got bigger exhaust ports, titanium rods, Pistal pistons and rings, STM clutch and kit cams."

Martin was happy enough despite the niggling problems and said: "The bikes are mint – very little different to what I've run in BSB. I can't run a race seat, it's not comfy, so we've changed that. The motor is fast. Mehew – we wanted him to build us something fast – so we've gone up on cam lift and bigger ports. It's mint off the bottom too – though a little harder to ride. But you can get that back with Motec.

"Hutchinson set off in front of me for practice and I caught him no problem, so that was good. Tuesday night I got stuck behind him from Ginger Hall to Ramsey. There's just one line through there, fast and flowing, and I was having to roll it off – and it looked like he was pushing hard.

"[Phillip] McCallen once told me that he'd go up to rivals just before the race, tap them on the helmet and say, 'if you get in my way I'm going to knock you off'. They thought he was joking, but he kept deadpan and then they'd wonder if he was saying it for real. I think I'll try that on race day!

"McGuinness, say what you like about him, he's fast. Been fast all practice, hasn't he? I thought Rutter would be the man but I've followed him a couple of times and he looks lost. He's thrupenny-bitting it and held me up at the end of the first lap on Friday!"

Bruce Anstey set the Superstock pace and Martin said of this rival: "I passed him on the superbike on Saturday and Monday. His bike doesn't handle. But he's the man in superstock though.

"My superstocker is bad. We can't get it to handle at all. It could be that we run the same tyre on supersport and superstock, but we run a 5.5-inch rim on the supersport and 6-inch on the superstocker. That changes the profile of the tyres and it's the only thing can think of. That makes the difference.

"Last year we had the same problem with the stocker because we concentrated so much time on getting the superbike right. I can ride the stocker but not for four laps. It's so physically demanding that I'm knackered."

Martin appeared to struggle at the North West on his Supersport CBR600RR but it wasn't known at the time that he had a hole from a stone in the top of the radiator in the second race. The temperature went up to 105 degrees C and the electronics knocked power right off it to try and save the engine from overheating.

But at the TT Martin was happy and had only one comment: "My supersport bike is mint!"

Opposite: Guy Martin encountered a number of problems with his Hydrex Honda during practice week, including a minor tumble, a kinked breather pipe, a holed radiator and poor handling – but as always he kept smiling.
© Stephen Davison

Above: Guy Martin on his mint Supersport bike.
© Double Red

IAN LOUGHER
STOBART HONDA
BLACK HORSE FINANCE HONDA

Best laps

Bennetts
SUPERBIKE 3rd, 128.140mph, Thursday
PokerStars
SUPERSTOCK 17th, 120.232mph, Friday
PokerStars
SUPERSPORT 5th, 120.962mph, Thursday

Above: Ian Lougher clocked over 128mph on the Stobart Honda to put him right in the frame as one of the favourites for the two Superbike events.

© Stephen Davison

Opposite: The Hondas were hit harder than most by the last-minute introduction of FIM-spec Superstock rules allowing quickshifters and different ECUs – and Ian Lougher wasn't happy.

© Stephen Davison

Ian Lougher was one of three riders to lap at over 128mph on Thursday in Superbike practice, continuing the blistering pace he showed in 2006 when he finished second and fourth in the two superbike races and lapped at 128.12mph.

In 2007 the 43-year-old veteran, with seven TT wins and 25 TT podiums to his credit, was even faster on what was virtually a BSB-spec Stobart Honda. Lougher's bike was built specially for the roads but featured the same suspension spec – KR swing-arm and linkage, Ohlins gas forks and shock – that Shane Byrne and Tom Sykes run in BSB.

The engine was very similar spec too, but with HRC kit pistons rather than the super-trick, specially made, lightweight ones used in BSB. It also featured HRC kit electronics rather than the more complex Magneti Marelli systems used in BSB, but only because there's no call for traction control on the bumpy TT course.

Chief technician Phil Borley said: "It's not so much about acceleration at the TT whereas it is in BSB. So we're less worried about the amount of reciprocating mass in the TT. Instead of using special lightweight pistons as in BSB, this engine has kit pistons, which are heavier. We're not looking for tenths of a second, we're looking for smooth power delivery."

The bike also had a different fuel tank and a more conventional airbox than used in BSB, and it was also fitted with a starter motor, the internal gears to drive it helping in the overall engine mass package.

Lougher said: "The latest Ohlins forks are that little bit more supple than the conventional forks I used last year, and a smaller diameter, so there's a bit more flex to give me more feel. We've also got an Ohlins shock this year after starting pre-season testing in Spain with a Showa unit. We were still making changes at the end of the week. One click makes such a huge difference these days and the really amazing thing is that we're almost identical on set-up to the short-circuit bikes at the TT now.

"This is also my first year on Dunlops and it seems the suspension set-up is therefore a bit more critical. But ultimately I've more grip now. The fronts are amazing.

"This engine is a lot easier to use. It's a lot smoother but still fast enough. It's showing 206bhp on the dyno! Last year's was a bit fierce getting on the gas and I was always fighting the front end – it came up everywhere.

"We've no fancy electronics. I believe they're too complex for here, too many things to go wrong. But the other issue is that there's never enough time at the TT to experiment with stuff like that.

"But the bike is good. I went as fast on Tuesday as I did in the first race last year, and then did 128mph on Thursday!"

Lougher was running his own Supersport and Superstock bikes in Black Horse livery but was struggling with the CBR600, just as he had earlier in the year when he took in the Brands Hatch and Thruxton BSB races.

He said: "We initially had the same fork problems that we had then, but we're getting there. We must be. I was third quickest on Tuesday, from a standing start.

"We used some K-Tech 20mm fork cartridges – not the 25mm ones used in Supersport though. They make it stiffer at the top end of the stroke whereas the 20mm internals soak up the bumps better, though they're not quite so good on the brakes as the 25mm ones."

Lougher, like a lot of competitors, was dismayed that the TT regulations for Superstock changed at the last minute to allow quickshifters and different ECUs, as per the FIM regulations.

He said: "When the TT rules first came out the FIM hadn't released theirs, and BSB rules don't allow quickshifters or ignition boxes. So that's how we built our bike. Then the FIM rules came out. The Hondas don't really gain anything with extra revs – certainly not like the Suzukis and Yamahas do. But the good thing about the Honda, especially here, is the handling. Jimmy [Moore, Lougher's American team-mate for the TT] loves it compared to his other bikes. He finds it much easier to ride.

"I didn't really get enough time on the bike in practice because I was concentrating on the superbike. But we know we'll struggle on it anyway [against the Suzukis and Finnegan's MV Agusta] even though it handles well and is deceptively fast."

A lot was made of John Crellin hitting a seagull on the first night of practice but Lougher had a better tale. He hit two pigeons and even knew the species!

He said: "I hit them at Bishopscourt on the first night and they were Barbary Doves. They always travel in pairs. I came on them just after Rhencullen, at the next fast left. I was the first on the road and caught one of them with my arm. It smashed the screen and fairing."

So how did Lougher know they were Barbary Doves? "I know a thing or two about birds – the ones with feathers. My dad was into them and I showed Australian Finches when I when I was about ten years old!"

"WE'VE NO FANCY ELECTRONICS. I BELIEVE THEY'RE TOO COMPLEX FOR HERE, TOO MANY THINGS TO GO WRONG…"

JIMMY MOORE
BLACK HORSE FINANCE HONDA

Best laps

Bennetts
SUPERBIKE 50th, 116.406mph, Thursday
PokerStars
SUPERSTOCK 38th, 116.406mph, Thursday
PokerStars
SUPERSPORT 41st, 114.645mph, Thursday

Two-time AMA Superstock Champion Jimmy Moore was almost in shock after Tuesday practice following a big moment on the Mountain during practice on his Black Horse Finance Honda CBR600RR.

TT rookie Moore had learned the basics of the course by playing video games and watching DVDs. He got his first look at the course over the winter when team boss Ian Lougher took him for some laps by car.

But after his scare he said of the course: "It's absolutely scary. Scary, scary, scary and more scary. I feel like the racer in me wants to go faster and faster all the time, but there's no room for error. There's a delicate balance of learning. On short circuits you learn by overdoing it. Here you can't do that.

"My big scare on the Mountain on Tuesday was only my second lap on the 600. At the end of the Mountain Mile I kept the power on too long. It was windy, Ian reckons, but I basically ran out of pavement. I was topped out in sixth and the road was turning the wrong

way. I've no idea how close I was to running off the track. But I stayed on it, brushed off the incident and carried on like nothing ever went wrong."

Moore came to the 2007 TT after talking to fellow American Mark Miller, who did the race for the first time in 2006.

"It just sounded so cool," Moore said. "Why do it? Why do people go to the moon? Because it's there. Because I grew up riding street bikes and only took up racing to take my aggression off the street. This race lets me take that aggression back to the street!"

Moore won his two Superstock titles in 2001/02 but then suffered a 175mph crash at Brainerd, Minnesota. It broke almost every bone in the left side of his body. "There are trees at the end of the run-off which normally you would never reach. But the grass run-off was wet and I never slowed at all. I hit one of the trees in my side and broke my arm, all my ribs down one side, my hip, fractured some vertebrae, collapsed a lung and

ruptured my spleen. It took a year and half before I could race again."

After those kind of injuries and seeing the unyeilding Manx walls, you could imagine that Moore might be more than a little concerned at the prospect of racing on the Island. But he said: "Man, if that Brainerd crash didn't put me off, nothing's going to. I've always wanted to race here. Even when I was a kid I watched re-runs of the TT. What makes the place so unique has never left my mind. I've got to do this."

Later during that same lap with the scare on the 600, Moore made another error and went straight on at Signpost. He said: "Yeah, I made a mistake there too, but I still did close to 112mph. I reckon that excursion lost me 30secs. I could have been in the region of 115mph."

Moore ended practice with respectable 117mph laps and added: "Every time I went out I learned, but I'm more aggressive than I should be.

"You don't make mistakes twice here. For example between Gooseneck and Joey's there are two lefts. Originally I was slowing too much and had no drive to the second left.

"I watched Ian's video to see what he does. Second left is steep uphill. So once you're committed to the first corner you can get on the throttle and now I'm screaming it up to Joey's.

"I kept picking areas where I was weak and tried to figure out what I was doing wrong, but my brush with mortality reminded me not to make those mistakes.

"I'm having a good time but Tuesday was freaky. It was good that I brushed it off and got it together. I'm having a good time but have to remember what's important. I'm not here to go fast. I need to be able to talk about it when we're done.

"My mother is here and we were talking one night and I told her, 'you know, if I make one mistake here I may not be coming home with you'. It was harsh but I had to be honest with her. That's how it is here."

But Moore reckoned he wasn't chasing the course and riding aggressively like he would on a short circuit, but riding more in a streetbike style

"The way I'm riding the TT course is like chasing your friends on a Sunday morning ride," he concluded. "I'm sat in the middle of the road, streetbiking it. Forget the whole knee-out thing. That's overdoing it. Like you're threading the eye down Bray Hill. One thing goes wrong there and you're just a stain…"

Left: TT rookie Jimmy Moore reckoned he was 'streetbiking' it out on the TT course with his Black Horse Finance Hondas.
© **Double Red**

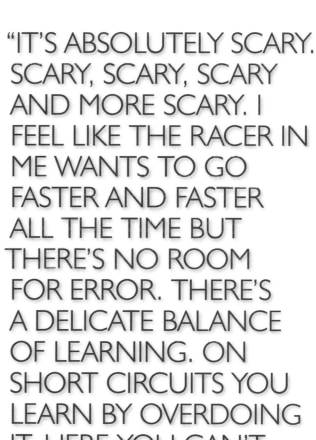

"IT'S ABSOLUTELY SCARY. SCARY, SCARY, SCARY AND MORE SCARY. I FEEL LIKE THE RACER IN ME WANTS TO GO FASTER AND FASTER ALL THE TIME BUT THERE'S NO ROOM FOR ERROR. THERE'S A DELICATE BALANCE OF LEARNING. ON SHORT CIRCUITS YOU LEARN BY OVERDOING IT. HERE YOU CAN'T DO THAT."

MARTIN FINNEGAN
ALPHA BOILERS KLAFFI HONDA
ALPHA BOILERS MV AGUSTA

Best laps

Bennetts
SUPERBIKE 5th, 127.2092mph, Thursday
PokerStars
SUPERSTOCK 3rd, 124.325mph, Friday
PokerStars
SUPERSPORT 15th, 119.731mph, Thursday

After his disappointing 2006 season, Martin Finnegan looked totally rejuvenated as he set third quickest time on the MV Agusta in Superstock practice and fifth quickest time in Superbike on the Klaffi Honda.

Finnegan's MV Agusta was backed by the factory, and three of their top men – Federico Toti (team manager), Giorgio Gattoni (chief race mechanic) and Angelo Merlini (head of the engine department) – were flown in to supervise the exercise. Merlini joined Cagiva in 1989 and worked on the 500 GP project with Randy Mamola, Eddie Lawson and John Kocinski, as well as with Garelli when Luca Cadalora and Ezio Gianola were the riders.

Finnegan was delighted with the MV Agusta R312 and said: "There's no comparison with a Japanese four-cylinder bike. It requires a different riding style though, because the chassis is like a Ducati – it's so positive. It turns easy, holds a line. It's not at all soft and squirmy like a Japanese bike.

"The power delivery is good but probably not as smooth as a Japanese bike – but that's only mapping stuff. It's a bit harsh down low. Until the Italians got here we made changes after talking to them by 'phone and e-mail. We've tested, but of course not using big gears and that changes things – unlike here there's not a corner below 5,000rpm on the short circuits we tested at."

Toti was overawed by the whole TT experience. He said: "Coming here it's like trying to watch a new world! For us this is so different. We've learned one thing: the TT is completely crazy! I love the TT now I can see it first-hand so it's good to be able to support a rider here and help Martin in his adventures. I saw Bray Hill for the first time on Tuesday and it's just impossible. It's amazing."

The TT version of the MV differed very little from the bikes the factory race in European Superstock. The suspension was softer and the balance of the bike was altered to take weight off the front.

"The bike is more level here," said Toti, "because there's a lot more fast, flowing bends and not so much heavy braking or corners where you throw the bike on its side. This is so different for us. You know, places like Mugello or Monza, even though they are fast tracks, have only one or two very high-speed corners. Here, most of the corners are very high-speed."

The engine, as per Superstock rules, was stock but the factory fitted an Arrow exhaust and Power Commander.

"The bike has a lot of power in high rpm," Toti added, "but we also have a lot of good torque all through the curve. Top speed is good too. We were second fastest through the speed trap. We knew we would be because of the speeds we've achieved at places like Monza and Mugello."

Finnegan's Klaffi Honda, however, was a very different machine from his 2006 bike and he looked very competitive with his 127.20mph lap on Thursday.

"The Klaffi Honda was a pig last year," said Finnegan.

It wheelied everywhere. The bike was based on the thing Alex Barros raced in WSB but was too harsh for the Mountain course.

"Now we've gone in a different direction. Klaffi built the bike again but we told them what we needed. I've got Bill Simpson and K-Tech working on suspension. They've altered the shimming in the forks and we've got Ohlins internals in stock Fireblade forks – last year we ran Showa stuff.

"I've also gone for 305mm discs instead of 320mm. It makes the bike easier to turn and really there are no hard braking places here to worry about.

"Chris Mehew has done the engine. It has a much smoother power delivery. He's done that with different camshafts but it has a similar compression ratio to last year. Gearbox is HRC, same as last year, but with different ratios. We have an STM slipper clutch – it makes the job that bit easier.

"The electronics are kit HRC. There's not that much difference in the mapping – just enough to calm the wheelies – but we've done that with suspension as well as engine characteristics. Last year I wrestled the bike all the time. Now it's easier to ride and the potential is there."

Opposite: Martin Finnegan's new Klaffi Honda Superbike was much more forgiving than the 'pig' he had to ride the previous year.
© Stephen Davison

Below: The TT experience was a whole new world for the MV Agusta staff.
© Double Red

"THERE'S NO COMPARISON WITH A JAPANESE FOUR-CYLINDER BIKE. IT REQUIRES A DIFFERENT RIDING STYLE THOUGH, BECAUSE THE CHASSIS IS LIKE A DUCATI – IT'S SO POSITIVE. IT TURNS EASY, HOLDS A LINE. IT'S NOT AT ALL SOFT AND SQUIRMY LIKE A JAPANESE BIKE."

MICHAEL RUTTER
ISILON MSS DISCOVERY KAWASAKI

Best laps

Bennetts
SUPERBIKE 7th, 125.003mph, Thursday
PokerStars
SUPERSPORT 8th, 120.434mph, Thursday

Below: Michael Rutter knew where he was going but just needed more laps to get into the sort of rhythm that's vital for TT speed.

© Stephen Davison

"ON MY FIRST LAP I GOT TO GINGER HALL AND THOUGHT, 'THIS IS IT THEN' AND GRITTED MY TEETH."

There was no fairy-tale return to the TT for Michael Rutter during practice week. After seven years away from the event, the harsh realities of racing around the 37.73-mile Mountain course came flooding back.

His Superbike blew up on Monday in the very first practice session. A lambda sensor plug fell out of the left-side exhaust header on Tuesday. The clutch started slipping virtually from the start of his first lap on Thursday. And then the bike, with a rebuilt engine, mysteriously went on to three cylinders just before the off on Friday after it had run perfectly well hours earlier at Jurby airfield, where the team went to bed in tyres and brakes.

Even so, Rutter's best Superbike lap of the week was 125.00mph on Thursday, eclipsing his previous personal best of 123.95mph in 2000 – the last time he raced on the Island.

His 600, the same one Stuart Easton normally races in British Supersport, ran like clockwork throughout practice and Rutter posted a very healthy 120.43mph lap on Thursday.

Rutter joked: "The Superbike is coming on and I'm hoping for a top-six finish, though the way things have gone in practice a finish will be good!

"Seriously, though, we've had a few problems but that happens at the TT. The Superbike feels good now and the Supersport bike is just great."

Rutter admitted he needed more time on the bike to get fully back into the rhythm of riding the TT course again.

"It's weird. I know where I'm going but to go fast I need a lot of laps to get confident," he explained. "Initially, I think it was worse than being a newcomer. If you're new, you've no idea what's around the next corner. I know what's coming if I screw up.

"Tuesday, when I was out on the 600, was the first time I started to do everything automatically – which is what you need to do here. But sit up on a 600 and you've lost all your speed here. The amazing thing is that, in terms of speed, the 600s are now like the Superbikes were when I last rode here.

"The bikes and the tyres have improved so much that the handling is so much better now. Where we used to spend all week trying to get the bikes going straight, now we can take them out of the truck after a BSB race and they go straight as an arrow. I set off down Bray Hill and it was perfect.

"On my first lap I got to Ginger Hall and thought, 'this is it then' and gritted my teeth. The run from there to Ramsey is the bumpiest and it used to be that the bikes were lock-to-lock through there. I held it flat and the bike went straight as a die.

"In fact I thought maybe I'd run through there too slowly and was expecting it to get ugly on my second lap, but it was perfect again. The track hasn't changed there, so it must be purely down to the bikes improving."

100 Racing Years : 110% Racing Effort

The Isle of Man TT is the most demanding road race event in the world. Making the task that little bit easier are the sponsors and numerous team supporters. Our sincere thanks to you all.

WWW.MSSDISCOVERYRACING.COM

Kawasaki
Let the good times roll.

WWW.KAWASAKI.CO.UK

BRUCE ANSTEY
RELENTLESS SUZUKI by TAS

Best laps

Bennetts
SUPERBIKE 6th, 126.461mph, Thursday
PokerStars
SUPERSTOCK 2nd, 125.338mph, Tuesday
PokerStars
SUPERSPORT 1st, 122.620mph, Tuesday

Below: Bruce Anstey had a lot of suspension problems with his Superbike and, as a last resort, fitted the shock out of his superstocker to try to cure it.

© Stephen Davison

"WE WEREN'T FAR OFF WITH THE SUPERBIKE AT THE NORTH WEST. THE MOTOR IS STRONG, IT'S THE FASTEST THING OUT THERE."

Kiwi Bruce Anstey looked fiercely competitive on his TAS Relentless Suzukis in the Supersport and Superstock classes all through practice despite going down with the 'flu mid-week, but he struggled to get his Superbike sorted.

He topped the Supersport leaderboard with his 122.61mph lap on Thursday, although John McGuinness came close on Friday with a 122.42mph lap on the Padgetts Honda. Anstey, the king of the Superstock class on the roads, having won the last three TT races with the TAS crew, clocked over 125mph on his GSX-R1000 on Tuesday and Thursday, but his 125.33mph best was beaten by HM Plant Honda's Ian Hutchinson on Friday with a lap of 125.57mph.

But the Kiwi had trouble sorting the handling of his Superbike, right up to the final session on Friday, and on the night could have done with one more lap before the session was red-flagged due to a three-bike crash at the Black Dub. Anstey's woe was a strange irony since the team had built its own Superbike specially for the roads after a nightmare 2006 with ex-Rizla bikes. The team came in for a fair amount of flak following the spate of technical problems, but it was a fact that the revvy BSB bikes with their high-compression motors didn't suit the sustained high-speed running of the road course, and the slipper clutches broke.

Over the past winter, as well as developing their own British Supersport bikes, the team built complete Superbikes in-house. Team boss Phillip Neil said: "It was quickly forgotten we had the fastest bike at last year's TT. It's overlooked that Bruce set the second fastest lap of the Senior. He clipped the wall on the first lap and not surprisingly was unnerved. So much so he was going to pull in after the first lap. But he composed himself and had a sensational ride, setting the second fastest lap ever on the final lap. He did 129mph on that last lap. That's unheard of.

"This year's bikes were still built to the minimum weight limit like the Rizla bikes [in the past weight wasn't such an issue for the team] but we're going to run stock clutches, which we know are very robust, and build our engines in-house."

Last year's ex-Rizla bikes turned 206bhp on the dyno, but now the engines, rebuilt by TAS for the end-of-season Sunflower International at Bishopscourt, were showing 214! Neil said: "It's one thing getting big horsepower figures but the important issue is making the bike rideable and we've much more experience with the Motec system we started to use on the road for the first time last year."

As it turned out, handling was the big issue this year, and Anstey said: "We weren't that far off with the Superbike at the North West from the very start. The motor is really strong, it's the fastest thing out there, but we've just got to get it to handle here and we'll be okay.

"We've been struggling with suspension all week and the bike is unstable in corners, so I'm lacking confidence and can't push it. It's slowly getting better but if you try to change too much in one go... well you just can't do that here."

The team finally suspected something amiss with the shock and at the last minute on Friday swapped the unit from Anstey's Superstock bike. This transformed the bike, but he still failed to improve on the 126.46mph he did on Thursday.

"It's getting better," Anstey said. "I could have done with another lap. We've sorted mid-corner stability but now we need to regain some stability going into the corner."

But the Kiwi was well happy with his other two bikes – as his times showed. He said: "The superstocker and 600 are both going really well."

SUFFER FOR YOUR ART. NO HALF MEASURES.

Right: Adrian Archibald was hampered by the same handling problems that plagued team-mate Bruce Anstey.
© Double Red

ADRIAN ARCHIBALD
RELENTLESS SUZUKI by TAS

Best laps

Bennetts
SUPERBIKE 8th, 124.792mph, Thursday
PokerStars
SUPERSTOCK 5th, 123.964mph, Friday
PokerStars
SUPERSPORT 25th, 116.842mph, Tuesday

"THIS YEAR THE TEAM HAVE BUILT A BIKE SPECIALLY FOR THE ROADS. IT HAS A NICE, SMOOTH POWER DELIVERY, AND IS NOWHERE NEAR AS AGGRESSIVE AS LAST YEAR'S BIKE."

Adrian Archibald only did one lap on the Relentless Suzuki GSX-R600 Supersport bike but clocked 116.84mph. He was quick on the Superstock at 123.96mph, but was still getting up to speed on the Superbike with a best of 124.79mph.

Archibald came back to the TAS team late last year after a disastrous North West 200 with a privateer Yamaha outfit. With no testing and a pile of problems with the ex-Rizla GSX-R1000 Superbike, Archie's form was lacking at the TT on a BSB bike with its lightweight, revvy engine internals.

This year's TAS bike was built in-house with heavier, more standard internals so that if the rider rolled the throttle and then wound it back on, he didn't lose so much momentum and was able to enjoy a much smoother ride.

"Last year we had a short-circuit bike [an ex-Rizla Suzuki] and had a lot of problems," said Archibald. "This year the team have built a bike specially for the roads. It has a nice, smooth power delivery, and is nowhere near as aggressive as last year's bike."

Despite that, Archibald's bike wasn't handling as well as he would have liked and the team were still dialling in the WP shock right up to the end of Friday practice.

Archibald was only 25th quickest on the Supersport bike simply because he spent most of practice trying to dial in the Superbike.

STEVE PLATER

AIM OPTOMA LOANS YAMAHA

Best laps

Bennetts
SUPERBIKE 18th, 121.384mph, Thursday
PokerStars
SUPERSTOCK 29th, 118.401mph, Thursday
PokerStars
SUPERSPORT 28th, 116.555mph, Tuesday

Above: Steve Plater was the fastest ever Newcomer in practice week, lapping at 121.38mph on the AIM Yamaha Superbike – but it took a whole different mentality to ride the same machine he's used to running in BSB.

© Double Red

Opposite: Rather than getting blown away by the atmosphere or the beauty of the TT course, Steve Plater was very workmanlike in the way he went about learning the way round.

© Double Red

Steve Plater became the fastest newcomer in TT history during practice when he lapped the tortuous 37.73-mile course at a very impressive 121.38mph on the AIM Optoma Loans Yamaha R1 Superbike.

Plater arrived at the TT with plenty of road-racing background, having won three races at the North West 200 in the past two years (two wins on HM Plant Hondas in 2006 and one win this year on the AIM Yamaha) plus victory in last winter's Macau GP on the AIM bike.

But the TT was a new experience for the man who's also racing this year in BSB with AIM and Kawasaki France in World Endurance.

"My 121mph lap didn't feel that fast," said Plater. "I know Mick Grant, who's been helping me, was concerned that I was pushing too hard, but it didn't feel that way at all. I'm enjoying riding the Superbike around here. It's more stable than the Supersport and Superstock bikes – but you'd expect that because it's built as a real racing machine whereas the other two are more like road bikes. Besides, the Superbike is what I know. I've done thousands of miles on them and I'm riding my North West bike here."

Plater's team arrived with two very different Superbikes: the one that won the North West, the second being his BSB bike.

"The TT bike has different geometry at the rear to make it softer," said Plater. "It also has different engine internals, with stock rods and pistons, a kit gearbox and a Steve Mellor cylinder head – which all adds up to an engine that has linear power delivery and none of the harshness you get with a short-circuit bike."

There were those who feared for Plater, feeling that he might not be able to curb his aggressive riding style for the TT, which requires a much smoother style, especially for a newcomer.

But Plater proved otherwise and said: "I've done Macau and the North West and I don't care what people say, they are short circuits. Michael [Rutter] and I broke the Macau lap record four times between us in the race last year, then he slagged me off for pushing my luck.

"If I'm comfy I don't feel like I'm riding hard and, hand on heart, I think I could have gone harder at Macau. If Michael had been in front of me I would have definitely gone harder.

"It's a different world here, though, and all along I just wanted to come and learn. Lap times, results – they mean nothing to me. It's all about being safe and gaining some track knowledge. The real pressure came at the North West because expectations were high. But here I'm chilling out and learning. I did a lap in a car with Finnegan and even he admits he's still learning his way around and isn't as strong as he could be over the Mountain.

"It was great that we rookies have to follow the travelling marshals on our first lap. I can imagine I would have been mega-nervous setting out on my own, but following them takes all that apprehension away. I wasn't as nervous as I thought. In 2003 and 2006 I was here watching the riders setting off and thought 'they must be so nervous'. But it's not like that at all once you set off because you have to be so focussed."

Plater has gone about learning the TT course in a very methodical way. In the build-up to the fortnight, he made four low profile trips to the Island to get an idea of the course layout, and was up at six each morning to do car laps with Grant, the seven-time TT winner.

"Here you don't sit the bike up and get on the gas hard, spinning the tyre on exits like you do on short circuits. It's much smoother than that, at the TT you're in fifth where you'd be in third. Like Ginger Hall to Ramsey – in the rough corners – if I throw it in the bike becomes

unstable, but go a gear higher and it cruises through. Certain sections I've been attacking – mainly the slower stuff. That's why Grantie's here to help me understand where I can do that.

"There's more to come. I expect to hit a brick wall – metaphorically and not for real I hope – and then struggle to pick up any more time. But if I can do this sort of pace and continue to learn then I'll be happy. The Supersport bike is great but I can't get comfy on the superstocker. It's strange because the bars, pegs, seat...everything's the same as the Superbike but I haven't felt comfy all week."

Plater came to the TT looking at a three-year programme to learn not just the way round the track but how the whole thing works. "I said to myself before I got here that I'd only come with the AIM Yamaha guys," he revealed. "I wouldn't come on my own or with a less experienced team. I've too much on my plate to learn my way around here. To get this chance with this team is brilliant.

"I thought I'd come and have a go, just to see if I like it. I wanted to see if I could ride 'relaxed'. See if I get on with the organisers. See if they want me to come back to race. Then we'll take it from there."

"HERE YOU DON'T SIT THE BIKE UP AND GET ON THE GAS HARD, SPINNING THE TYRE ON EXITS LIKE YOU DO ON SHORT CIRCUITS. IT'S MUCH SMOOTHER THAN THAT, AT THE TT YOU'RE IN FIFTH WHERE YOU'D BE IN THIRD…"

CONOR CUMMINS
JMf MILLSPORT YAMAHA

Best laps

Bennetts
SUPERBIKE 11th, 122.925mph, Thursday
PokerStars
SUPERSTOCK 10th, 121.763mph, Thursday
PokerStars
SUPERSPORT 10th, 120.053mph, Monday

Twenty-year-old Manxman Conor Cummins came to the 2007 TT with a lot of local hope resting on him after his brilliant debut in 2006, when he lapped at a stunning 120.08mph on his own Superstock Yamaha R1.

Riding Yamahas for JMf Millsport Motorsport, of Ballymoney in Northern Ireland, his pre-TT build-up couldn't have been better, with a Supersport race on the short circuit at Bishopscourt, Northern Ireland, and top three finishes in the shorter Irish road races on his Superstock.

At the North West 200 he finished eighth in Superbike, retired on the 600 when the gear rod snapped in two, and in Superstock, after starting 17th in the grid, was up

Below: Conor Cummins overcame an unfortunate collision on Tuesday to post some competitive lap times by the end of the week on the JMf Millsport Yamaha.

© Double Red

to third when the gear lever pedal snapped off and he ended up fifth.

"In Ireland we've been running the superstocker," Cummins said, "because my Superbike has only just been finished." His Superbike's spec included a Race Techniques engine, customer Ohlins gas forks and shock, modified stock swing arm and Micron exhaust.

"I'm still not used to the Superbike – or the course. I might live here but it's a whole different world on a racing bike. Guthrie's, Mountain, places that matter for speed, I still need to get my head around.

"In my first run out on Saturday I did 118mph from a standing start on the superstocker that still wasn't handling quite right. I have my handlebars set forward and I think that makes it a bit unstable. We had to do some suspension work to overcome that. The 600 is great and I did 120mph on Monday and felt comfortable.

"Tuesday was a disaster though. The steering damper popped a shim out at Ramsey and I had to stop. Then I was trying to get by someone at Laurel Bank. It wasn't a hot-headed move at all, the move was on, but we touched and the other guy went down. I pulled in because I didn't feel like I was fit to carry on. I'd nosed in front but his handlebar caught my right leg. I'm just glad he was okay but I had to stop to make sure he was going to be all right."

Cummins overcame that incident to post top-ten times over 120mph in Superbike and Superstock on the Millsport R1s.

"I'M STILL NOT USED TO THE SUPERBIKE – OR THE COURSE. I MIGHT LIVE HERE BUT IT'S A WHOLE DIFFERENT WORLD ON A RACING BIKE. GUTHRIE'S, MOUNTAIN, PLACES THAT MATTER FOR SPEED, I STILL NEED TO GET MY HEAD AROUND."

Yamaha YZF R1
A Legendary Performance

With a brand new engine including a 4-valve head, amazing variable intake stacks, improved mapping, plus a fly-by-wire throttle all helping to churn out 180* horses, you would think that you have quite an animal on your hands.

Perceptions are deceptive, because while this bike is one of the sharpest tools in the box, it's also one of the most refined, enabling you, the rider, to enjoy every corner and every bit in between.

Check out our website for more info on our authorised dealer network and full range of models, accessories and rider benefits.

* Without direct air induction

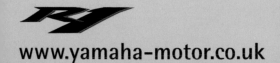

www.yamaha-motor.co.uk

MARK MILLER
APRILIA UK
WOLF MAN/YOSHIHARU
HONDA

Best laps

Bennetts
SUPERBIKE 40th, 114.893mph, Thursday
PokerStars
SUPERSTOCK 37th, 116.445mph, Friday
PokerStars
SUPERSPORT 49th, 116.445mph, Friday

Below: Mark Miller returned for a second year at the TT with last-minute deals to ride an Aprilia factory bike in the Superbike and Superstock races and a Japanese-entered Honda in Supersport.

© Stephen Davison

American Mark Miller returned to the TT for a second time with a last-minute ride in the Superbike and Superstock classes on a factory Aprilia alongside his team-mate, Cumbrian bike dealer Dave Milling.

The two machines, built to Stocksport regulations, were spare bikes, built for last year's Bol d'Or, while a third bike won the Superstock class at the prestigious 24-hour race.

Miller also got a ride in the Supersport class on a CBR600 run in the colours of Wolfman/Yoshiharu, a Japanese-based team that ran out of the Padgetts' awning in the TT paddock.

The 32-year-old Californian, twice a podium finisher at the Macau GP as well as being a top class AMA pro racer, made an impressive TT debut in 2006 riding a Superstock-spec TAS Suzuki GSX-R750 and lapped at a fraction of a second under the 120mph mark.

He said: "I guess I'm back here as an underdog again after running the stock GSX-R750 last year. TAS were going to run me again right up to the last minute but they just didn't have the resources this time, which, looking at their set-up, I can totally understand.

"Then the Aprilia thing happened at the last minute thanks to Paul Phillips [TT and Motorsport Development Manager] putting me with them. The bike showed up with short-circuit stuff and was way too stiff, but K-Tech helped us dial in the suspension. It only has 135bhp at the rear wheel but mid-range is so much fun. Out of corners it's unbelievable, but it's not quick. I'm just gonna do wheelies and stuff to entertain the fans. There are so many people coming up to us and saying how great it is that Aprilia are here and how they love the sound of the bike.

"The weather was bad for the first two days and I felt green. I knew where to go but wasn't confident to commit to corners. There's a tiny finite threading of the needle where to commit. I wasn't comfy for a while."

The Honda came with Bridgestones, just about the only bike in the paddock to be running the Japanese tyres, and it took the American some time to gain confidence in them.

"The 600 is brilliant – it's even got more horsepower than the Aprilia," he joked. "The bike arrived with expensive Showa equipment and was overly stiff. It's also on Bridgestones, which no-one else is running here, so we're out on a limb there. It was horrifying to ride on my first lap. But Padgetts came up with some spare stuff that McGuinness uses and it was better straight off."

Miller came into the TT with limited racing under his belt this year because he's pursuing another career.

"I've been working on a film, a short 16-minute thing," he revealed, "for a Spielberg contest looking for young directors. There were real actors in it too! But I did Macau and some races in the US as well."

His movie industry connections could help promote the TT in the future. Miller explained: "Dan Younger, one of my crew here this time, is a real film director. He has worked on some feature-length movies and is working on a new TT movie. Meryl Streep is already signed and they're trying to get Brad Pitt. The script is done – it was finished last week. There's not going to be any computer-generated stuff – all real footage using on-bike cameras. I'm working with Dan so the thing comes across how it really is here."

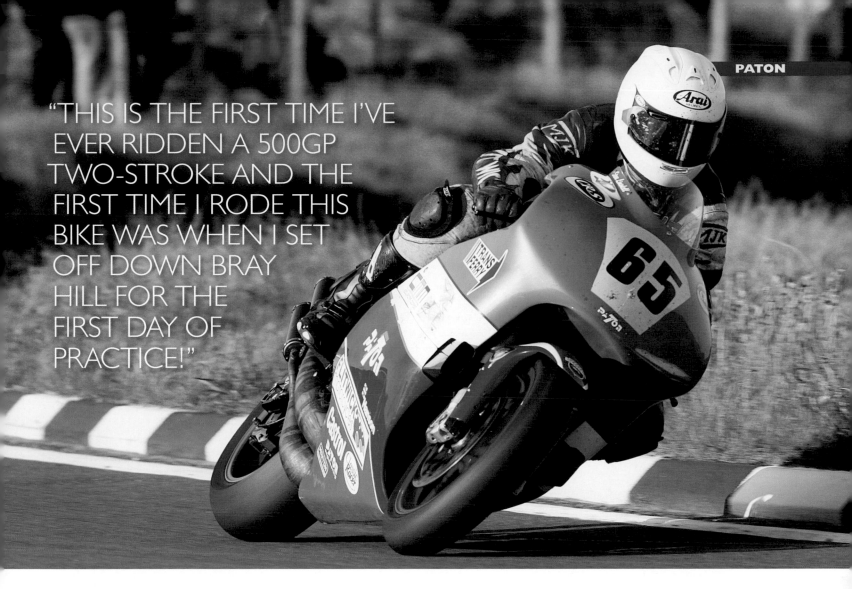

"THIS IS THE FIRST TIME I'VE EVER RIDDEN A 500GP TWO-STROKE AND THE FIRST TIME I RODE THIS BIKE WAS WHEN I SET OFF DOWN BRAY HILL FOR THE FIRST DAY OF PRACTICE!"

STEVE LINSDELL
SQUADRA CORSE CMM PATON

Best laps

PokerStars
SENIOR 35th, 108.355mph, Thursday

Above: Steve Linsdell, never one for convention, opted to run an ex-GP500 Paton two-stroke in the Senior class.
© Double Red

Experienced TT campaigner Steve Linsdell gave two-stroke fans a rare treat at the TT in the otherwise four-stroke dominated, production-based races when he entered the Senior TT on the Italian-built GP500 Paton.

Linsdell, who has a penchant for running different bikes at the TT and once raced a hub-centre-steered Yamaha GTS1000, said: "I wanted to ride the Paton because it's different. It's available because Giovanni Cabassi [the owner of the bike] backed it. We wanted to see something different on the circuit – and to remind people that Paton ran in GPs right up until 2001.

The PG500RC is the last of a long line of Paton GP bikes and Linsdell's machine was built from spares produced for the team's world championship effort in 2001. The engine is fed by four 36mm Keihin carburettors and has a six-speed gearbox.

The few non-GP parts on the bike include steel brakes to replace the original Brembo carbon stoppers, steel expansion pipes instead of the original titanium ones, and new ignition rotors because the original type is no longer available. The added weight meant that the TT bike, with 190bhp on tap, tipped the scales at 132kg whereas the GP version weighed 124kg.

"I'm basically a four-stroke man," said Linsdell. "The only time I've raced two-strokes was back in 1996 and 1997 when I ran a TZ250, but it was too small for me.

"This is the first time I've ever ridden a 500GP two-stroke and the first time I rode this bike was when I set off down Bray Hill for the first day of practice!

"It made me burst out laughing because it was like fast-forwarding the video game. I've had limited time on it though. We did two laps on three cylinders and two other half laps, but we've been plagued with carburation problems. Even so, there's nothing like this 500 when the power comes in!"

The bike was being maintained at the TT by Roberto Pattoni, son of Giuseppe, the original constructor of a range of exotic twin-cylinder Grand Prix machines including the 500cc BIC500 eight-valve twin and GP500 two-strokes.

The Paton link with Giovanni Cabassi started when the latter embarked on the single-cylinder CRS programme four years ago and asked Roberto's company to look after the technical development. "I wanted a road-legal Manx Norton," said Cabassi. "We've made 34 since last September."

Linsdell also finished second in the 2006 Manx GP Classic Senior race on a replica of one of the sixties four-stroke Paton 500cc twins, lapping at 105.66mph.

Bennetts
SUPERBIKE
Fastest Laps – All Sessions

Pos	No	Rider	Machine	Entrant	Lap Time	Speed	Run
1	3	John McGuinness	2007 Honda Fireblade 1000cc	HM Plant Honda Racing	17 32.24	129.084	Thur, 31st May Practice
2	8	Guy Martin	2007 Honda 1000cc	Hydrex Honda	17 39.78	128.166	Thur, 31st May Practice
3	7	Ian Lougher	2007 Honda CBR 1000cc	Stobart Motorsport	17 40.00	128.140	Thur, 31st May Practice
4	6	Ian Hutchinson	2007 Honda CBR 1000cc	HM Plant Honda Racing	17 44.93	127.547	Thur, 31st May Practice
5	4	Martin Finnegan	2007 Honda CBR 1000cc	Alpha Boilers Racing	17 47.06	127.292	Thur, 31st May Practice
6	5	Bruce Anstey	2007 Suzuki GSXR 1000cc	Relentless by TAS Racing	17 54.07	126.461	Thur, 31st May Practice
7	1	Michael Rutter	2007 Kawasaki ZX10 R 1000cc	MSS Discovery Kawasaki	18 06.60	125.003	Thur, 31st May Practice
8	2	Adrian Archibald	2007 Suzuki GSXR 1000cc	Relentless by TAS Racing	18 08.44	124.792	Thur, 31st May Practice
9	9	Ryan Farquhar	2007 Honda Fireblade 1000cc	Mark Johns Motors	18 12.59	124.317	Fri, 1st June Practice
10	14	Paul Hunt	2006 Yamaha R1 1000cc	John Alsop	18 16.20	123.908	Thur, 31st May Practice
11	10	Conor Cummins	2007 Yamaha YZF R1 1000cc	Team Millsport Racing	18 24.96	122.925	Thur, 31st May Practice
12	20	Mark Parrett	2007 Yamaha R1 1000cc	Ripley Land	18 31.21	122.235	Fri, 1st June Practice
13	23	James McBride	2007 Yamaha R1 1000cc		18 32.18	122.127	Thur, 31st May Practice
14	27	Ian Pattinson	2006 Suzuki GSXR 1000cc	Martin Bullock Raceteam	18 32.27	122.117	Thur, 31st May Practice
15	17	Nigel Beattie	2007 Yamaha R1 1000cc	CD Racing/Millsport Racing	18 32.70	122.071	Fri, 1st June Practice
16	36	Michael Weynand	2007 Kawasaki ZX10R 1000cc	Bolliger Kawasaki/SK Support	18 34.82	121.839	Tue, 29th May Practice
17	24	Dan Stewart	2006 Yamaha R1 1000cc	Wilcock Consulting	18 36.58	121.647	Fri, 1st June Practice
18	31	Steve Plater*	2007 Yamaha R1 1000cc	AIM Racing	18 38.99	121.384	Thur, 31st May Practice
19	13	Ian Armstrong	2004 Yamaha R1 1000cc	Canteen Smithy	18 39.73	121.304	Tue, 29th May Practice
20	25	Chris Palmer	2005 Yamaha R1 1000cc	Solway Slate & Tile	18 41.81	121.079	Fri, 1st June Practice
21	19	John Barton	2006 Honda CBR 1000cc	Marks Bloom Racing	18 48.37	120.375	Tue, 29th May Practice
22	26	Les Shand	2006 Honda CBR 1000cc	Barron Transport	18 48.43	120.369	Thur, 31st May Practice
23	35	Phil Stewart	2007 Yamaha R1 1000cc		18 50.46	120.153	Fri, 1st June Practice
24	30	Liam Quinn	2006 Yamaha R1 1000cc	Team Racing	18 53.06	119.878	Thur, 31st May Practice
25	28	Gary Johnson*	2007 Yamaha R1 1000cc	Speedfreak Racing	18 53.69	119.810	Fri, 1st June Practice
26	33	Mark Buckley	2006 Yamaha YZF R1 1000cc	Crossan Motorcycles	18 53.86	119.792	Fri, 1st June Practice
27	15	Gary Carswell	2007 Kawasaki ZX10R 1000cc	Bolliger Kawasaki/SK Support	18 57.40	119.420	Thur, 31st May Practice
28	29	John Burrows	2006 Honda CBR 1000cc	H.M. Sports Motorhomes	18 57.60	119.399	Thur, 31st May Practice
29	18	Shaun Harris	2007 Suzuki K7 1000cc	Blacks Bike Shop	19 00.19	119.128	Thur, 31st May Practice
30	49	Craig Atkinson	2004 Suzuk GSXR 1000cc	Martin Bullock Raceteam	19 01.14	119.029	Thur, 31st May Practice
31	36	Stephen Oates	2007 Suzuki GSXR 1000c	Hallett Aviation Racing	19 01.40	119.002	Thur, 31st May Practice
32	16	Davy Morgan	2005 Honda 1000cc	Investasure	19 05.13	118.614	Tue, 29th May Practice
33	37	James Edmeades	2007 Yamaha R1 1000cc	Speedfreak Racing	19 05.29	118.597	Fri, 1st June Practice
34	51	Stefano Bonetti	Suzuki GSXR 1000cc		19 05.64	118.561	Thur, 31st May Practice
35	39	Roger Maher*	2006 Yamaha R1 1000cc		19 07.39	118.380	Fri, 1st June Practice
36	43	Michael Dunlop	2004 Yamaha 1000cc		19 08.90	118.225	Fri, 1st June Practice
37	42	Paul Owen	2006 Kawasaki ZX10R 1000cc	Back to Normal	19 11.21	117.987	Mon, 28th May
38	38	Jim Hodson	2007 Yamaha R1 1000cc	Pete Beale Racing	19 13.97	117.705	Thur, 31st May Practice
39	39	Victor Gilmore	2007 Yamaha R1 1000cc		19 14.47	117.654	Tue, 29th May Practice
40	45	Keith Amor*	2005 Honda CBR 1000cc	Robinson Concrete	19 14.54	117.647	Thur, 31st May Practice
41	52	Paul Dobbs	2003 Suzuki GSXR 1000cc	Dave East Engineering	19 14.81	117.619	Thur, 31st May Practice
42	22	Dean Silvester	2006 Yamaha R1 1000cc	CSC Racing	19 15.55	117.545	Thur, 31st May Practice
43	21	Chris Heath	2004 Honda CBR 1000cc		19 18.90	117.204	Tue, 29th May Practice
44	50	Frank Spenner	2004 Yamaha R1 1000cc	ADAC Hessen-Thueringen	19 20.28	117.065	Thur, 31st May Practice
45	58	Stephen Harper	2006 Suzuki GSXR 1000cc		19 24.30	116.661	Thur, 31st May Practice
46	53	George Spence	2006 Yamaha YZF R1 1000cc		19 24.32	116.659	Tue, 29th May Practice
47	59	David Milling	2006 Aprilia RSV 1000cc	Aprilia UK	19 24.65	116.625	Fri, 1st June Practice
48	47	Tim Poole	2007 Yamaha YZF R1 1000cc	Bill Smith Motorcycles	19 25.66	116.525	Tue, 29th May Practice
49	40	Mark Miller	Aprilia 1000cc	Wolfman/Yoshiharu/Padgetts	19 26.45	116.445	Fri, 1st June Practice
50	54	Jimmy Moore*	2007 Honda CBR 1000cc	Team Black Horse Racing	19 26.85	116.406	Thur, 31st May Practice
51	55	Paul Shoesmith	2007 Yamaha R1 1000cc	Speedfreak Racing	19 28.09	116.282	Thur, 31st May Practice
52	62	Adrian McFarland	2005 Yamaha R1 1000cc	Team Hardship Racing	19 28.49	116.242	Thur, 31st May Practice
53	69	David Paredes	Yamaha R1 1000cc	Bill Smith Motorcycles	19 29.42	116.150	Thur, 31st May Practice
54	68	Steve Kuenne	2006 Yamaha YZF 1000cc	Dave Sandlan	19 29.96	116.096	Thur, 31st May Practice
55	56	Alan Bud Jackson	2005 Suzuki GSXR 1000cc	BDS Fuels	19 33.49	115.747	Thur, 31st May Practice
56	41	Tim Maher	2005 Suzuki GSXR 1000cc		19 35.26	115.573	Fri, 1st June Practice
57	74	Martin Hamberg	2006 Yamaha R1 1000cc	Hallett Aviation Racing	19 36.12	115.489	Thur, 31st May Practice
58	66	Chris McGahan	2007 Yamaha R1 1000cc	McKinstry Skip Hire	19 44.74	114.648	Fri, 1st June Practice
59	71	Fabrice Miguet	2006 Suzuki GSXR 1000cc		19 45.52	114.572	Thur, 31st May Practice
60	44	Dave Madsen-Mygdal	2007 Yamaha R1 1000cc	CSC Racing	19 45.64	114.561	Thur, 31st May Practice
61	63	John Crellin	2002 Suzuki GSX 1000cc	J Richards	19 46.48	114.480	Tue, 29th May Practice
62	46	Paul Duckett	2005 Kawasaki ZX10 RR 1000cc	Wilson & Collins	19 51.37	114.010	Thur, 31st May Practice
63	81	Sandor Bitter	2006 Suzuki GSXR 1000cc		19 51.63	113.986	Fri, 1st June Practice
64	77	Alan Connor	2006 Suzuki GSXR 1000cc	Dunshaughlin RRSC	19 54.21	113.739	Tue, 29th May Practice
65	64	Karsten Schmidt	2006 Suzuki GSXR 1000cc		19 54.68	113.694	Thur, 31st May Practice
66	60	Thomas Schoenfelder	2005 Suzuki GSXR 1000cc	ADAC Hessent-Thueringen	19 55.27	113.638	Thur, 31st May Practice
67	86	Chris Petty	2006 Suzuki GSXR 1000cc	York Suzuki Centre	19 55.76	113.592	Thur, 31st May Practice
68	61	Daniel Jansen	2005 Kawasaki ZX10 1000cc		19 55.92	113.576	Thur, 31st May Practice
69	89	Mike Hose	2003 Aprilia RSV 1000cc	Mike Hose Motorcycles	19 59.64	113.224	Thur, 31st May Practice
70	85	Ian Mackman*	2006 Suzuki GSXR 1000cc	Bill Smith Motorcycles	20 00.14	113.177	Thur, 31st May Practice
71	57	Andrew Marsden	2004 Yamaha R1 1000cc	Austin Powered Racing	20 00.92	113.103	Thur, 31st May Practice
72	67	Dirk Kaletsch	2004 Honda CBR 1000cc		20 01.90	113.012	Tue, 29th May Practice
73	88	David Hewson*	2004 Kawasaki ZX10 1000cc		20 05.94	112.632	Thur, 31st May Practice
74	80	Marc Ramsbotham*	2006 Suzuki K6 1000cc		20 13.96	111.888	Thur, 31st May Practice
75	65	Christer Miinin*	2006 Suzuki GSXE 1000cc	Martin Bullock Raceteam	20 16.35	111.669	Fri, 1st June Practice
76	90	John Nisill*	2006 Yamaha R1 1000cc	PR Haulage/CJN Services	20 47.77	108.857	Fri, 1st June Practice
77	75	Antonio Maeso*	2007 Yamaha R1 1000cc		20 48.86	108.761	Thur, 31st May Practice
78	73	Bob Collins*	2007 Suzuki GSXR 1000cc	2Bob Racing	21 15.71	106.472	Fri, 1st June Practice

SUPERSTOCK
Fastest Laps – All Sessions

Pos	No		Rider	Machine	Entrant	Lap Time	Speed	Run
1	6		Ian Hutchinson	2007 Honda CBR 1000cc	HM Plant Honda Racing	18 01.69	125.570	Fri, 1st June Practice
2	5		Bruce Anstey	2007 Suzuki GSXR 1000cc	Relentless by TAS Racing	18 03.70	125.338	Tue, 29th May Practice
3	4		Martin Finnegan	2007 MV Agusta 1000cc	Alpha Boilers Racing	18 05.37	125.145	Mon, 4th June Practice
4	8		Guy Martin	2007 Honda 1000cc	Hydrex Honda	18 09.98	124.616	Mon, 4th June Practice
5	3		John McGuinness	2007 Honda Fireblade 1000cc	HM Plant Honda Racing	18 12.79	124.295	Thur, 31st May Practice
6	2		Adrian Archibald	2007 Suzuki GSXR 1000cc	Relentless by TAS Racing	18 15.72	123.963	Fri, 1st June Practice
7	10		Mark Parrett	2007 Yamaha R1 1000cc	C & C Ltd	18 27.78	122.613	Thur, 31st May Practice
8	12	#	James McBride	2007 Yamaha R1 1000cc		18 32.18	122.127	Thur, 31st May Practice
9	14	#	Ian Pattinson	2006 Suzuki GSXR 1000cc	Martin Bullock Raceteam	18 32.27	122.117	Thur, 31st May Practice
10	16		Conor Cummins	2007 Yamaha YZF R1 1000cc	Team Millsport Racing	18 35.51	121.763	Thur, 31st May Practice
11	9		Paul Hunt	2007 Yamaha 1000cc	Peter Beale	18 36.16	121.692	Tue, 29th May Practice
12	1		Ryan Farquhar	2007 Kawasaki ZX10 1000cc	Harker Racing	18 37.03	121.598	Mon, 4th June Practice
13	17		Nigel Beattie	2007 Yamaha R1 1000cc	CD Racing/Millsport Racing	18 41.68	121.094	Fri, 1st June Practice
14	11		Gary Carswell	2000 Suzuki GSXR 1000cc		18 42.82	120.970	Thur, 31st May Practice
15	13		Ian Armstrong	2007 Suzuki GSX K7 1000cc	Powersport Bikes	18 44.80	120.758	Thur, 31st May Practice
16	21		Dan Stewart	2007 Yamaha R1 1000cc	Wilcock Consulting	18 47.59	120.458	Mon, 4th June Practice
17	7		Ian Lougher	2007 Honda CBR 1000cc	Team Blackhorse Racing	18 49.72	120.232	Fri, 1st June Practice
18	28	#	Phil Stewart	2007 Yamaha R1 1000cc		18 50.46	120.153	Fri, 1st June Practice
19	30	#	Liam Quinn	2006 Yamaha R1 1000cc	Team Racing	18 53.06	119.878	Thur, 31st May Practice
20	29	#	Gary Johnson*	2007 Yamaha R1 1000cc	Speedfreak Racing	18 53.69	119.810	Fri, 1st June Practice
21	24		Chris Palmer	2007 Yamaha R1 1000cc	NCT Racing	18 54.26	119.750	Tue, 29th May Practice
22	22		Davy Morgan	2007 Suzuki GSXR 1000cc	Blacks Bike Breaker	18 54.35	119.741	Fri, 1st June Practice
23	26		John Burrows	2006 Suzuki GSXR 1000cc	H.M. Sports Motorhomes	18 56.10	119.556	Mon, 4th June Practice
24	25		Les Shand	2007 Yamaha YZF R1 1000cc	Leeds Parcel Company	18 58.49	119.306	Thur, 31st May Practice
25	46		Keith Amor*	2007 Honda CBR 1000cc	Site Welding Services Ltd/Uel	18 58.94	119.259	Mon, 4th June Practice
26	33		Mark Buckley	Suzuki GSXR 1000cc	P.R.F. Racing	18 59.71	119.178	Mon, 4th June Practice
27	15	#	Shaun Harris	2007 Suzuki K7 1000cc	Blacks Bike Shop	19 00.19	119.128	Thur, 31st May Practice
28	41	#	Craig Atkinson	2004 Suzuki GSXR 1000cc	Martin Bullock Raceteam	19 01.14	119.029	Thur, 31st May Practice
29	37	#	Stephen Oates	2007 Suzuki GSXR 1000cc	Hallett Aviation Racing	19 01.40	119.002	Thur, 31st May Practice
30	34	#	James Edmeades	2007 Yamaha R1 1000cc	Speedfreak Racing	19 05.29	118.597	Fri, 1st June Practice
31	37	#	Stefano Bonetti*	Suzuki GSXR 1000cc		19 05.64	118.561	Thur, 31st May Practice
32	31		Steve Plater*	2007 Yamaha R1 1000cc	AIM Racing	19 07.18	118.401	Thur, 31st May Practice
33	36	#	Victor Gilmore	2007 Yamaha R1 1000cc		19 14.47	117.654	Tue, 29th May Practice
34	20	#	Dean Silvester	2007 Yamaha R1 1000cc	CSC Racing	19 15.55	117.545	Thur, 31st May Practice
35	19		John Barton	2007 Suzuki K7 1000cc	Marks Bloom Racing	19 19.21	117.173	Mon, 4th June Practice
36	61	#	Stephen Harper	2006 Suzuki GSXR 1000cc		19 24.30	116.661	Thur, 31st May Practice
37	39	#	David Milling	2006 Aprilia RSV 1000cc	Aprilia UK	19 24.65	116.625	Fri, 1st June Practice
38	38	#	Mark Miller	Aprilia 1000cc	Wolfman/Yoshiharu/Padgetts	19 26.45	116.445	Fri, 1st June Practice
39	50	#	Jimmy Moore*	2007 Honda CBR 1000cc	Team Blackhorse Racing	19 26.85	116.406	Thur, 31st May Practice
40	57	#	Paul Shoesmith	2007 Yamaha R1 1000cc	Speedfreak Racing	19 28.09	116.282	Thur, 31st May Practice
41	51		David Paredes	Yamaha R1 1000cc	Bill Smith Motorcycles	19 29.42	116.150	Thur, 31st May Practice
42	52	#	Steve Kuenne	2006 Yamaha YZF 1000cc	Dave Sandlan	19 29.96	116.096	Thur, 31st May Practice
43	54		David Coughlan	2006 Suzuki GSXR 1000cc	R&C duetiny	19 30.90	116.003	Mon, 28th May
44	49		George Spence	2005 Yamaha YZF R1 1000cc		19 31.78	115.916	Thur, 31st May Practice
45	35		Jim Hodson	2007 Yamaha R1 1000cc	Pete Beale Racing	19 33.19	115.777	Tue, 29th May Practice
46	53	#	Alan Bud Jackson	2005 Suzuki GSXR 1000cc	BDS Fuels	19 33.49	115.747	Thur, 31st May Practice
47	42	#	Tim Maher	2005 Suzuki GSXR 1000cc		19 35.26	115.573	Fri, 1st June Practice
48	72	#	Martin Hamberg	2006 Yamaha R1 1000cc	Hallett Aviation Racing	19 36.12	115.489	Thur, 31st May Practice
49	65	#	Chris McGahan	2007 Yamaha R1 1000cc	McKinstry Skip Hire	19 44.74	114.648	Fri, 1st June Practice
50	68	#	Fabrice Miguet	2006 Suzuki GSXR 1000cc		19 45.52	114.572	Thur, 31st May Practice
51	44	#	Dave Madsen-Mygdal	2007 Yamaha R1 1000cc	CSC Racing	19 45.64	114.561	Thur, 31st May Practice
52	59	#	John Crellin	2002 Suzuki GSX 1000cc	J Richards	19 46.48	114.480	Tue, 29th May Practice
53	81	#	Sandor Bitter	2006 Suzuki GSXR 1000cc		19 51.63	113.986	Fri, 1st June Practice
54	74	#	Alan Connor	2006 Suzuki GSXR 1000cc	Dunshaughlin RRSC	19 54.21	113.739	Tue, 29th May Practice
55	63	#	Karsten Schmidt	2006 Suzuki GSXR 1000cc		19 54.68	113.694	Thur, 31st May Practice
56	55	#	Thomas Schoenfelder	2005 Suzuki GSXR 1000cc	ADAC Hessent-Thueringen	19 55.27	113.638	Thur, 31st May Practice
57	88	#	Chris Petty	2007 Suzuki GSXR 1000cc	York Suzuki Centre	19 55.76	113.592	Thur, 31st May Practice
58	62	#	Daniel Jansen	2005 Kawasaki ZX10 1000cc		19 55.92	113.576	Thur, 31st May Practice
59	76	#	Mike Hose	2003 Aprilia RSVR 1000cc	Mike Hose Motorcycles	19 59.64	113.224	Thur, 31st May Practice
60	87	#	Ian Mackman*	2006 Suzuki GSXR 1000cc	Bill Smith Motorcycles	20 00.14	113.177	Thur, 31st May Practice
61	84		Robert Barber*	2005 Suzuki GSXR 750cc		20 00.35	113.157	Thur, 31st May Practice
62	43	#	Christer Miinin*	2006 Suzuki GSXE 1000cc	Martin Bullock Raceteam	20 00.88	113.108	Thur, 31st May Practice
63	66	#	Dirk Kaletsch	2004 Honda CBR 1000cc		20 01.90	113.012	Tue, 29th May Practice
64	85	#	David Hewson*	2006 Kawasaki ZX10 1000cc		20 05.94	112.632	Thur, 31st May Practice
65	89		Mike Crellin	Honda CBR 1000cc		20 09.85	112.268	Tue, 29th May Practice
66	14		Carl Rennie	Suzuki GSXR 1000cc	PRF Racing Team	20 11.45	112.121	Mon, 28th May
67	73		Derran Slous	2005 Suzuki GSXR 750cc		20 13.59	111.922	Fri, 1st June Practice
68	80	#	Marc Ramsbotham*	2006 Suzuki K6 1000cc		20 13.96	111.888	Thur, 31st May Practice
69	58		Andrew Marsden	2004 Yamaha R1 1000cc	Austin Powered Racing	20 15.18	111.776	Tue, 29th May Practice
70	86		Alan Chamley	2006 Suzuki GSXR 1000cc	BDS Fuels	20 33.09	110.153	Tue, 29th May Practice
71	82	#	John Nisill*	2006 Yamaha R1 1000cc	PR Haulage/CJN Services	20 47.77	108.857	Fri, 1st June Practice
72	78	#	Antonio Maeso*	2007 Yamaha R1 1000cc		20 48.86	108.761	Thur, 31st May Practice
73	67	#	Bob Collins*	2007 Suzuki GSXR 1000cc	2Bob Racing	21 15.71	106.472	Fri, 1st June Practice

* Denotes newcomer riders
\# Denotes riders entered in a linked qualifying class

PokerStars
SUPERSPORT
Fastest Laps – All Sessions

Pos	No	Rider	Machine	Entrant	Lap Time	Speed	Run
1	5	**Bruce Anstey**	2007 Suzuki GSXR 600cc	Relentless by TAS Racing	18 27.72	122.620	Thur, 31st May Practice
2	3	**John McGuinness**	2007 Honda CBR 600cc	Padgetts Honda	18 29.50	122.423	Fri, 1st June Practice
3	8	**Guy Martin**	2007 Honda 600cc	Hydrex Honda	18 31.26	122.228	Thur, 31st May Practice
4	1	**Ryan Farquhar**	2007 Kawasaki ZX6 600cc	Harker Racing	18 32.80	122.060	Thur, 31st May Practice
5	7	**Ian Lougher**	2007 Honda CBR 600cc	Team Black Horse Racing	18 42.90	120.962	Thur, 31st May Practice
6	9	**Martin Finnegan**	2007 Honda CBR 600cc	Alpha Boilers Racing	18 45.70	120.661	Tues, 5th June
7	6	**Ian Hutchinson**	2007 Honda CBR 600cc	HM Plant Honda Racing	18 46.08	120.620	Tues, 5th June
8	13	**Shaun Harris**	2006 Suzuki GSXR 600cc	Blacks Bike Shop	18 46.65	120.560	Fri, 1st June Practice
9	11	**Nigel Beattie**	2007 Yamaha R6 600cc	CD Racing/Millsport Racing	18 47.58	120.460	Thur, 31st May Practice
10	12	**Michael Rutter**	2007 Kawasaki ZX6 R 600cc	MSS Discovery Kawasaki	18 47.82	120.434	Thur, 31st May Practice
11	14	**Dan Stewart**	2006 Yamaha R6 600cc	Wilcock Consulting	18 51.15	120.079	Thur, 31st May Practice
12	22	**Ian Pattinson**	2006 Honda 600cc	Martin Bullock Raceteam	18 51.18	120.076	Tues, 5th June
13	10	**Conor Cummins**	2007 Yamaha YZF R6 600cc	Team Millsport Racing	18 51.40	120.053	Mon, 28th May
14	17	**Paul Hunt**	2007 Triumph Daytona 675cc	Kevin Cringle	18 53.51	119.829	Thur, 31st May Practice
15	16	**Mark Parrett**	2007 Yamaha R1 600cc	Vixen Racing	18 54.42	119.733	Thur, 31st May Practice
16	15	**Chris Palmer**	2005 Honda CBR 600cc	Solway Slate & Tile	18 58.26	119.330	Thur, 31st May Practice
17	21	**Ian Armstrong**	2006 Honda CBR 600cc	Padgetts Honda	18 58.30	119.326	Thur, 31st May Practice
18	25	**James McBride**	2006 Yamaha R6 600cc		18 58.44	119.310	Thur, 31st May Practice
19	32	**Phil Stewart**	2004 Honda 600RR 600cc		19 02.91	118.844	Thur, 31st May Practice
20	33	**Adrian McFarland**	2006 Yamaha R6 600cc	Team Hardship Racing	19 10.10	118.101	Thur, 31st May Practice
21	40	**Paul Dobbs**	2005 Triumph Daytona 675cc	Action Triumph	19 12.47	117.858	Mon, 4th June Practice
22	28	**Keith Amor***	2005 Honda RR 600cc	Wilson Craig/Uel Duncan Racing	19 13.05	117.799	Tues, 5th June
23	30	**Jimmy Moore***	2007 Honda CBR 600cc	Team Black Horse Racing	19 14.45	117.657	Tues, 5th June
24	23	**Chris Heath**	Yamaha 600cc	Webtech Software	19 15.73	117.525	Tue, 29th May Practice
25	41	**Liam Quinn**	2006 Yamaha R6 600cc	Team Racing	19 18.00	117.295	Tue, 29th May Practice
26	2	**Adrian Archibald**	2007 Suzuki GSXR 600cc	Relentless by TAS Racing	19 18.90	117.205	Mon, 4th June Practice
27	27	**William Dunlop**	2006 Kawasaki 600cc	Lilley Racing	19 20.34	117.059	Thur, 31st May Practice
28	34	**Manfred Vogl**	2007 Yamaha R6 600cc		19 23.13	116.778	Tue, 29th May Practice
29	42	**Victor Gilmore**	2006 Yamaha R6 600cc		19 25.17	116.574	Thur, 31st May Practice
30	31	**Steve Plater***	2007 Yamaha R6 600cc	AIM Racing	19 25.36	116.555	Tue, 29th May Practice
31	44	**Roy Richardson**	2006 Yamaha R6 600cc	Ian Barnes Racing	19 25.48	116.542	Thur, 31st May Practice
32	24	**Paul Owen**	2004 Honda CBR 600cc	Rapid Racing	19 26.22	116.469	Thur, 31st May Practice
33	37	**Stephen Oates**	2006 Suzuki GSXR 600cc	Hallett Aviation Racing	19 27.23	116.368	Tue, 29th May Practice
34	20	**Davy Morgan**	2007 Honda 600cc	Autotech	19 29.06	116.186	Thur, 31st May Practice
35	35	**Craig Atkinson**	2006 Honda CBR 600cc	Martin Bullock Raceteam	19 29.19	116.173	Thur, 31st May Practice
36	39	**Mark Buckley**	2006 Honda CBR 600cc	Crossan Motorcycles	19 32.55	115.840	Thur, 31st May Practice
37	18	**Gary Carswell**	2006 Honda CBR RR 600cc	Crossan Motorcycles	19 33.81	115.715	Tues, 5th June
38	42	**Michael Dunlop**	2006 Yamaha R6 600cc		19 35.94	115.506	Thur, 31st May Practice
39	48	**Stefano Bonetti**	Honda CBR 600cc		19 37.25	115.377	Mon, 4th June Practice
40	26	**Les Shand**	2007 Yamaha R6 600cc	McKinstry Skip Hire	19 38.10	115.295	Tues, 5th June
41	49	**Alan Oversby**	2006 Honda CBR 600cc	W.A. Corless	19 39.01	115.206	Mon, 4th June Practice
42	19	**Dean Silvester**	2007 Yamaha R6 600cc	CSC Racing	19 39.90	115.118	Thur, 31st May Practice
43	78	**Stephen Harper**	Honda 600cc		19 41.47	114.965	Tues, 5th June
44	46	**Tim Poole**	2007 Triumph 675cc	Bill Smith Motorcycles	19 42.00	114.914	Tue, 29th May Practice
45	43	**Mark Miller**	Honda 600cc	Wolf Man/Yo Shiharu/Padgetts	19 42.21	114.893	Thur, 31st May Practice
46	59	**Frank Spenner**	2006 Yamaha R6 600cc	ADAC Hessen-Thueringen	19 49.33	114.205	Fri, 1st June Practice
47	45	**Phil Harvey**	2006 Yamaha YZF-R6 600cc	theFSD.com	19 51.47	114.000	Thur, 31st May Practice
48	36	**John Barton**	2005 Kawasaki ZXR 600cc	Marks Bloom Racing	19 53.03	113.852	Tue, 29th May Practice
49	50	**Karsten Schmidt**	2004 Ducati 750cc		19 54.72	113.690	Fri, 1st June Practice
50	52	**Dave Madsen-Mygdal**	2007 Yamaha R6 600cc	CSC Racing	19 57.04	113.470	Tues, 5th June
51	56	**Chris McGahan**	2007 Yamaha R6 600cc	Manx Glass and Glazing	19 58.09	113.371	Tues, 5th June
52	29	**John Burrows**	2007 Honda RR 600cc	H.M. Sports Motorhomes	20 00.69	113.125	Tues, 5th June
53	38	**Jim Hodson**	2006 Honda CBR 600cc	Alan Gibbon	20 03.49	112.862	Thur, 31st May Practice
54	54	**David Milling**	2006 Honda 600cc	Dave Milling Motorcycles	20 03.52	112.859	Thur, 31st May Practice
55	57	**Mike Hose**	2005 Honda CBR 600cc	RJP Racing	20 03.72	112.840	Mon, 4th June Practice
56	47	**Tim Maher**	2007 Kawasaki ZX6R 600cc	Clarkes Hardware	20 05.56	112.668	Mon, 4th June Practice
57	68	**Roger Maher***	2006 Yamaha 600 600cc		20 06.22	112.607	Tue, 29th May Practice
58	51	**Alan Bennie**	2005 Honda CBR 600cc		20 06.51	112.579	Tue, 29th May Practice
59	76	**David Coughlan**	2005 Yamaha R6 600cc	ATM Construction	20 07.92	112.448	Tue, 29th May Practice
60	62	**Alan Bud Jackson**	2004 Yamaha R6 600cc	Oddfellows Arms	20 12.85	111.991	Thur, 31st May Practice
61	65	**John Crellin**	Honda CBR 600cc	J Richards	20 15.01	111.791	Thur, 31st May Practice
62	28	**Carl Rennie**	Suzuki GSXR 600cc	PRF Racing Team	20 16.27	111.676	Mon, 28th May
63	71	**Paul Shoesmith**	2004 Yamaha R6 600cc	Speedfreak Racing	20 16.88	111.620	Fri, 1st June Practice
64	74	**Etienne Godart**	Honda 600cc	Martin Bullock Raceteam	20 21.30	111.216	Thur, 31st May Practice
65	60	**Derran Slous**	2005 Honda R6 600cc		20 21.76	111.174	Tues, 5th June
66	81	**Alan Connor**	2006 Suzuki GSXR 600cc	Dunshaughlin RRSC	20 26.18	110.774	Fri, 1st June Practice
67	70	**Mike Crellin**	Yamaha R6 600cc		20 28.02	110.607	Tues, 5th June
68	53	**Paul Duckett**	2007 Triumph 675 RR 675cc	Investasure	20 29.01	110.518	Thur, 31st May Practice
69	79	**Robert Barber***	2007 Triumph Daytona 675cc		20 29.86	110.442	Thur, 31st May Practice
70	63	**Phil Gilmour**	2004 Yamaha R6 600cc	Austin Powered Racing	20 31.59	110.286	Thur, 31st May Practice
71	82	**Ian Mackman***	2006 Triumph 675cc	Bill Smith Motorcycles	20 34.39	110.036	Tues, 5th June
72	84	**Angelo Conti***	2007 Triumph Daytona 675cc		20 34.87	109.994	Tues, 5th June
73	67	**Thomas Schoenfelder**	2002 Suzuki GSXR 500cc	ADAC Hessent-Thueringen	20 37.30	109.778	Fri, 1st June Practice
74	89	**Chris Petty**	2005 Honda CBR 600cc	Dave Milling Motorcycles	20 49.27	108.726	Thur, 31st May Practice
75	88	**Wade Boyd**	2005 Kawasaki ZX6 600cc	Hallett Aviation Racing	20 50.66	108.605	Mon, 4th June Practice
76	66	**Kevin Murphy**	2004 Triumph Daytona 600cc	C & C Ltd	20 54.59	108.265	Thur, 31st May Practice
77	85	**John Nisill***	2007 Yamaha R6 600cc	Greenhey Engineering	21 04.06	107.454	Tues, 5th June
78	75	**Marc Ramsbotham***	Kawasaki 600cc		21 24.15	105.773	Mon, 28th May
79	90	**Alan Chamley**	2004 Kawasaki ZXRR 600cc	Bob Jackson Racing	24 05.45	93.969	Mon, 28th May

Bavaria Beer
SIDECAR
Fastest Laps – All Sessions

Pos	No	Rider	Machine	Entrant	Lap Time	Speed	Run
1	2	Nick Crowe/Dan Sayle	2007 Honda 600RR 600cc	A J Groundworks	19 48.25	114.309	Tues, 5th June
2	1	Dave Molyneux/Rick Long	2007 Honda CBR 600cc	HM Plant Honda Racing	20 04.39	112.778	Fri, 1st June Practice
3	4	Klaus Klaffenbock/Christian Parzer	Honda CBR 600cc	Alpha Boilers Racing	20 14.53	111.835	Tues, 5th June
4	7	John Holden/Andrew Winkle	2007 Suzuki K6 600cc		20 21.09	111.235	Fri, 1st June Practice
5	3	Steve Norbury/Scott Parnell	2007 Yamaha YZF R6 600cc	Lockside Engineering	20 32.66	110.191	Fri, 1st June Practice
6	16	Allan Schofield/Peter Founds	2006 Suzuki K6 600cc		20 32.93	110.167	Fri, 1st June Practice
7	5	Simon Neary/Stuart Bond	2005 Yamaha R6 600cc	Neary Racing	20 47.61	108.871	Thur, 31st May Practice
8	12	Greg Lambert/Gary Partridge	2007 Honda RR 600cc	Dave Hudspeth Carpets	20 51.80	108.506	Fri, 1st June Practice
9	25	Nigel Connole/Jamie Winn	2005 Honda RR 600cc		20 57.73	107.995	Fri, 1st June Practice
10	24	Conrad Harrison/Kerry Williams	2003 Honda CBR RR 600cc	Printing Roller Services	21 02.78	107.562	Fri, 1st June Practice
11	10	Gary Bryan/Ivan Murray	2006 Yamaha R6 600cc		21 03.19	107.528	Fri, 1st June Practice
12	14	Tony Elmer/Darren Marshall	2006 Yamaha R6 600cc	D.L. Elmer	21 04.60	107.408	Thur, 31st May Practice
13	9	Phil Dongworth/Stuart Castles	2007 Honda CBR RR 600cc		21 08.26	107.098	Thur, 31st May Practice
14	19	Glyn Jones/Chris Lake	2006 Honda RR 600cc	DSC Racing	21 08.83	107.049	Tues, 5th June
15	8	Andy Laidlow/Patrick Farrance	2006 Suzuki GSXR 600cc		21 10.52	106.907	Thur, 31st May Practice
16	11	Gary Horspole/Mark Cox	2007 Honda CBR RR 600cc		21 11.54	106.822	Fri, 1st June Practice
17	6	Roy Hanks/Dave Wells	Suzuki K6 600cc	Rose Hanks	21 15.04	106.528	Thur, 31st May Practice
18	21	Dave Wallis/Philip Iremonger	2000 Honda RR 600cc	Compass	21 21.61	105.982	Fri, 1st June Practice
19	46	Douglas Wright/Dipash Chauhan*	2006 Suzuki Honda 600cc	Dougie Wright & Eddy Wright	21 25.42	105.668	Fri, 1st June Practice
20	15	Roger Stockton/Pete Alton	2007 Yamaha R6 600cc		21 32.00	105.130	Tues, 5th June
21	18	Bill Currie/Philip Bridge	2007 Yamaha R6 600cc		21 32.59	105.082	Fri, 1st June Practice
22	20	Kenny Howles/Doug Jewell	2007 Suzuki GSXR 600cc	Clive Price Racing	21 34.82	104.901	Thur, 31st May Practice
23	36	Mark Halliday/Mark Holland	2004 Kawasaki ZX6RR 600cc	Hazel's Fashions of Tamworth	21 42.81	104.258	Fri, 1st June Practice
24	17	Tony Baker/Fiona Baker-Milligan	2003 Yamaha R6 600cc		21 43.54	104.200	Fri, 1st June Practice
25	52	Steven Coombes/Darren Hope	2006 Honda Ireson RR 600cc	Clive Price Racing	21 51.67	103.553	Tues, 5th June
26	29	Brian Kelly/Dicky Gale	2005 Honda DMR 600cc		21 53.39	103.418	Thur, 31st May Practice
27	23	Tony Thirkell/Roy King	2005 Honda 600 RR 600cc	Merlin Race Paint	22 04.64	102.539	Tues, 5th June
28	37	Rod Bellas/Geoff Knight	2007 Honda 600cc		22 05.87	102.444	Fri, 1st June Practice
29	43	Steve Pullan/Kevin Morgan	2006 Suzuki K3 600cc		22 08.81	102.218	Thur, 31st May Practice
30	26	Mike Cookson/Diane Noakes	1998 Honda CBR 600cc		22 10.56	102.083	Fri, 1st June Practice
31	28	Howard Baker/Nigel Barlow	2005 Honda CBR 600cc	D & J Bikespares, Lincoln	22 12.40	101.942	Thur, 31st May Practice
32	41	Francois Leblond/Sylvie Leblond	2000 Honda CBR 600cc		22 18.53	101.476	Mon, 28th May
33	34	Nev Jones/Joe Shardlow	2007 Suzuki GSXR 600cc		22 19.84	101.376	Mon, 28th May
34	22	Mick Harvey/Steve Taylor	2007 Suzuki K6 600cc	theFSD.com	22 22.60	101.168	Fri, 1st June Practice
35	39	Peter Farrelly/Jason Miller	2002 Yamaha R6 600cc		22 23.38	101.109	Tues, 5th June
36	27	Eddy Wright/Martin Hull	2006 Honda 600 RR 600cc		22 27.47	100.802	Thur, 31st May Practice
37	31	Neil Kelly/Jason O'Connor	1998 Honda CBR 600cc		22 32.86	100.401	Thur, 31st May Practice
38	30	Peter Nuttall/Neil Wheatley	2005 Honda RR 600cc		22 33.69	100.339	Mon, 28th May
39	38	Alan Langton/Christian Chaigneau	1997 Yamaha R6 600cc	Ray Sansbury	22 33.72	100.337	Thur, 31st May Practice
40	59	John Saunders/Loic Ansquer	2004 Yamaha YZF 600cc		22 34.47	100.281	Thur, 31st May Practice
41	33	Bryan Pedder/Rod Steadman	2002 Yamaha Thundercat 600cc	Bill & Neil Coxon	22 43.45	99.621	Fri, 1st June Practice
42	32	Stephen Ramsden/James Coward	1997 Yamaha Thundercat 600cc		22 46.19	99.421	Thur, 31st May Practice
43	53	Dylan Lynch/Aaron Galligan	2006 Honda R6 600cc		22 48.22	99.273	Tues, 5th June
44	71	Matthew Sayle/Aki Alto*	2000 Yamaha Thundercat 600cc		22 50.03	99.142	Tues, 5th June
45	54	Mike Roscher/Michael Hildebrand*	1997 Yamaha Thundercat 600cc		22 50.47	99.110	Tues, 5th June
46	56	Keith Walters/James Hibberd	2006 Honda CBR 600cc		22 52.16	98.989	Tues, 5th June
47	42	Wal Saunders/Eddy Kiff	2006 Yamaha R6 600cc	Dialled In Racing	23 05.80	98.014	Thur, 31st May Practice
48	35	Andrew Thompson/Steve Harpham	2006 Yamaha R6 600cc		23 09.24	97.771	Thur, 31st May Practice
49	49	Brian Alflatt/Herve Chenu	2004 Honda CBR 600cc		23 10.76	97.665	Fri, 1st June Practice
50	50	Michael Thompson/Bruce Moore	2001 Yamaha Thundercat 600cc		23 12.22	97.562	Fri, 1st June Practice
51	55	Dick Tapken/Willem Vandis	2001 Suzuki GSXR 600cc	Dialled In Racing	23 15.00	97.368	Fri, 1st June Practice
52	45	Wayne Lockey/Stuart Stobbart	2000 Yamaha R6 600cc		23 17.43	97.199	Thur, 31st May Practice
53	47	Geoff Smale/Karl McGrath	1999 Honda Ireson 600cc	Selfdrive Hire Ltd	23 19.46	97.058	Thur, 31st May Practice
54	40	Alan Warner/Bert Vloemans	2000 Kawasaki Ireson 600cc	Dialled In Racing	23 29.11	96.393	Fri, 1st June Practice
55	63	Jean-Louis Hergott/Christophe Darras	2005 Suzuki GSXR 600cc		23 30.30	96.312	Thur, 31st May Practice
56	48	Claude Montagnier/Laurent Seyeux	2007 Kawasaki ZXR 600cc		23 30.32	96.310	Fri, 1st June Practice
57	60	Peter Allebone/Bob Dowty	2005 Kawasaki ZX6 600cc		23 35.70	95.944	Mon, 28th May
58	64	Eckhard Rossinger/Peter Hoss*	2003 Suzuki GSXR 600cc		23 39.79	95.668	Thur, 31st May Practice
59	67	Ian Salter/Deborah Salter	2006 Honda CBR 600cc		23 41.06	95.582	Thur, 31st May Practice
60	66	Masahito Watanabe/Hideyuki	2007 Honda PC47E 600cc	Rising Sun Racing	23 49.25	95.034	Fri, 1st June Practice
61	70	Colin Smith/Tony Palacio	2003 Honda RR 600cc		23 54.39	94.694	Tues, 5th June
62	44	Dick Hawes/Tim Dixon	Yamaha R6 600cc	Dialled In Racing	24 01.45	94.230	Fri, 1st June Practice
63	68	Robert Handcock/Mathew Buckley*	1998 Yamaha R6 600cc		24 07.26	93.852	Thur, 31st May Practice
64	58	Ruth Laidlow/Mike Killingsworth	2007 Suzuki GSXR 600cc	Action Motorcycles	24 07.43	93.841	Tues, 5th June
65	62	David Hirst/Paul Lowther*	2003 Honda R6 600cc		24 09.36	93.716	Tues, 5th June
66	52	Nick Houghton/Paul Thomas	2007 Yamaha YZF R6 600cc		24 13.59	93.443	Mon, 28th May
67	74	Arthur Belsey/Tony Belsey*	2002 Yamaha 600cc		25 50.61	87.596	Tues, 5th June

* Denotes newcomer riders

PokerStars
SENIOR
Fastest Laps – All Sessions

Pos	No.	Rider	Machine	Entrant	Lap Time	Speed	Run
1	3	John McGuinness	2007 Honda Fireblade 1000cc	HM Plant Honda Racing	17 33.35	128.948	Wed, 6th June
2	8	Guy Martin	2007 Honda 1000cc	Hydrex Honda	17 40.66	128.060	Wed, 6th June
3	7	Ian Lougher	2007 Honda CBR 1000cc	Stobart Motorsport	17 42.78	127.804	Wed, 6th June
4	6	Ian Hutchinson	2007 Honda CBR 1000cc	HM Plant Honda Racing	17 43.47	127.721	Wed, 6th June
5	4	Martin Finnegan	2007 Honda CBR 1000cc	Alpha Boilers Racing	17 50.29	126.907	Wed, 6th June
6	2	Adrian Archibald	2007 Suzuki GSXR 1000cc	Relentless by TAS Racing	17 51.08	126.814	Wed, 6th June
7	1	Michael Rutter	2007 Kawasaki ZX10 R 1000cc	MSS Discovery Kawasaki	18 02.36	125.492	Wed, 6th June
8	11	Steve Plater*	2007 Yamaha R1 1000cc	AIM Racing	18 15.29	124.011	Wed, 6th June
9	17	Nigel Beattie	2007 Yamaha R1 1000cc	CD Racing/Millsport Racing	18 34.00	121.929	Wed, 6th June
10	12	Keith Amor*	2005 Honda CBR 1000cc	Robinson Concrete	18 35.08	121.810	Wed, 6th June
11	24	Dan Stewart	2006 Yamaha R1 1000cc	Wilcock Consulting	18 35.42	121.773	Wed, 6th June
12	15	Gary Carswell	2007 Kawasaki ZX10R 1000cc	Bolliger Kawasaki/SK Support	18 36.26	121.681	Wed, 6th June
13	25	Chris Palmer	2005 Yamaha R1 1000cc	Solway Slate & Tile	18 37.84	121.509	Wed, 6th June
14	10	Conor Cummins	2007 Yamaha YZF R1 1000cc	Team Millsport Racing	18 41.40	121.124	Wed, 6th June
15	20	Mark Parrett	2007 Yamaha R1 1000cc	Ripley Land	18 43.44	120.904	Wed, 6th June
16	5	Bruce Anstey	2007 Suzuki GSXR 1000cc	Relentless by TAS Racing	18 51.56	120.036	Tues, 5th June
17	29	John Burrows	2006 Honda CBR 1000cc	H.M. Sports Motorhomes	18 53.87	119.792	Wed, 6th June
18	37	Roger Maher*	2006 Yamaha R1 1000cc		19 00.63	119.082	Wed, 6th June
19	30	Liam Quinn	2006 Yamaha R1 1000cc	Team Racing	19 02.41	118.896	Wed, 6th June
20	53	George Spence	2006 Yamaha YZF R1 1000cc		19 05.46	118.580	Wed, 6th June
21	32	David Coughlan	2005 Yamaha R1 1000cc	Ridge Developments	19 11.90	117.917	Thur, 31st May Practice
22	31	Jimmy Moore*	2007 Honda CBR 1000cc	Team Black Horse Racing	19 12.65	117.840	Wed, 6th June
23	26	Les Shand	2006 Honda CBR 1000cc	Barron Transport	19 19.10	117.184	Wed, 6th June
24	72	Marc Ramsbotham*	2006 Suzuki K6 1000cc		19 26.23	116.468	Wed, 6th June
25	57	Alan Bud Jackson	2005 Suzuki GSXR 1000cc	BDS Fuels	19 28.97	116.195	Wed, 6th June
26	49	Craig Atkinson	2004 Suzuki GSXR 1000cc	Martin Bullock Raceteam	19 36.14	115.486	Wed, 6th June
27	46	Paul Duckett	2005 Kawasaki ZX10 RR 1000cc	Wilson & Collins	19 39.82	115.126	Wed, 6th June
28	54	Stephen Harper	2006 Suzuki GSXR 1000cc		19 40.81	115.029	Wed, 6th June
29	66	John Crellin	2002 Suzuki GSX 1000cc	J Richards	19 44.86	114.636	Thur, 31st May Practice
30	52	Paul Dobbs	2003 Suzuki GSXR 1000cc	Dave East Engineering	19 59.18	113.267	Tue, 29th May Practice
31	74	David Hewson*	2006 Kawasaki ZX10 1000cc		20 09.20	112.329	Wed, 6th June
32	41	Tim Maher	2005 Suzuki GSXR 1000cc		20 14.72	111.818	Tues, 5th June
33	58	Andrew Marsden	2004 Yamaha R1 1000cc	Austin Powered Racing	20 15.93	111.707	Wed, 6th June
34	21	Chris Heath	2004 Honda CBR 1000cc	Webtech Software	20 24.64	110.913	Mon, 28th May
35	65	Steve Linsdell	2001 Paton PG500RC 500cc	Squadra Corse CMM	20 53.55	108.355	Thur, 31st May Practice
36	75	Bob Collins*	2007 Suzuki GSXR 1000cc	2Bob Racing	21 18.01	106.281	Wed, 6th June

© Double Red

© Jon Stroud

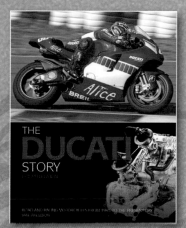

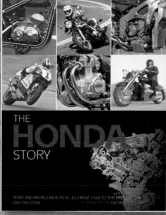
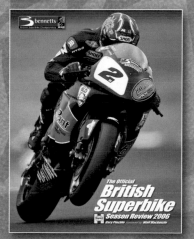
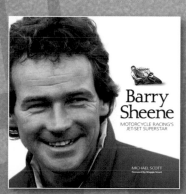
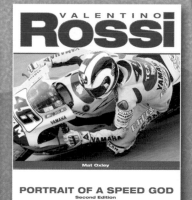
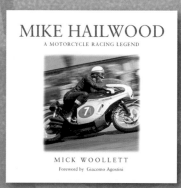
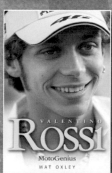

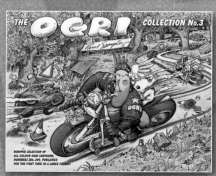

Bennetts
SUPERBIKE TT
John McGuinness reigns supreme

Mylchreests GROUP VOLVO

Nobles Hospital H A&E

© Mac McDiarmid

SUPERBIKE TT

SETTING A NEW SUPERBIKE LAP RECORD AND A NEW RACE RECORD, THE HM PLANT HONDA STAR RIPPED THE OPPOSITION TO BITS IN MONDAY'S BENNETTS SUPERBIKE TT RACE AS HE WON HIS 12TH TT

By Dave Fern & Gary Pinchin

Opposite: Guy Martin pushed as hard as he dared on the Hydrex Honda but couldn't quite match the flying John McGuinness.

© Stephen Davison

Below: Michael Rutter's ride on the MSS Kawasaki ended very early with a blown motor.

© Double Red

The rain and mist, as well as the tyre controversies of Saturday, had all but gone and the first race action of the fortnight was able to get underway, but not without two further hour-long delays owing to damp and misty conditions.

As Michael Rutter, back racing on the Island after a break of seven years, powered his Isilon MSS Discovery Kawasaki away from the Glencrutchery Road startline at 12.45pm, the riders in the Bennetts Superbike TT Race had been advised of some damp patches on the course (at Greeba, from the Hairpin to the Waterworks at Ramsey, and from Kate's through to the Creg), but all the riders put behind them the wrangles over the forbidden use of 'cut-slick' tyres that had allegedly posed a major threat to the participation of some of the major players had the race gone ahead as originally scheduled.

The emphasis was on racing, and it wasn't long before all attention was being focussed firmly on John McGuinness, the winner of the race for the previous three years, on the first two occasions for Yamaha and last year aboard the same HM Plant Honda Fireblade on which he was now charging ahead. The Lancastrian ruled supreme, just as he had done in practice when he came close to matching his lap record. Despite a few anxieties about a little dampness in places on the Mountain Course, he was up and running as only he can be, the back end of his Fireblade hanging out of shape at times as he powered relentlessly on.

McGuinness was away third on the road, following Rutter and the Relentless Suzuki ridden by Adrian Archibald, and soon he was making inroads on them. But while he had an untroubled run over the first nine miles or so to Glen Helen, others were already having problems. Local rider Nigel Beattie couldn't get his Yamaha off the startline because of a rear wheel problem. As he snicked his bike into gear, one of the wheel adjuster brackets sheared off, and luckily was spotted by an eagle-eyed marshal.

Bruce Anstey was having to make adjustments to his Suzuki, its problem later found to be a blown ignition amplifier box.

Soon Rutter ground to a halt with a blown engine. It was probably for the good since Rutter was hiding the fact that he was riding with a suspected broken scaphoid in his left wrist, caused when he highsided out of the Russell's chicane in the previous weekend's BSB round at Snetterton. He said: "Each time I braked it hurt when my hand was forced onto the bar. It was hard to use the clutch too. But I was still gutted when the thing stopped. I felt well on it other than my wrist."

McGuinness was flying, already by then 2secs up on Guy Martin on the Hydrex Honda with Ian Hutchinson in close contention on the second HM Plant bike. Ian Lougher, Ryan Farquhar, Archibald and Martin Finnegan were packed in adrift of them with local hero Paul Hunt riding strongly. Anstey stopped at Crosby, his Relentless Suzuki team boss Phillip Neil reporting: "We had an ignition amplifier go – a forty-quid part. It's not the first time either, as we had one fail on Michael Laverty's supersport bike at Snetterton."

The race leader had pulled another 0.5sec on Martin by the time they reached Ramsey for the first time, but the Hydrex rider was hounding him all the way and giving no chance for any thought of relaxation. However, the dash over the Mountain saw McGuinness use the 210bhp of the factory Fireblade to the full, opening up more of a lead on his favourite section.

McGuinness was leading on the road by now and as they powered into the second lap he was running 4.5secs clear of Martin with Hutchinson another 5secs down. Finnegan was 15secs further back with Lougher not too far adrift and just holding off the attentions of Farquhar with Archibald and Conor Cummins running strongly. But Hunt was out: he had crashed at Kerrowmoar, fortunately without serious injury.

At the front Martin was giving little away and McGuinness was having to ride hard to maintain his

MIST AND OIL CAUSE RESCHEDULING

'Mist on the Mountain' is an ever-present problem for racers and spectators alike and the weather pays scant regard to the occasion, whether or not it be the opening race day of the fortnight.

However, the prevailing conditions overhead weren't the initial cause of the hold-up ahead of the scheduled running of the Bennetts Superbike TT Race on Saturday. Rather, with ten minutes to go, race officials called for a half-hour delay as marshals dealt with an alleged oil spillage at the Bungalow.

The explanation was that the one-way system in operation over the Mountain caused delays for the team of marshals to reach their positions and sort themselves out ready for the action, and it was only when they inspected the road in front of them that they discovered the drops of oil on the racing line.

It was necessary to call in a mechanical sweeper to deal with the problem, and that brought about frustrations for the riders and their teams who were assembled on the dummy grid on Glencrutchery Road.

While the oil problem was being resolved, the weather, which had been on the grey and gloomy side all morning, closed in again and light rain began to fall on the damp patches that were already the cause of considerable anxiety among some of the riders. In addition low cloud and mist reduced visibility to almost nil in some places, particularly at Brandywell.

Local weather forecasters were called into play and they opined that conditions would worsen through the day, and into Sunday. So at 12.20pm the decision was made to postpone the race until Monday morning, and to re-schedule Monday's programme by moving the PokerStars Superstock race to Tuesday.

"It's unbelievable. We've built up for this for a year, and then this happens," said John McGuinness. "Safety is paramount around here so this has to be the right decision. It feels as though ten tons of cement have been lifted off my back right now, but, that said, I'm ready to go when they say."

advantage. By the time they reached Parliament Square in Ramsey the gap between them was just 4.8secs. Hutchinson, still feeling the effects of the shoulder injury sustained in a crash during a British Supersport race the previous month, was third, though losing ground on the front-running duo, but he was still well ahead of Finnegan, Farquhar, Lougher and Cummins.

Again over the Mountain, McGuinness set a fearsome pace that was to almost double his advantage. Incredibly, that second lap was achieved in a time of 17m 38.85secs, a Superbike record of 128.279mph – and that included slowing down for his pit-stop.

McGuinness was well in control and his pit crew were just as slick, refuelling, popping in a new rear wheel, and getting him out in 44secs. That increased by 7secs his advantage over Martin, whose stop had been somewhat slower. Hutchinson was running third, 20secs down, but ahead of Finnegan by a similar margin. Farquhar, Lougher, Cummins, Archibald, Ian Armstrong and Mark Parrett completed the top ten.

Others were having problems. Wigan's Jim Hodson withdrew, suffering from rib injuries he sustained in Friday night's horrifying crash at the Black Dub with Belgian rider Michael Weynand and Ballymoney's Victor Gilmore. Also out was Paul Owen, while Jamie Edmeades tipped off at Ballacraine and Dave Milling incurred a 10secs penalty

"IT WAS A DIFFERENT BIKE TO PRACTICE… IT JUST WOULDN'T HANDLE. THE FRONT WAS OFF THE GROUND EVERYWHERE. IT WAS LIKE A DIFFERENT BIKE BUT WE'VE CHANGED NOTHING."

IAN LOUGHER

Right: Ian Lougher pushes on at Union Mills: after comfortably doing 128mph in practice, he struggled with handling problems in the race.
© Double Red

Below: Martin Finnegan finished fourth on the Klaffi Honda, admitting after the race that he'd been too cautious on the opening lap.
© Dave Purves

Below: Chris Palmer, better known as a 125, 250 or 600 rider, hustles his Yamaha R1 through the top of Barregarrow on his way to a respectable 13th place.
© **Double Red**

for a stop-box offence as he pitted the works Aprilia.

It was a trouble-free run for McGuinness, who was 17.83secs clear at Glen Helen on the third lap, but pushing on with unrelenting pace he added a further 4secs to that as he completed half distance. Parrett didn't get that far as he tumbled at Cruickshanks. The top six were running in order as a pattern developed, with 66secs separating them, though further back Steve Plater was beginning to put together a determined challenge for a top ten finish.

By the fourth lap, in bright sunshine and with the course now dry, McGuinness, more confident, was forging away. Martin wasn't taking it lying down, and he was doing his best to stay in contention as he lived up to his comments that he wasn't out there to make up the numbers. He was

gaining a lot of fans with his hard-charging performance, though that left him 25.68secs down as they pitted for the second time.

Again the HM Plant pit crew provided a rapid turn-around for their man, getting him back on track in just 40secs, in the process increasing his lead over Martin to 36secs. Their speed almost equalled that of McGuinness, whose fourth lap had been completed at 127.207mph. Hutchinson was a solid third, from Finnegan, Lougher, Farquhar, Archibald, Cummins, Armstrong and Plater.

Martin had ground to make up and that showed from the off as he pegged back 5secs on McGuinness in the opening 10 miles of the fifth lap, and on the Sulby Straight he was surprisingly 10mph faster than the leader. Round

Top: Everyone is a photographer as Dan Stewart crests Ballaugh Bridge on his way to 12th place on his Yamaha.
© Double Red

Bottom left: Local hero Paul Hunt, seen here at Ago's Leap, crashed out at Kerrowmoar, thankfully without serious injury.
© Double Red

Bottom right: At Braddan, and Guy Martin has caught and passed Ian Hutchinson on the road; they finished second and third respectively.
© Double Red

Opposite: The TT pit stops are probably the most stressful time for the teams during the races, but everything looks cool and calm as laid-back Ian Hutchinson takes a sip of energy drink to see him through another two laps.
© Double Red

PLATER'S IMPRESSIVE TT DEBUT

Steve Plater is not only one of the top BSB short-circuit racers but has also won races at the North West 200 and the Macau Grand Prix. However, 2007 was his first time at the TT and he quickly got to grips with the demands of the Mountain Course.

His performance in the Bennetts Superbike TT Race was stunning. He gradually picked up pace and worked through the field with a confident, measured performance, illustrated in the early stages when, having been the 20th fastest rider at the Sulby speed trap on the opening lap, he was third best next time round at a speed of 185.4mph.

He progressed through the field, upping his pace again, with a top speed of 187.5mph on the fifth lap, on course to finishing as the top newcomer in the race, and tenth overall, having completed the race at an average speed of 123.141mph.

It was a ride that left the Lincolnshire rider well pleased with his efforts.

"That was spot-on. I am well happy with that. I learned quite a lot through the race and found some

different lines by following some of the faster guys.

"I got caught out twice. Once at May Hill when someone held up a chalkboard for me on the first lap – I was so busy reading it that I was distracted and missed my turning point. Then I made a mistake at the 13th Milestone, which isn't the place to do that.

"I got on okay with the pit-stops. Having done quite a bit of endurance racing I'm used to those but found them not really long enough.

I really could have done with more time to have a cup of tea and a slice of cake!

"I wasn't actually aiming for any position for this race. I had top 15 in my mind but really wasn't too bothered. I just wanted to finish the race, using it as a few more laps of practice. I just want to learn more and more this year."

Right: Steve Plater's tenth place was an outstanding result for a TT rookie – even if he reckoned he was more intent on getting laps under his belt than worrying about where he finished.

© Dave Purves

"I GOT CAUGHT OUT TWICE. ONCE AT MAY HILL WHEN SOMEONE HELD UP A CHALKBOARD FOR ME ON THE FIRST LAP – I WAS SO BUSY READING IT THAT I WAS DISTRACTED AND MISSED MY TURNING POINT."

STEVE PLATER

SUPERBIKE TT

the lap Martin continued to make inroads into the leader's advantage, paring it back to 27.44secs at Ramsey and then taking out another a second on the dash over the Mountain. Chris Heath and Shaun Harris both retired, while Daniel Jansen crashed at Union Mills and suffered a leg injury.

McGuinness pepped up things a little on the sixth and final dash through Glen Helen but again Martin came back at him. But the result was never in doubt as the HM Plant Honda rider completed the 12th victory of his TT career.

"It's unbelievable," said McGuinness. "I'm not getting any younger, and they made me work for this one. I'd trained hard all winter to be ready for them and it's well worth it all.

"I had to ride really hard and gave it everything. In places it was a bit damp, and they're not really my conditions, but here we are and enjoying it.

"To win this race is a tremendous feeling. It will go down in the history books as the first win in the Centenary event and that means an awful lot for me and for Honda – this victory is a testament to their preparation."

The success put him third in the list of all-time winners and rightly he was given a tremendous reception around the course by the tens of thousands of spectators who had enjoyed his winning performance.

"I've never seen so many. Seeing them all there waving to me on that last lap left me feeling really emotional. Winning is always special, this one is even more so. I'm just glad that I could put on such a show for them and give them the victory."

Again, McGuinness, in giving Honda their 131st win on the Island, had used his tried and tested strategy of throwing everything into the race from the off.

"It has worked well before, so why not again? I got my head down and went for it, riding as hard as I could, though being a bit careful in the damp bits. I had a few moments on the first lap, including a big slide at the 13th Milestone when the back end of the bike came round on me, but I kept it going."

Martin took second. "Maybe I didn't push hard enough on the first lap," he said. "I'm disappointed as I want to win races, but happy with second and I have a lot to learn, but now, there's Friday and the Senior race. That's the one to win. If you win a six-lap race around here, then you really are someone."

Hutchinson took third and said: "I'm fairly pleased with that. I was a bit conscious of the conditions on the first couple of laps and had a few slides. At Ramsey on the final lap the front end tucked in a bit but I held on, though it probably didn't look too professional."

Finnegan, Lougher and Farquhar completed an all-Honda top six. Finnegan said: "I messed up the first lap, by taking it a bit too easy for the first few miles, but after that I was okay. We made a few small changes to the bike and the rear suspension was pumping a bit on the last lap."

Lougher, after doing 128mph in practice, was devastated with his performance in the race. "It was a different bike to practice," he said. "It just wouldn't handle. The front was off the ground everywhere. It was like a different bike but we've changed nothing. It was hard to

Opposite: Keith Amor was another impressive rookie: without Cameron Donald, he had the full attention of the Uel Duncan Honda team.
© Double Red

Top: The congregation get a chance to worship Conor Cummins as the emerging Manx hero finishes eighth on the JMf Millsport Yamaha.
© Mac McDiarmid

Below: The stop box. Brake.
Stop. Foot down. Accelerate.
One tiny mistake here can
incur enough of a time penalty
to lose a race. Experienced
McGuinness takes no risks.
© Double Red

"IT'S UNBELIEVABLE, I'M NOT GETTING ANY YOUNGER, AND THEY MADE ME WORK FOR THIS ONE. I'D TRAINED HARD ALL WINTER TO BE READY FOR THEM AND IT'S WELL WORTH IT ALL."

JOHN MCGUINNESS

hang on to and at places like Bray Hill and Rhencullen I was having to shut off, and at places where you wouldn't expect it the thing was tankslapping – so I couldn't ever settle. The weird thing is it seemed to settle on the third and fourth lap and then it was just as bad again in the fifth and sixth laps."

Archibald was seventh but frustrated by the handling of his GSX-R1000. Relentless team-mate Anstey had solved his suspension woes with an Ohlins shock but never got the chance to prove its worth in the race. Archibald stuck with his WP unit and said: "Any time I tried to push it the bike got out of shape. I also had a fork seal go when a stone hit but the bike wasn't great to begin with."

Cummins was next home and delighted with his eighth place: "I enjoyed the ride but I've got a sore neck just down to the buffeting you get around here. The bike has been really good and I did better than I expected. I would have been happy with a top-15 finish so this is a bonus!"

Ian Armstrong was ninth with Plater, on his debut in the event, tenth on the AIM Yamaha. John Barton, Dan Stewart and Chris Palmer ran just ahead of second best newcomer Keith Amor aboard the Uel Duncan Honda, with Davy Morgan completing the top 15 finishers.

Top: Relief. McGuinness gets his race week off to a winning start.
© **Stephen Davison**

Right: Ryan Farquhar lacks the motocross technique here, landing the Mark Johns Honda on its nose at Ballaugh Bridge – he finished sixth.
© **Double Red**

Opposite: Ian Pattinson pushing hard at Braddan on Martin Bullock's Suzuki GSX-R1000.
© **Mac McDiarmid**

SUPERBIKE TT

RESULTS

Monday 4th June

LAP ONE

Pos	Rider	Time	Speed
1	John McGuinness	17 42.79	127.804
2	Guy Martin	17 47.30	127.264
3	Ian Hutchinson	17 53.58	126.519
4	Martin Finnegan	18 08.84	124.745
5	Ian Lougher	18 12.89	124.283
6	Ryan Farquhar	18 13.07	124.263
7	Adrian Archibald	18 17.06	123.811
8	Conor Cummins	18 21.01	123.367
9	Ian Armstrong	18 30.52	122.311
10	Mark Parrett	18 37.77	121.517
11	Dan Stewart	18 46.54	120.571
12	Davy Morgan	18 49.11	120.297
13	Chris Palmer	18 54.49	119.726
14	Shaun Harris	18 55.08	119.664
15	James McBride	18 55.56	119.614
16	Stephen Oates	18 55.75	119.593
17	John Barton	18 56.56	119.508
18	Ian Pattinson	18 57.74	119.384
19	Mark Buckley	18 58.46	119.308
20	Steve Plater*	19 00.33	119.112

LAP TWO

Pos	Rider	Time	Speed
1	John McGuinness	17 38.85	128.279
2	Guy Martin	17 44.84	127.557
3	Ian Hutchinson	17 58.33	125.962
4	Martin Finnegan	18 03.19	125.396
5	Ryan Farquhar	18 12.85	124.288
6	Ian Lougher	18 21.45	123.318
7	Conor Cummins	18 18.97	123.595
8	Adrian Archibald	18 32.06	122.141
9	Ian Armstrong	18 26.73	122.730
10	Mark Parrett	18 37.84	121.509
11	Dan Stewart	18 40.38	121.234
12	James McBride	18 38.83	121.401
13	Davy Morgan	18 45.61	120.670
14	John Barton	18 41.32	121.132
15	Stephen Oates	18 44.37	120.804
16	Ian Pattinson	18 45.23	120.711
17	Steve Plater*	18 45.03	120.733
18	Chris Palmer	18 51.02	120.093
19	Gary Carswell	18 55.94	119.573
20	Mark Buckley	19 01.68	118.973

LAP THREE

Pos	Rider	Time	Speed
1	John McGuinness	18 29.05	122.473
2	Guy Martin	18 40.60	121.210
3	Ian Hutchinson	18 41.52	121.111
4	Martin Finnegan	18 44.77	120.761
5	Ian Lougher	18 43.52	120.895
6	Ryan Farquhar	19 02.19	118.919
7	Conor Cummins	19 19.90	117.104
8	Adrian Archibald	19 17.61	117.335
9	Ian Armstrong	19 29.25	116.167
10	Dan Stewart	19 46.25	114.502
11	John Barton	19 38.60	115.245
12	Steve Plater*	19 31.17	115.976
13	Davy Morgan	19 48.17	114.317
14	Ian Pattinson	19 46.17	114.510
15	Chris Palmer	19 43.90	114.730
16	Stephen Oates	19 53.18	113.837
17	James McBride	19 59.75	113.213
18	Gary Carswell	19 48.92	114.245
19	Gary Johnson*	19 39.98	115.111
20	Mark Buckley	19 52.61	113.891

LAP FOUR

Pos	Rider	Time	Speed
1	John McGuinness	17 47.78	127.207
2	Guy Martin	17 51.92	126.715
3	Ian Hutchinson	17 59.61	125.813
4	Martin Finnegan	17 56.89	126.130
5	Ian Lougher	18 06.94	124.964
6	Ryan Farquhar	18 09.31	124.692
7	Adrian Archibald	18 10.03	124.610
8	Conor Cummins	18 24.02	123.031
9	Ian Armstrong	18 29.50	122.423
10	Steve Plater*	18 30.21	122.344
11	John Barton	18 33.46	121.987
12	Dan Stewart	18 41.86	121.074
13	Davy Morgan	18 39.89	121.287
14	James McBride	18 29.59	122.412
15	Chris Palmer	18 43.11	120.939
16	Ian Pattinson	18 45.72	120.659
17	Stephen Oates	18 54.56	119.719
18	Keith Amor*	18 39.14	121.369
19	Gary Carswell	18 51.59	120.033
20	Mark Buckley	18 53.56	119.825

LAP FIVE

Pos	Rider	Time	Speed
1	John McGuinness	18 39.08	121.375
2	Guy Martin	18 39.87	121.289
3	Ian Hutchinson	18 40.61	121.209
4	Martin Finnegan	18 46.77	120.546
5	Ian Lougher	18 58.89	119.263
6	Ryan Farquhar	19 01.20	119.022
7	Adrian Archibald	18 57.68	119.390
8	Conor Cummins	19 24.70	116.620
9	Ian Armstrong	19 35.90	115.509
10	Steve Plater*	19 21.07	116.985
11	John Barton	19 28.23	116.268
12	Dan Stewart	19 34.89	115.609
13	Davy Morgan	19 43.28	114.790
14	Chris Palmer	19 34.94	115.605
15	Ian Pattinson	19 36.27	115.474
16	James McBride	19 53.47	113.810
17	Gary Carswell	19 20.67	117.026
18	Keith Amor*	19 30.28	116.065
19	Stephen Oates	19 53.55	113.802
20	Gary Johnson*	19 46.63	114.465

LAP SIX

Pos	Rider	Time	Speed
1	John McGuinness	17 53.63	126.513
2	Guy Martin	17 52.58	126.637
3	Ian Hutchinson	18 03.68	125.339
4	Martin Finnegan	17 55.24	126.323
5	Ian Lougher	18 10.55	124.550
6	Ryan Farquhar	18 16.15	123.914
7	Adrian Archibald	18 12.82	124.292
8	Conor Cummins	18 30.40	122.323
9	Ian Armstrong	18 35.76	121.736
10	Steve Plater*	18 23.03	123.141
11	John Barton	18 31.76	122.174
12	Dan Stewart	18 36.27	121.681
13	Chris Palmer	18 25.89	122.823
14	Keith Amor*	18 17.60	123.750
15	Davy Morgan	18 37.59	121.536
16	Gary Carswell	18 33.11	122.026
17	Ian Pattinson	18 42.94	120.958
18	James McBride	18 37.41	121.556
19	Stephen Oates	18 51.51	120.041
20	Gary Johnson*	19 09.27	118.186

THE HIGHS

JOHN McGUINNESS
HM Plant Honda
Made his intentions plain from the start, riding hard and fast. Might have had the best bike on the Island, but it still takes a great rider to bring the best out of it and he used those qualities to the full with a stylish winning ride.

GUY MARTIN
Hydrex Honda
Fast talker, fast rider. Always good for a great soundbite, but equally good on the course with his own brand of riding pushing him ever closer to the first victory he's so desperate to achieve on the Island. Again, so near, but no cigar!

IAN HUTCHINSON
HM Plant Honda
Still nursing a shoulder injury from a crash on the mainland, and that made throwing the big bike round this course painful and difficult. Had a few scary moments in the damp and then taking back-markers on the final lap.

MARTIN FINNEGAN
Alpha Boilers Honda
Hard and unrelenting ride, but not able to make any real challenge for a top-three finish – noticeable that his privateer Fireblade lacked the punch of the two factory HM Plant machines.

IAN LOUGHER
Stobart Honda
Overcame the hard-riding Ryan Farquhar to take fifth place but his hopes of achieving a 'big-bike' win never looked achievable despite his smooth riding in an unequal contest against the McGuinness Fireblade.

THE LOWS

MICHAEL RUTTER
Isilon MSS Kawasaki
Unhappy return to the Island with machine problems more problematic than the wrist injury sustained in a crash during a Bennetts British Superbike race the previous month.

BRUCE ANSTEY
Relentless Suzuki by TAS
Sidelined just six miles into the opening lap by an ignition amplifier failure.

PAUL HUNT
John Alsop Yamaha
Local firefighter who was determined to fly the Manx flag, but in his 21st year of racing the course he tipped off Kerrowmoar, suffering a leg injury that ruled him out of the remainder of the festival.

ADRIAN ARCHIBALD
Relentless Suzuki by TAS
Struggled throughout with a handling problem, therefore not able to push hard but held on amid several scary moments.

NIGEL BEATTIE
JMf Millsport Yamaha
Didn't make the start thanks to an eagle-eyed scrutineer who spotted a broken wheel adjuster that could have proved highly dangerous had he set off down Bray Hill.

Pos	No	Rider	Machine	Entrant	Time	Speed	Replica
1	3	John McGuinness	2007 Honda Fireblade 1000cc	HM Plant Honda Racing	01 48 11.17	125.550	Silver
2	8	Guy Martin	2007 Honda 1000cc	Hydrex Honda	01 48 37.11	125.051	Silver
3	6	Ian Hutchinson	2007 Honda CBR 1000cc	HM Plant Honda Racing	01 49 17.33	124.284	Silver
4	4	Martin Finnegan	2007 Honda CBR 1000cc	Alpha Boilers Racing	01 49 35.71	123.936	Silver
5	7	Ian Lougher	2007 Honda CBR 1000cc	Stobart Motorsport	01 50 34.23	122.843	Silver
6	9	Ryan Farquhar	2007 Honda Fireblade 1000cc	Mark Johns Motors	01 50 54.77	122.464	Silver
7	2	Adrian Archibald	2007 Suzuki GSXR 1000cc	Relentless by TAS Racing	01 51 27.25	121.869	Silver
8	10	Conor Cummins	2007 Yamaha YZF R1 1000cc	Team Millsport Racing	01 52 19.00	120.933	Silver
9	13	Ian Armstrong	2004 Yamaha R1 1000cc	Canteen Smithy	01 53 07.65	120.066	Silver
10	31	Steve Plater*	2007 Yamaha R1 1000cc	AIM Racing	01 53 30.84	119.657	Silver
11	19	John Barton	2006 Honda CBR 1000cc	Marks Bloom Racing	01 53 49.94	119.323	Bronze
12	24	Dan Stewart	2006 Yamaha R1 1000cc	Wilcock Consulting	01 54 06.19	119.040	Bronze
13	25	Chris Palmer	2005 Yamaha R1 1000cc	Solway Slate & Tile	01 54 13.34	118.915	Bronze
14	45	Keith Amor*	2005 Honda CBR 1000cc	Robinson Concrete	01 54 21.21	118.779	Bronze
15	16	Davy Morgan	2005 Honda 1000cc	Investasure	01 54 23.65	118.737	Bronze
16	15	Gary Carswell	2007 Kawasaki ZX10R 1000cc	Bolliger Kawasaki/SK Support	01 54 33.53	118.566	Bronze
17	27	Ian Pattinson	2006 Suzuki GSXR 1000cc	Martin Bullock Raceteam	01 54 34.06	118.557	Bronze
18	23	James McBride	2007 Yamaha R1 1000cc		01 54 34.61	118.548	Bronze
19	36	Stephen Oates	2007 Suzuki GSXR 1000cc	Hallett Aviation	01 55 12.92	117.891	Bronze
20	28	Gary Johnson*	2007 Yamaha R1 1000cc	Speedfreak Racing	01 55 43.39	117.373	Bronze
21	35	Phil Stewart	2007 Yamaha R1 1000cc		01 55 47.05	117.311	Bronze
22	26	Les Shand	2006 Honda CBR 1000cc	Barron Transport	01 56 34.80	116.511	Bronze
23	52	Paul Dobbs	2003 Suzuki GSXR 1000cc	Dave East Engineering	01 56 44.25	116.353	Bronze
24	49	Craig Atkinson	2004 Suzuki GSXR 1000cc	Martin Bullock Raceteam	01 56 49.69	116.263	Bronze
25	43	Michael Dunlop	2004 Yamaha 1000cc		01 57 14.17	115.859	Bronze
26	40	Mark Miller	Aprilia 1000cc	Wolfman/Yoshiharu/Padgetts	01 57 15.61	115.835	Bronze
27	53	George Spence	2006 Yamaha YZF R1 1000cc		01 57 46.92	115.321	Bronze
28	41	Tim Maher	2005 Suzuki GSXR 1000cc		01 57 59.20	115.121	Bronze
29	70	David Coughlan	2005 Yamaha 1000cc	Marks Bloom Racing	01 57 59.51	115.116	Bronze
30	58	Stephen Harper	2006 Suzuki GSXR 1000cc		01 58 14.66	114.871	Bronze
31	44	Dave Madsen-Mygdal	2007 Yamaha R1 1000cc	CSC Racing	01 58 20.52	114.776	Bronze
32	50	Frank Spenner	2004 Yamaha R1 1000cc	ADAC Hessen-Thueringen	01 58 34.97	114.543	Bronze
33	54	Jimmy Moore*	2007 Honda CBR 1000cc	Team Black Horse Racing	01 58 39.11	114.476	Bronze
34	68	Steve Kuenne	2006 Yamaha YZF 1000cc	Dave Sandlan	01 58 54.00	114.237	Bronze
35	69	David Paredes	Yamaha R1 1000cc	Bill Smith Motorcycles	01 59 06.06	114.044	
36	55	Paul Shoesmith	2007 Yamaha R1 1000cc	Speedfreak Racing	01 59 09.53	113.989	
37	39	Roger Maher*	2006 Yamaha R1 1000cc		01 59 16.01	113.886	
38	46	Paul Duckett	2005 Kawasaki ZX10 RR 1000cc	Wislon & Collins	01 59 26.55	113.718	
39	66	Chris McGahan	2007 Yamaha R1 1000cc	McKinstry Skip Hire	01 59 32.05	113.631	
40	71	Fabrice Miguet	2006 Suzuki GSXR 1000cc		01 59 43.09	113.456	
41	74	Martin Hamberg	2006 Yamaha R1 1000cc	Hallett Aviation Racing	01 59 57.51	113.229	
42	59	David Milling	2006 Aprilia RSV 1000cc	Aprilia UK	02 00 17.77	112.911	
43	65	Christer Miinin*	2006 Suzuki GSXE 1000cc	Martin Bullock Raceteam	02 00 22.05	112.844	
44	77	Alan Connor	2006 Suzuki GSXR 1000cc	Dunshaughlin RRSC	02 00 27.36	112.761	
45	56	Alan Bud Jackson	2005 Suzuki GSXR 1000cc	BDS Fuels	02 00 39.77	112.568	
46	60	Thomas Schoenfelder	2005 Suzuki GSXR 1000cc	ADAC Hessent-Thueringen	02 00 43.34	112.513	
47	80	Marc Ramsbotham*	2006 Suzuki K6 1000cc		02 00 47.12	112.454	
48	64	Karsten Schmidt	2006 Suzuki GSXR 1000cc		02 01 18.49	111.969	
49	57	Andrew Marsden	2004 Yamaha R1 1000cc	Austin Powered Racing	02 01 45.13	111.561	
50	81	Sandor Bitter	2006 Suzuki GSXR 1000cc		02 02 35.54	110.797	
51	86	Chris Petty	2006 Suzuki GSXR 1000cc	York Suzuki Centre	02 02 49.96	110.580	
52	85	Ian Mackman*	2006 Suzuki GSXR 1000cc	Bill Smith Motorcycles	02 03 03.75	110.373	
53	88	David Hewson*	2006 Kawasaki ZX10 1000cc		02 03 12.43	110.244	
54	67	Dirk Kaletsch	2004 Honda CBR 1000cc		02 03 42.85	109.792	
55	75	Antonio Maeso*	2007 Yamaha R1 1000cc		02 09 09.62	105.162	

RETIREMENTS

Time	No	Rider	Machine	Entrant	Location
12:54:05	5	Bruce Anstey	2007 Suzuki GSXR 1000cc	Relentless by TAS Racing	**Crosby Village Cross Roads** (4.50 miles)
13:06:58	17	Nigel Beattie	2007 Yamaha R1 1000cc	CD Racing/Millsport Racing	**Grandstand** (0 miles)
13:12:17	30	Liam Quinn	2006 Yamaha R1 1000cc	Team Racing	**Quarterbridge** (1.25 miles)
13:17:24	42	Paul Owen	2006 Kawasaki ZX10R 1000cc	Back to Normal	**Pits** (0.01 miles)
13:23:52	1	Michael Rutter	2007 Kawasaki ZX10 R 1000cc	MSS Discovery Kawasaki	**Glen Helen** (9.25 miles)
13:24:18	90	John Nisill	2006 Yamaha R1 1000cc	PR Haulage/CJN Services	**Quarterbridge** (1.25 miles)
13:28:40	18	Shaun Harris	2007 Suzuki K7 1000cc	Blacks Bike Shop	**Pits** (0.01 miles)
13:32:36	38	Jim Hodson	2007 Yamaha R1 1000cc	Pete Beale Racing	**Pits** (0.01 miles)
13:38:45	47	Tim Poole	2007 Yamaha YZF R1 1000cc	Bill Smith Motorcycles	**Pits** (0.01 miles)
13:43:53	89	Mike Hose	2003 Aprilia RSVR 1000cc	Mike Hose Motorcycles	**Pits** (0.01 miles)
13:45:30	20	Mark Parrett	2007 Yamaha R1 1000cc	Ripley Land	**May Hill Cruickshanks Corner** (24.00 miles)
13:46:06	35	Phil Stewart	2007 Yamaha R1 1000cc		**Ballagarey Corner** (3.50 miles)
13:52:46	21	Chris Heath	2004 Honda CBR 1000cc		**Signpost Corner** (36.50 miles)
13:54:01	62	Adrian McFarland	2005 Yamaha R1 1000cc	Team Hardship Racing	**Creg Ny Baa** (34.50 miles)
13:58:54	37	James Edmeades	2007 Yamaha R1 1000cc	Speedfreak Racing	**Ballacraine** (7.50 miles)
14:15:14	29	John Burrows	2006 Honda CBR 1000cc	H.M. Sports Motorhomes	**Braddan Bridge** (Church) (1.75 miles)
14:17:27	63	John Crellin	2002 Suzuki GSX 1000cc	J Richards	**Pits** (0.01 miles)
14:30:05	33	Mark Buckley	2006 Yamaha YZF R1 1000cc	Crossan Motorcycles	**Westwood** (Civil Defence) (13.20 miles)
14:49:35	14	Paul Hunt	2006 Yamaha R1 1000cc	John Alsop	**Kerrowmoar** (Civil Defence) (20.25 miles)
15:09:12	61	Daniel Jansen	2005 Kawasaki ZX10 1000cc		**Union Mills** (Strang Road) (2.60 miles)

* Denotes newcomer riders

PokerStars
SUPERSTOCK TT

Bruce Anstey owns
Superstock – again

SUPERFAST BRUCE SETS STUNNING EARLY PACE FOR HIS FOURTH SUCCESSIVE WIN IN THE CLASS

By Dave Fern & Gary Pinchin

Bruce Anstey shattered his own race and lap records as he romped to victory in the four-lap PokerStars Superstock TT Race at unbelievable speeds on what was little more than a road-going Suzuki GSX-R1000. His best lap of 128.400mph aboard the Relentless-backed, TAS-prepared bike was even faster than John McGuinness had recorded as he won the previous afternoon's Superbike race on the fully-tuned, slick-shod Honda Fireblade.

For the previous three years the reserved Kiwi had won this race in its various guises as Production 1000 TT and more recently Superstock TT, and in perfect conditions on Tuesday 5 June he left no-one under any illusions that he was all set to maintain the record.

Anstey's performance was remarkable, and one that helped power him to his sixth victory on the Island, and his fourth in this class, as he packed the power to lead throughout, breaking the challenge of 12-time TT race winner McGuinness by shattering the record on the opening lap from a standing start, and then going even faster next time round.

Anstey wasn't messing around from the moment the flag dropped. He was riding at his best, and by the time he had covered the ten miles or so to the first timing sector, and first of the outposts of the Manx Radio commentary

team, he was running almost 4secs ahead of the HM Plant Honda in the hands of McGuinness.

The pace was stunning, his lead swelling to 7.83secs on the dash to Ramsey. Although McGuinness is often quickest over the Mountain, on this occasion the Lancastrian had no answer, even though he himself was running inside the record. As McGuinness crossed the line to start his second lap, he was 12.96secs adrift, Anstey having put in a staggering time of 17min 38.70secs (128.297mph) from a standing start.

Ian Hutchinson on the second HM Plant bike was holding third, some 4secs up on Martin Finnegan, who was giving MV Agusta a competitive return to the Island after a break of three decades. Guy Martin was fifth on the Hydrex Honda from Ryan Farquhar on Kenny Harker's Kawasaki, but there was no luck for Anstey's team-mate Adrian Archibald, who pitted after one lap reporting that his Suzuki was "wobbling a bit at the front". In fact what he really meant was that it was scaring him witless with huge tankslappers. "We've had trouble all weekend with the handling. It was unstable everywhere. As soon as I set off it tankslapped down Bray Hill and was much the same everywhere."

Anstey, however, was having no such problems and was upping the tempo and forging further ahead. He had opened up a further 5secs as he tore through Glen Helen, was 20.33secs up at Ramsey and as he pitted for the half-distance fuelling halt he was running 23 seconds clear of McGuinness. There was no surprise when the timing

Top: Seen at Governor's Bridge, Ian Hutchinson led Martin Finnegan on the road after two laps; Hutchinson finished third, over 20secs up on the MV Agusta rider.
© Double Red

Opposite: Bruce Anstey set a sensational pace from the start and even John McGuinness had no response to the Relentless Suzuki rider's opening lap of 128.29mph – the pair are seen approaching Gooseneck.
© Jon Stroud

PHENOMENAL ROAD BIKES

The speeds recorded during the race were phenomenal considering that the bikes were little more that standard road-going machines with key ignitions and very few modifications permitted. But that did pose a question – were they all strictly legal?

The answer was 'yes', as each of the bikes examined at post-race scrutineering passed without problem.

So why the queries? Simply the incredible opening lap. John McGuinness raised the record to 126.74mph, but that lasted only a few seconds before Bruce Anstey completed his lap and shattered the new record.

The Relentless Suzuki rider, who had been clocked at 182.90mph through the Sulby speed trap, completed the first lap in 17min 38.70secs, an amazing average speed of 128.297mph, and that wasn't the end of it. There was more to come on the second lap, completed at 128.400mph.

"He really pulled our pants down on that first lap," said a bemused McGuinness, who finished the race in second place aboard the HM Plant Honda. "Bruce is the 'super Superstocker'. He beat me fair and square, but I can tell you that it wasn't for the lack of trying. There was no way I could have ridden any harder or faster.

"My bike never missed a beat and when you consider that you can go into a shop and buy the thing, turn the key and ride it, the speeds have been amazing. I broke the record, but Bruce was still faster."

Those thoughts were echoed by his team-mate Ian Hutchinson: "When I got the minus five signal on my board, I just couldn't believe it. Things like that really deflate you, especially as it came so early in the race."

Anstey, a man of few words, let his speed and race victory do most of the talking: "They were two good, hard, fast laps and I got past them [McGuinness and Hutchinson] a lot quicker than I thought I would."

Right: John McGuinness might be on it, but still leaves himself acres of room coming out of Creg-ny-Baa as he chases Bruce Anstey on the road.
© Double Red

Below: Gary Johnson, top rookie finisher in the Superstock race with 12th place, leads 20th-placed Chris Palmer at Gooseneck.
© Jon Stroud

screens flashed up his lap time and a record-breaking lap at 128.400mph.

Hutchinson was 18secs down on the leading duo, but 10secs up on Finnegan. Conor Cummins was fifth, but the Manx rider had difficulty re-starting his bike after pitting for fuel. Guy Martin and Ryan Farquhar didn't make it that far, running out of fuel at the Creg and at Bedstead respectively. Farquhar said: "I couldn't believe it. In practice we had 2 litres of fuel left." Martin was equally bemused: "My bike used more fuel than my superbike so we're not sure what has happened."

Enjoying a really fast 'splash and dash', Anstey was quickly back on track. He and McGuinness had basically spent the same time in pit lane, but there was a fractional increase in Anstey's lead early on into that third lap and that had swelled by 1sec to 24secs as they powered through Ramsey. Anstey's Suzuki was awesome over the Mountain section, giving McGuinness no opportunity to hit back and, by the end of the third lap the Kiwi was 27.31secs clear.

Behind them Hutchinson continued to ride hard, a further 27secs down, running just ahead of Finnegan, Mark Parrett and Cummins, whose Yamaha had stalled as he left the pits, leaving him trying to make up the lost time on his third lap. Nevertheless, Cummins was proclaimed the fastest ever Manx rider around the course with a lap at 124.212mph – and, like Anstey, he was to better that. James McBride, Ian Pattinson, Dan Stewart and Ian Armstrong were packed in behind.

There was no chance of pegging anything back on Anstey. He was flying, extending his lead lap by lap and that despite coming across a lot of traffic as he carved through the backmarkers. At Glen Helen his lead was 29secs; at Ballaugh Bridge, 32secs; at Ramsey 33secs. He

Right: After the disappointment of not starting the Superbike race, Nigel Beattie bounced back to claim 13th place in the Superstock race on his R1.
© Dave Purves

Below: Martin Finnegan's MV Agusta was fast, but not fast enough to run with the HM Plant Honda he expected to be able to beat. Fourth was a good result for the Italian manufacturer, returning to the Isle of Man for the first time since the 1970s.
© Stephen Davison

"I COULDN'T BELIEVE IT. IN PRACTICE WE HAD TWO LITRES OF FUEL LEFT."

RYAN FARQUHAR

TOO MUCH DASH, NOT ENOUGH SPLASH

The super-fast pace took its toll on several competitors as they failed to reach the halfway house 'splash and dash' refuelling halt. Guy Martin ground to a halt at the Creg, while Ryan Farquhar stopped at Bedstead.

In the Superstock and Supersport races at the TT, it's always a fine balancing act to have just enough fuel on board to get to the line but not so much that you're unduly weighed down or the handling of the bike is affected. The emphasis is to do anything and everything possible to get that judgement as accurate as possible.

The regulations for the event mean that bikes have to run with tanks of standard size, as per the manufacturer's specification, but 'it is permitted to modify the standard manufacturer's tank provided the silhouette of the tank remains as homologated'.

Some teams use squeezy bottles to try and force in more fuel, but, despite the calculations, things can work out incorrectly – as Martin discovered when his Hydrex Honda spluttered to a halt.

"Damn it, I thought," said Martin. "The fuel light had come on at Ginger Hall and I knew that I was going to really struggle to get back. The lads had been trying to get a bit more fuel in, and I thought they'd squeezed enough in, brimming it."

His demise wasn't lost on McGuinness. "I caught sight of him sitting on the grass – looked like he was having a picnic. Sympathy for him? No [with a laugh]. We've all been there, haven't we? It happens over here, part of the learning experience."

Left: Ryan Farquhar's run on the Kenny Harker Kawasaki ended prematurely when he ran out of fuel on the second lap – even though he had run two laps of practice without problem.
© Jon Stroud

Right: Guy Martin's Hydrex Honda also ran dry before he could get back to the pits at the end of the second lap.
© Double Red

"McBRIDE GOT ME JUST AFTER THE PIT STOP SO I JUST STUCK WITH HIM FOR A LAP, PULLING WHEELIES AND HAVING FUN."

IAN LOUGHER

was comfortably clear, but his speed was unrelenting as he concentrated hard. At the Bungalow, he was running 35.46secs ahead of McGuinness and by the end of the race his winning margin was up to 40.30secs.

A man of few words, Anstey summed up his performance: "The bike was really going well, although I was a little bit nervous early on. I knew that I had to put in a really good first lap, and then push on hard because the opposition was strong. I was concentrating hard, and was able to take John McGuinness on the second lap.

"The first two were good laps, breaking the record in both of them. I'd got my head down and was going for it and the speed was no problem.

"I was brought up on production machines but the Relentless Suzuki was just awesome. If I'm a bit picky we could have had the handling a bit better but I suppose we were doing Superbike-type lap times out there – which

Left: James McBride finished seventh on his Yamaha.
© **Double Red**

Below: Ian Lougher struggled to 14th place with his stock Honda lacking power against the Suzukis and Yamahas.
© **Double Red**

Opposite: Ian Pattinson (14) has made up a lot of time on Gary Carswell as the Suzuki-mounted duo round Gooseneck in a battle for eighth place.
© **Jon Stroud**

shows how good the showroom GSX-R1000 Suzuki really is. It's nice to win a Centenary TT race."

McGuinness had given everything, and he was fulsome in his praise for the winner's performance: "I'm second, but that's not for the lack of trying – Bruce's speed was absolutely incredible. I was trying really hard, pushing on, but there was no staying with him. My bike never missed a beat, it was good enough to win the race, but on this occasion the jockey wasn't good enough.

"Isn't it amazing that these bikes have a key ignition and you could fire one up and take it down to the shops. This is a testament to the bikes. But also to Anstey, he's the King of the Superstockers, a super superstocker!"

HM Plant Honda team-mate Ian Hutchinson took a solid third. He said: "It was all right, but I knew Anstey would be the man to beat. I rode the wheels off my bike but couldn't do anything to stop him. I was steady to Glen Helen on the first lap but I got minus five after that on my pit board and thought, 'he must be on it if he's that far ahead of me already.'

"I was with Finnegan after the pit stops and was ahead of him on the road but he started dicing with me. I didn't want to battle with him. Why did he do that when he knew I was already ahead of him on time?"

Finnegan finished fourth on the MV Agusta and said: "I lost the front at Gorselea twice and that was it – the bike was good though. But it's funny how the Hondas weren't even in the top seven in 2006 but were so fast this year."

Cummins finished fifth on his Yamaha with a final lap at 124.332mph, although ninth-placed fellow Manxman Gary Carswell went even quicker with his 124.621mph last lap to become fastest-ever Manx rider around the course. Cummins, though, was happy with his performance: "I'm really chuffed with that. I kept smooth all the way around. The bike was fantastic and so was the team. The only thing wrong was me messing up the pit stop. It wouldn't fire up but I got my head down and made the time up."

Mark Parrett and James McBride, also riding Yamahas, followed Cummins home, with Suzuki riders Ian Pattinson and Gary Carswell ahead of tenth-placed Dan Stewart.

Ian Armstrong was just ahead of Gary Johnson and Nigel Beattie, while Steve Plater continued to impress in his 'rookie' year on the Island, taking 15th place, running only a couple of seconds down on the experienced Ian Lougher, who was again at a loss to explain quite what went wrong and said: "Second lap I was going to pull out but that wouldn't have been fair with all the Black Horse people here. The bike wasn't competitive so I just thought, 'I'll bring it home.' McBride got me just after the pit stop so I just stuck with him for a lap, pulling wheelies and having fun."

They had ridden hard, but had been left far behind in the wake of the amazing Anstey, who had rounded his race off with a last lap at an average speed of 125.771mph, ensuring a record-breaking end to his victory – the race-winning time of 1hr 11mins 56.29secs was a staggering 65secs inside the previous record.

The only sad note at what had been a great sporting event was the news that another highly popular Kiwi, Shaun Harris, who returned to the event after a two-year break, had been seriously injured in a heavy crash at Union Mills and had been airlifted to the Nobles Hospital in Douglas.

Opposite & below: Bruce Anstey is, according to McGuinness, 'Mr Super Superstocker'. This was the Kiwi's fourth consecutive Superstock TT victory.
© Stephen Davison

LAP ONE

Pos	Rider	Time	Speed
1	Bruce Anstey	17 38.70	128.297
2	John McGuinness	17 51.66	126.746
3	Ian Hutchinson	17 55.41	126.303
4	Martin Finnegan	18 00.71	125.685
5	Guy Martin	18 01.89	125.547
6	Ryan Farquhar	18 06.17	125.052
7	Conor Cummins	18 10.78	124.523
8	Mark Parrett	18 18.33	123.667
9	James McBride	18 22.12	123.242
10	Dan Stewart	18 25.34	122.883
11	Gary Johnson	18 25.56	122.859
12	Ian Lougher	18 33.21	122.015
13	Ian Pattinson	18 34.23	121.903
14	Adrian Archibald	18 35.61	121.752
15	Phil Stewart	18 37.10	121.590
16	Shaun Harris	18 37.11	121.589
17	Nigel Beattie	18 37.18	121.581
18	Ian Armstrong	18 37.22	121.577
19	Stephen Oates	18 39.11	121.371
20	Gary Carswell	18 43.37	120.911

LAP TWO

Pos	Rider	Time	Speed
1	Bruce Anstey	17 37.85	128.400
2	John McGuinness	17 48.05	127.174
3	Ian Hutchinson	18 02.70	125.453
4	Martin Finnegan	18 07.17	124.937
5	Conor Cummins	18 13.52	124.212
6	James McBride	18 18.17	123.686
7	Mark Parrett	18 22.91	123.154
8	Dan Stewart	18 27.47	122.647
9	Ian Pattinson	18 25.40	122.877
10	Ian Armstrong	18 32.54	122.088
11	Gary Johnson	18 44.61	120.778
12	Stephen Oates	18 35.19	121.798
13	Nigel Beattie	18 40.22	121.252
14	Phil Stewart	18 40.32	121.240
15	Gary Carswell	18 37.38	121.559
16	Steve Plater	18 36.12	121.697
17	Ian Lougher	18 51.90	120.000
18	Mark Buckley	18 40.37	121.235
19	Keith Amor	18 48.24	120.389
20	Chris Palmer	18 47.95	120.420

LAP THREE

Pos	Rider	Time	Speed
1	Bruce Anstey	18 39.78	21.299
2	John McGuinness	18 43.93	120.851
3	Ian Hutchinson	18 52.92	119.892
4	Martin Finnegan	19 04.46	118.683
5	Mark Parrett	19 04.05	118.726
6	Conor Cummins	19 23.50	116.741
7	James McBride	19 21.50	116.942
8	Ian Pattinson	19 13.02	117.802
9	Dan Stewart	19 31.56	115.938
10	Ian Armstrong	19 21.35	116.957
11	Gary Johnson	19 29.21	116.171
12	Gary Carswell	19 21.22	116.970
13	Ian Lougher	19 27.39	116.352
14	Nigel Beattie	19 35.55	115.544
15	Stephen Oates	19 39.58	115.149
16	Steve Plater	19 30.37	116.055
17	Mark Buckley	19 33.76	115.721
18	Keith Amor	19 31.93	115.901
19	Les Shand	19 29.27	116.165
20	Chris Palmer	19 45.30	114.594

LAP FOUR

Pos	Rider	Time	Speed
1	Bruce Anstey	17 59.97	125.771
2	John McGuinness	18 12.96	124.276
3	Ian Hutchinson	18 07.88	124.855
4	Martin Finnegan	18 06.27	125.041
5	Conor Cummins	18 12.46	124.332
6	Mark Parrett	18 18.36	123.665
7	James McBride	18 19.38	123.550
8	Ian Pattinson	18 11.89	124.397
9	Gary Carswell	18 09.93	124.621
10	Dan Stewart	18 28.95	122.484
11	Ian Armstrong	18 32.39	122.105
12	Gary Johnson	18 36.73	121.630
13	Nigel Beattie	18 28.73	122.508
14	Ian Lougher	18 36.32	121.675
15	Steve Plater	18 35.83	121.728
16	Stephen Oates	18 46.19	120.608
17	Mark Buckley	18 40.33	121.240
18	Keith Amor	18 39.60	121.319
19	Les Shand	18 45.89	120.641
20	Chris Palmer	18 44.95	120.742

THE HIGHS

BRUCE ANSTEY

Relentless Suzuki by TAS

Took the race by the scruff of the neck from the start, forging clear with an incredible pace that broke any thoughts of challenges to his supremacy.

JOHN McGUINNESS

HM Plant Honda

Rode as hard, briefly bettering the record, as he could but unable to make any impression in the runaway lead being opened up by the dominant Anstey.

IAN HUTCHINSON

HM Plant Honda

Pushed on hard but admitted feeling a bit deflated when he kept seeing signals saying how far he was adrift – even so an impressive ride.

MARTIN FINNEGAN

Alpha Boilers MV Agusta

Shrugged aside the hype surrounding the return to the Island of this legendary marque, getting on with a solid job and missing out on a podium finish by less than 20secs.

CONOR CUMMINS

JMf Millsport Yamaha

Growing force, following his eight place in the Bennetts Superbike race with another maturing performance on the Yamaha R1.

THE LOWS

ADRIAN ARCHIBALD

Relentless Suzuki by TAS

"I knew as soon as I went down Bray Hill that my race was over. I couldn't even hook sixth gear until I was over Ago's leap – I was filling the road with the bike."

GUY MARTIN

Hydrex Honda

Had high expectations and began swiftly but early on into the second lap was having anxieties as the fuel light gave early warning that he would soon be out of gas.

RYAN FARQUHAR

McAdoo Kawasaki

Running sixth and looking at one point that he would be challenging Finnegan for better things, but spluttered forlornly to a halt at Bedstead.

IAN LOUGHER

Stobart Honda

Never able to match the pace of the leading runners and that left this highly experienced campaigner frustrated and annoyed to be so far back.

SHAUN HARRIS

Black Bike Shop Suzuki

Back on the Island after a two-year break but involved in a heavy crash at Union Mills that hospitalised him with serious injuries – but he was on the mend in hospital in Leeds as this book went to press.

RACE RESULTS

Pos	No	Rider	Machine	Entrant	Time	Speed	Replica
1	5	Bruce Anstey	2007 Suzuki GSXR 1000cc	Relentless by TAS Racing	01 11 56.29	125.875	Silver
2	3	John McGuinness	2007 Honda Fireblade 1000cc	HM Plant Honda Racing	01 12 36.59	124.710	Silver
3	6	Ian Hutchinson	2007 Honda CBR 1000cc	HM Plant Honda Racing	01 12 58.91	124.075	Silver
4	4	Martin Finnegan	2007 MV Agusta 1000cc	Alpha Boilers Racing	01 13 18.61	123.519	Silver
5	16	Conor Cummins	2007 Yamaha YZF R1 1000cc	Team Millsport Racing	01 14 00.26	122.360	Silver
6	10	Mark Parrett	2007 Yamaha R1 1000cc	C & C Ltd	01 14 03.65	122.267	Silver
7	12	James McBride	2007 Yamaha R1 1000cc		01 14 21.17	121.787	Silver
8	14	Ian Pattinson	2006 Suzuki GSXR 1000cc	Martin Bullock Raceteam	01 14 24.54	121.695	Silver
9	11	Gary Carswell	2000 Suzuki GSXR 1000cc		01 14 51.91	120.953	Silver
10	21	Dan Stewart	2007 Yamaha R1 1000cc	Wilcock Consulting	01 14 53.32	120.915	Silver
11	13	Ian Armstrong	2007 Suzuki GSX K7 1000cc	Powersport Bikes	01 15 03.51	120.642	Silver
12	29	Gary Johnson*	2007 Yamaha R1 1000cc	Speedfreak Racing	01 15 16.11	120.305	Silver
13	17	Nigel Beattie	2007 Yamaha R1 1000cc	CD Racing/Millsport Racing	01 15 21.68	120.157	Silver
14	7	Ian Lougher	2007 Honda CBR 1000cc	Team Black Horse Racing	01 15 28.81	119.968	Silver
15	31	Steve Plater*	2007 Yamaha R1 1000cc	AIM Racing	01 15 30.20	119.931	Silver
16	32	Stephen Oates	2007 Suzuki GSXR 1000cc	Hallett Aviation Racing	01 15 40.08	119.670	Bronze
17	33	Mark Buckley	2006 Yamaha YZF R1 1000cc	Crossan Motorcycles	01 15 40.90	119.649	Bronze
18	46	Keith Amor*	2007 Honda CBR 1000cc	Site Welding Services Ltd/Uel Duncan	01 15 46.37	119.505	Bronze
19	25	Les Shand	2007 Yamaha YZF R1 1000cc	Leeds Parcel Company	01 16 06.09	118.988	Bronze
20	24	Chris Palmer	2007 Yamaha R1 1000cc	NCT Racing	01 16 06.67	118.973	Bronze
21	48	Paul Dobbs	2003 Suzuki GSXR 1000cc	Dave East Engineering	01 16 32.94	118.293	Bronze
22	54	David Coughlan	2006 Suzuki GSXR 1000cc	R&C duetiny	01 16 45.01	117.983	Bronze
23	37	Stefano Bonetti	Suzuki GSXR 1000cc		01 17 01.97	117.550	Bronze
24	38	Mark Miller	Aprilia 1000cc	Wolfman/Yoshiharu/Padgetts	01 17 08.45	117.385	Bronze
25	50	Jimmy Moore*	2007 Honda CBR 1000cc	Team Black Horse Racing	01 17 09.47	117.359	Bronze
26	57	Paul Shoesmith	2007 Yamaha R1 1000cc	Speedfreak Racing	01 17 10.36	117.337	Bronze
27	45	Frank Spenner	2004 Yamaha R1 1000cc	ADAC Hessen-Thueringen	01 17 14.25	117.238	Bronze
28	40	Paul Owen	2006 Kawasaki ZX10R 1000cc	Back to Normal	01 17 15.47	117.208	Bronze
29	52	Steve Kuenne	2006 Yamaha YZF 1000cc	Dave Sandlan	01 17 33.17	116.762	Bronze
30	49	George Spence	2005 Yamaha YZF R1 1000cc		01 17 39.46	116.604	Bronze
31	26	John Burrows	2006 Suzuki GSXR 1000cc	H.M. Sports Motorhomes	01 17 39.99	116.591	Bronze
32	61	Stephen Harper	2006 Suzuki GSXR 1000cc		01 17 53.81	116.246	Bronze
33	30	Liam Quinn	2006 Yamaha R1 1000cc	Team Racing	01 18 00.60	116.077	Bronze
34	47	Tim Poole	2007 Yamaha YZF R1 1000cc	Bill Smith Motorcycles	01 18 00.80	116.073	Bronze
35	44	Dave Madsen-Mygdal	2007 Yamaha R1 1000cc	CSC Racing	01 18 06.87	115.922	Bronze
36	19	John Barton	2007 Suzuki K7 1000cc	Marks Bloom Racing	01 18 33.21	115.274	Bronze
37	34	James Edmeades	2007 Yamaha R1 1000cc	Speedfreak Racing	01 18 37.87	115.161	Bronze
38	87	Ian Mackman*	2006 Suzuki GSXR 1000cc	Bill Smith Motorcycles	01 18 38.86	115.136	Bronze
39	43	Christer Miinin	2006 Suzuki GSXE 1000cc	Martin Bullock Raceteam	01 18 38.94	115.134	Bronze
40	51	David Paredes	Yamaha R1 1000cc	Bill Smith Motorcycles	01 18 51.83	114.821	Bronze
41	59	John Crellin	Honda CBR 1000cc	J Richards	01 19 16.01	114.237	
42	80	Marc Ramsbotham*	2006 Suzuki K6 1000cc		01 19 18.61	114.175	
43	74	Alan Connor	2006 Suzuki GSXR 1000cc	Dunshaughlin RRSC	01 19 20.83	114.121	
44	53	Alan Bud Jackson	2005 Suzuki GSXR 1000cc	BDS Fuels	01 19 21.86	114.097	
45	55	Thomas Schoenfelder	2005 Suzuki GSXR 1000cc	ADAC Hessent-Thueringen	01 19 30.77	113.884	
46	65	Chris McGahan	2007 Yamaha R1 1000cc	McKinstry Skip Hire	01 19 32.22	113.849	
47	84	Robert Barber*	2005 Suzuki GSXR 750cc		01 19 52.03	113.378	
48	68	Fabrice Miguet	2006 Suzuki GSXR 1000cc		01 19 56.14	113.281	
49	89	Mike Crellin	Honda CBR 1000cc		01 20 49.35	112.038	
50	73	Derran Slous	2005 Suzuki GSXR 750cc		01 20 49.56	112.033	
51	50	Andrew Marsden	2004 Yamaha R1 1000cc	Austin Powered Racing	01 20 51.94	111.978	
52	88	Chris Petty	2007 Suzuki GSXR 1000cc	York Suzuki Centre	01 21 00.27	111.786	
53	85	David Hewson*	2006 Kawasaki ZX10 1000cc		01 21 39.06	110.901	
54	76	Mike Hose	2003 Aprilia RSVR 1000cc	Mike Hose Motorcycles	01 22 11.35	110.175	
55	78	Antonio Maeso*	2007 Yamaha R1 1000cc		01 23 23.79	108.580	
56	82	John Nisill*	2006 Yamaha R1 1000cc	PR Haulage/CJN Services	01 24 19.37	107.387	
57	67	Bob Collins*	2007 Suzuki GSXR 1000cc	2Bob Racing	01 24 26.33	107.240	

RETIREMENTS

Time	No	Rider	Machine	Entrant	Location
12:30:39	22	Davy Morgan	2007 Suzuki GSXR 1000cc	Blacks Bike Breaker	Ballacraine (7.50 miles)
12:35:15	2	Adrian Archibald	2007 Suzuki GSXR 1000cc	Relentless by TAS Racing	Pits (0.01 miles)
12:42:03	42	Tim Maher	2005 Suzuki GSXR 1000cc		Mountain Box (27.75 miles)
12:40:42	72	Martin Hamberg	2006 Yamaha R1 1000cc	Hallett Aviation Racing	Pits (0.01 miles)
12:52:10	8	Guy Martin	2007 Honda 1000cc	Hydrex Honda	Creg Ny Baa (34.50 miles)
12:54:48	1	Ryan Farquhar	2007 Kawasaki ZX10 1000cc	Harker Racing	Bedstead Corner (36.75 miles)
13:19:10	39	David Milling	2006 Aprilia RSV 1000cc	Aprilia UK	11th Milestone (11.00 miles)
13:31:27	63	Karsten Schmidt	2006 Suzuki GSXR 1000cc		Greeba Bridge (6.50 miles)
13:33:23	28	Phil Stewart	2007 Yamaha R1 1000cc		Pits (0.01 miles)
13:34:20	81	Sandor Bitter	2006 Suzuki GSXR 1000cc		Guthrie's Memorial (26.50 miles)
13:39:10	15	Shaun Harris	2007 Suzuki K7 1000cc	Blacks Bike Shop	Union Mills (Strang Road) (2.60 miles)
13:39:53	41	Craig Atkinson	2004 Suzuki GSXR 1000cc	Martin Bullock Raceteam	May Hill Cruickshanks Corner (24.00 miles)
13:56:27	66	Dirk Kaletsch	2004 Honda CBR 1000cc		Pits (0.01 miles)

* Denotes newcomer riders

PokerStars
SUPERSPORT TT

Ian Hutchinson claims
first TT win

HONDA'S MAN TAKES DRAMATIC POKERSTARS SUPERSPORT RACE AFTER ANSTEY'S PIT-STOP NIGHTMARE

By Dave Fern & Gary Pinchin

Ian Hutchinson scorched to an emotional first TT victory at record race pace aboard his HM Plant Honda in a highly dramatic PokerStars Supersport TT Race, finishing clear of last year's winner John McGuinness on the Padgetts Honda with Guy Martin's Hydrex Honda third.

The outcome of the race, however, turned around a problematic pit stop by Bruce Anstey. It was heartbreaking for the Kiwi, who had forged clear on the opening two laps, and was starting to contemplate a repeat of his winning ride in the previous day's PokerStars Superstock race when it all went wrong for him. His hard riding over the first two laps was undone by his Suzuki's reluctance to fire up after the half-distance refuelling halt.

His Honda rivals were quick to capitalise, with Hutchinson running a split second up on McGuinness after ten miles of the third lap, while Anstey put a high-speed damage-limitation exercise into play. To put it mildly, the loss of those vital seconds had been traumatic for the popular Kiwi, and he was left playing catch-up and reflecting what should have been. Hutchinson, by contrast, had no worries after his rapid pit stop, and he fully exploited the situation to take charge.

Anstey had started so well, powering to a record-breaking 124.055mph opening lap to emerge 2secs ahead of McGuinness. Hutchinson and Guy Martin disputed third place on that first lap, Martin's Honda fitted with an engine that he said he'd put together himself for the race. Nigel Beattie, Ryan Farquhar, Mark Parrett, Conor Cummins, Ian Lougher and Chris Palmer (the last named much more

suited to the smaller 600 than the 1000cc machines) were all well on the case, but there were problems for Michael Rutter, who retired at the Crosby Hotel with an oil leak.

Rutter's MSS Kawasaki team had borrowed an engine from Ryan Farquhar after blowing up their last one in practice. Rutter said: "My foot slipped off the peg going down Bray Hill starting the second lap but the leak wasn't so bad. But then it happened again and I thought it was best not to risk anything. I'm so disappointed with the way things have been going."

Adrian Archibald was also an early retirement, pulling out just into the second lap at Ballagarrie. He said: "There was water pouring out. I reckon it had done a head gasket. It started on the Mountain on the first lap and by Ballacraine on lap two I knew it was finished. The temperature was way up and I knew I had to stop." This was particularly frustrating for him and his Relentless Suzuki team, as the GSX-R600 had caught fire in the morning when a broken wire shorted onto the frame, forcing the team to replace the entire wiring loom before the race.

Back at the front of the race there was another record-breaking performance to come on that second lap, and again it was Anstey providing the magic as he charged round in 18min 06.27secs, a speed of 125.041mph. That saw him running 4.5secs up on McGuinness, aboard the Padgetts Honda, with Hutchinson a further 7secs down and only 0.5sec ahead of Martin. By now both of the Dunlop brothers, William and Michael, nephews of the legendary Joey, had pulled out with machine problems.

More dramas were unfolding in the pit lane. Anstey and his pit crew pushed his bike almost three-quarters of the way along it – around 200 yards – before it finally fired into life. "What can I say?" explained Anstey. "It's very disappointing but it's no-one's fault. The bike took a while to fire and it cost me the race – up to that point I was

Top: Once HM Plant Honda's Ian Hutchinson was leading on the road, Bruce Anstey had no chance to fight back from a disastrous pit stop.
© Mac McDiarmid

Top right: While Bruce Anstey is already setting the pace out on the road, back at the Grandstand there are still tense moments as the lower-order starters wait for their turn to be flagged off.
© Stephen Davison

Opposite: Guy Martin was third on the Hydrex Honda, acknowledging that he'd need to pull something out of the bag if he wanted to claim a TT victory in Friday's Senior.
© Double Red

"THE TT HAS HAD ITS DIPS, BUT IT IS RUNNING STRONG. NOW IT IS UPWARDS AND ONWARDS."

MURRAY WALKER

MURRAY STARTS THE RACE

Flagging away the leading riders in the PokerStars Supersport TT Race was a man who single-handedly transformed motorsport coverage on TV. With his insatiable enthusiasm and excitement, backed by an intimate knowledge of the sport on two and four wheels, Murray Walker brought racing to life.

Murray had been invited back to the Centenary celebrations, renewing a first-hand link that began way back in 1925 when, as a small boy, he accompanied his parents to the races. His father, Graham, was racing, and naturally Murray took a big interest in the action.

"I would have been about eight years old then," he recalled. "Dad had parked the bike outside the Castle Mona Hotel, and I quickly climbed on to it, and adopted a racing pose. I asked if I could do a bit more, but mum was stern and said, 'off!'"

Six years later, in 1931, Murray was at the TT again to cheer his father's victory, aboard a Rudge, in that year's Lightweight race.

Murray is one of life's real gentlemen and loves to be involved in any major motorsport event. He was delighted to be invited to the start-line to drop the flag to signal the start of the PokerStars Supersport race, seeing off the top riders as they charged into the four-lap race. Then he retired to the Media Office to study their progress on the timing screens. Attention to detail was just the same as when he was commentating, a career that took in lengthy stints describing the action on the Mountain Course, prior to his television work.

"I was involved in the commentary over here between 1949 and 1974, working at various locations including Ballaugh, Ramsey and Creg-ny-Baa. In 1962 I moved to *Grandstand*, and in those days the BBC was spending two to three hours a day, on national radio, covering the TT races."

Murray was able to re-live those times throughout the Centenary Festival as he relaxed among friends, as he savoured the Gala Dinner at the Villa Marina, and – most of all – as he watched races and in particular marvelled at John McGuinness breaking the magical 130mph mark as he completed a hat-trick of victories in the Senior TT.

"The week has been absolutely fabulous," Murray enthused after it was all over. "I was here when the first 80mph lap was set, then 90mph, then 100mph and so on, and now I am here when 130mph is topped for the first time. That is marvellous!

"The TT has had its dips, but it is running strong. Now it is upwards and onwards," said Murray with that knowing smile. He might not have followed in his father's footsteps as a winning motorcycle racer, but in terms of commentary he surpassed him to become one of motorsport's most respected figures.

John McGuinness ahead of Ryan Farquhar on the road through Laurel Bank.
© Double Red

SUPERSPORT TT

Right: Ian Hutchinson had been denied a rostrum place in the 2006 Supersport TT on a technicality outside his control, but this year there were no such problems and he earned a well-deserved first TT victory.
© Stephen Davison

Below: Bruce Anstey did everything right on the first two laps. His crew did everything right in the pits. Then the bike simply refused to fire on the button. It doesn't get any more frustrating.
© Double Red

Opposite: On the way to ninth place, Chris Palmer's Honda breaks the serenity as it howls through the verdant glade approaching Laurel Bank.
© Double Red

riding hard but cruising in control of the race. I had run two perfect laps, gradually easing away from both Hondas, and I was confident we would do the business. I couldn't fault the bike – we just got dealt a bad hand in the end. Everyone in the team is gutted, but that's racing."

Hutchinson was having no worries and was back on track, running 0.39secs up on McGuinness as they flashed through Glen Helen for the third time. Martin was third ahead of Anstey, who was riding hard and playing catch-up.

Hutchinson had the bit between his teeth and was 5secs up by the end of that third lap. McGuinness was second from Martin, Anstey, Parrett, Farquhar and Beattie. The pace was unrelenting but Hutchinson's HM Plant Honda was well in command, although McGuinness was giving it everything and on the final dash over the Mountain closed in dramatically.

The Lancastrian put in a final lap of 125.096mph to slice the deficit to just under 3secs, but Hutchinson held on to take that all-important first victory. He was finally able to dispel the bitter disappointment of his exclusion from the corresponding race of last year when his hard ride into second place came to nothing as a minor breach of the technical regulations, of which the rider knew nothing, was discovered at scrutineering.

"I just want to forget about that – at the time it killed me being disqualified – but now I have set the record straight by winning this Centenary TT race," reflected Hutchinson. "There are so many people over here this

year who have never been to the event before, and there has been so much close, safe racing that the event is on the crest of a wave.

"It was a perfect run, no problems. The pit stop was superb and I don't think I made a mistake all of the way through. I can still hardly believe that I've done it. On the final lap I knew that John was closing in on me, but felt comfortable that I could hold him. I didn't want to push too hard in case I made an error. I was concentrating really hard just to ensure that

"I WAS HAVING A BIT OF FUN WITH KEITH AMOR ON THAT LAST LAP AND IT WAS BRILLIANT, REALLY ENJOYABLE."

STEVE PLATER

Right: Steve Plater (31) and Keith Amor had a right ding-dong, short-circuit style, on the roads. Plater finished eighth, Amor 12th.
© Mac McDiarmid

DAMN THE BIKE!

Pit stops are a necessity, part of the TT scene, but the importance of them is heightened frequently. In the modern era of closely fought action, with little between the top riders, pit stops can be the decisive factor in the outcome of the race – and that's what happened in the PokerStars Supersport TT Race.

Bruce Anstey had a lead of over 4secs as he pitted to refuel his Relentless Suzuki by TAS, and though his pit stop was barely 3secs longer than those experienced by his main rivals John McGuinness and Ian Hutchinson, the drama was just beginning. The machine refused to fire on a number of occasions, while his pit team frantically pushed him most of the way down pit lane before his bike finally started and he was able to begin the third lap. That cost him his lead, putting him 23secs back on McGuinness.

But Anstey was full of fight, setting a searing pace as he clawed back time, but he had to be satisfied with fourth place despite his heroics over the final two laps. In the final 75 miles of racing, he hauled back the deficit from eventual winner Ian Hutchinson to just 14secs, but his valiant effort wasn't quite enough to warrant a podium position, losing out to Guy Martin in third place by just 2secs.

© Double Red

Right: Does it get any better than this? Fantastic weather. Beautiful Manx scenery. And John McGuinness absolutely flat-stick on the Padgetts Honda at Tower Bends.
© **Mac McDiarmid**

I took my first win, and I'm really delighted."

McGuinness had to settle for second best: "It was a fantastic race and Hutch deserved his victory."

Martin on the Hydrex Honda wasn't complaining about third: "It's good, mint, but I've got to try harder, and will be going for it in the Senior, no doubt about that."

Anstey, finishing fourth, took some consolation as he upped his own record on his final lap with an incredible time of 18min 05.35secs, an average speed of 125.147mph, although Martin out-paced him at 125.161mph. Anstey said: "My problem was that when I came out of the pits Hutchy was already by me. I could just see him in front and got my head down for the first couple of miles and caught him, but knew he'd tail me even once I got in front of him."

Nigel Beattie took fifth place: "After not being able to even start the Superbike race and then not getting into a rhythm for the Superstock, that was a good race. I saw Conor in front at Crosby– like a dot in the distance – and finally got him at Sulby on the second lap. We went into Ramsey but when I got to Parliament Square all the lights on the dash went out and a warning light flashed on. I was worried but it all came back up again so I got my head down and caught Conor again."

Beattie's JMf Millsport Yamaha team-mate and fellow Manxman Cummins finished sixth, Farquhar was seventh and Steve Plater was a strong eighth. "I was having a bit of fun with Keith Amor on that last lap and it was brilliant, really enjoyable," said Plater. "I was pushing a bit harder on the first lap this time. I set my stall out right from the start this time and it paid off. I'm happy with that result."

Chris Palmer and Ian Lougher completed the top ten, with Dan Stewart just holding off second-best newcomer Keith Amor in the scrap for 11th place with Martin Finnegan running adrift of them but ahead of Ian Pattinson and Jimmy Moore.

Above: Nigel Beattie finished fifth on the JMf Millsport Yamaha but leads Martin Finnegan here at Cronk-ny-Mona.
© Double Red

Bottom left: After the disappointment of the Superstock race, Ryan Farquhar finished seventh and top Kawasaki in Supersport.
© Jon Stroud

Bottom right: James McBride on his way to 19th place.
© Double Red

© Stephen Davison

TEAM-MATES OR RIVALS?

John McGuinness and Ian Hutchinson were HM Plant Honda teamsters for three of the races at the Isle of Man TT Races sponsored by Bennetts, but for the PokerStars Supersport race they lined up in opposing camps – the Yorkshireman continued with the factory team while the Lancastrian rode in the colours of the Padgetts Motorcycle team for whom he races in the Maxxis British Supersport series.

A war of the roses? Not really. Hutchinson had been snapped up during the close season by an astute Neil Tuxworth, the Honda Racing Manager looking to strengthen his resources for the future, while McGuinness, losing out on that contract, was still a vital part to the Honda effort as he was moved across to the Padgetts effort.

"Clive Padgett put together a very good package for me," reflected McGuinness. "It's a great team to be with, we're all as one, working together, and I really enjoy riding for them."

Meanwhile, Padgett enthused: "It's wonderful to see John up there on the podium. He's done a really good job and rode so well. Thanks to him, I've really enjoyed this race."

McGuinness might have done a little better but he was slightly hampered by losing a knee slider early in the race, and that left him with a bit of problem as he tried to get his knee down on the Mountain section, but he battled on, finishing less than 3secs down on Hutchinson.

"Ian has done a good job and I'm pleased for him," said McGuinness, adding with a grin, "but maybe I've taught him too much." If that was the case, it was a lesson well-learned by Hutchinson, who had overcome the bitter disappointment of his exclusion on a technicality the previous year.

"I can hardly believe it," said the rider from Bingley when he was greeted by the Manx Radio interviewer as he finished the race and was told that victory was his. "Thanks to Honda for giving me this chance."

"IAN HAS DONE A GOOD JOB AND I'M PLEASED FOR HIM, BUT MAYBE I'VE TAUGHT HIM TOO MUCH."
JOHN McGUINNESS

Right: John McGuinness tried so hard to give Clive Padgett a win but had to give best to his mate Ian Hutchinson on the rival HM Plant Honda.
© Mac McDiarmid

RESULTS

Wednesday 6th June

LAP ONE

Pos	Rider	Time	Speed
1	Bruce Anstey	18 14.90	124.055
2	John McGuinness	18 16.98	123.820
3	Guy Martin	18 20.24	123.453
4	Ian Hutchinson	18 20.59	123.414
5	Nigel Beattie	18 33.02	122.035
6	Ryan Farquhar	18 34.78	121.843
7	Mark Parrett	18 36.67	121.636
8	Conor Cummins	18 38.45	121.444
9	Ian Lougher	18 39.66	121.312
10	Chris Palmer	18 40.36	121.236
11	Adrian Archibald	18 42.71	120.983
12	Ian Pattinson	18 47.49	120.470
13	Michael Rutter	18 48.15	120.399
14	Dan Stewart	18 50.72	120.126
15	Steve Plater	18 51.81	120.009
16	Martin Finnegan	18 54.32	119.744
17	Roy Richardson	18 58.77	119.276
18	Ian Armstrong	18 59.92	119.155
19	James McBride	19 04.34	118.696
20	Keith Amor	19 05.28	118.598

LAP TWO

Pos	Rider	Time	Speed
1	Bruce Anstey	18 06.27	125.041
2	John McGuinness	18 08.68	124.763
3	Ian Hutchinson	18 11.96	124.390
4	Guy Martin	18 12.66	124.310
5	Ryan Farquhar	18 25.67	122.847
6	Mark Parrett	18 27.70	122.622
7	Nigel Beattie	18 34.66	121.856
8	Conor Cummins	18 34.95	121.824
9	Chris Palmer	18 35.93	121.718
10	Ian Lougher	18 44.60	120.779
11	Dan Stewart	18 36.08	121.701
12	Ian Pattinson	18 40.46	121.225
13	Steve Plater	18 41.84	121.076
14	Martin Finnegan	18 44.29	120.812
15	Ian Armstrong	18 49.20	120.287
16	Roy Richardson	18 53.56	119.825
17	Keith Amor	18 52.08	119.981
18	Jimmy Moore	18 50.22	120.178
19	James McBride	18 58.68	119.286
20	Les Shand	18 56.58	119.506

LAP THREE

Pos	Rider	Time	Speed
1	Ian Hutchinson	18 48.58	120.353
2	John McGuinness	19 00.50	119.095
3	Guy Martin	18 57.80	119.378
4	Bruce Anstey	19 11.76	117.931
5	Mark Parrett	19 26.86	116.405
6	Ryan Farquhar	19 31.57	115.937
7	Nigel Beattie	19 24.41	116.650
8	Conor Cummins	19 22.91	116.800
9	Chris Palmer	19 23.98	116.693
10	Steve Plater	19 15.55	117.544
11	Ian Lougher	19 28.46	116.246
12	Dan Stewart	19 33.87	115.710
13	Martin Finnegan	19 35.07	115.592
14	Keith Amor	19 22.21	116.870
15	Ian Pattinson	20 02.60	112.945
16	Ian Armstrong	19 44.33	114.687
17	Jimmy Moore	19 43.84	114.735
18	Roy Richardson	19 59.27	113.259
19	Les Shand	19 48.50	114.285
20	James McBride	19 55.25	113.640

LAP FOUR

Pos	Rider	Time	Speed
1	Ian Hutchinson	18 07.99	124.843
2	John McGuinness	18 05.79	125.096
3	Guy Martin	18 05.23	125.161
4	Bruce Anstey	18 05.35	125.147
5	Nigel Beattie	18 31.49	122.204
6	Conor Cummins	18 33.77	121.953
7	Ryan Farquhar	18 42.43	121.012
8	Steve Plater	18 25.74	122.840
9	Chris Palmer	18 34.93	121.827
10	Ian Lougher	18 42.22	121.035
11	Dan Stewart	18 41.33	121.131
12	Keith Amor	18 25.45	122.871
13	Martin Finnegan	18 51.88	120.002
14	Ian Pattinson	18 38.06	121.485
15	Jimmy Moore	18 39.02	121.381
16	Ian Armstrong	18 50.49	120.149
17	Roy Richardson	18 42.85	120.968
18	Les Shand	18 57.19	119.442
19	James McBride	18 53.67	119.813
20	Paul Dobbs	18 54.02	119.776

THE HIGHS

IAN HUTCHINSON
HM Plant Honda

Finally made the top step of the podium, beating the previous year's winner in the process and taking a result that laid to rest the bad memories of the 2006 race when he lost his second placing on a technicality.

JOHN McGUINNESS
Padgetts Honda

Rode as hard as he could but had to settle for second best, though left pondering what might have been but for a lost knee slider and then the heavy traffic he encountered in the closing stages at the most inopportune points.

GUY MARTIN
Hydrex Honda

"I'm not going to moan and complain, I'm third and I got the lap record so I'm happy really. Farquhar took some getting past as he's about ten foot wide when he's on the track – his elbows and knees stick out."

STEVE PLATER
AIM Yamaha

"I now have another silver trophy to add to the one I picked up for the Superbike race. As a newcomer I didn't expect too much but I've improved my lap times with each passing lap in this race."

JAMES McBRIDE
Yamaha

"I had a standard engine in the R6 and I just couldn't compete against the top-end speed of the likes of Steve Plater and Keith Amor. They caught and passed me on the Mountain, but I still got my Silver Replica."

THE LOWS

MARK PARRETT
Vixen Racing Yamaha

Running sixth at the half-distance pit stop but penalised 10secs for a 'stop-box' offence. Unperturbed by that, he rode hard to make up time only to be halted at Quarterbridge by a deflating rear tyre.

THE DUNLOPS
Michael (Honda) and William (Flynn Kawasaki)

Both retired in the early stages of the race with machine gremlins, William at Sulby, Michael at Ramsey.

BRUCE ANSTEY
Relentless Suzuki by TAS

Brilliantly hard riding, twice bettering the lap record in the opening two laps, but it was all undone when his bike was reluctant to fire up after the refuelling halt.

MICHAEL RUTTER
Isilon MSS Discovery Kawasaki

Another machine failure, as he was forced to pull out at Crosby – over the week, across all classes, he ended up with five engines needing rebuilds.

ADRIAN ARCHIBALD
Relentless Suzuki by TAS

Pulled out early into the second lap with an undisclosed machine problem. "What a week it's turning out to be for me – another retirement," he moaned.

RACE RESULTS

Pos	No	Rider	Machine	Entrant	Time	Speed	Replica
1	6	Ian Hutchinson	2007 Honda CBR 600cc	HM Plant Honda Racing	01 13 29.11	123.225	Silver
2	3	John McGuinness	2007 Honda CBR 600cc	Padgetts Honda	01 13 31.95	123.145	Silver
3	8	Guy Martin	2007 Honda 600cc	Hydrex Honda	01 13 35.92	123.035	Silver
4	5	Bruce Anstey	2007 Suzuki GSXR 600cc	Relentless by TAS Racing	01 13 38.27	122.969	Silver
5	11	Nigel Beattie	2007 Yamaha R6 600cc	CD Racing/Millsport Racing	01 15 03.59	120.640	Silver
6	10	Conor Cummins	2007 Yamaha YZF R6 600cc	Team Millsport Racing	01 15 10.08	120.466	Silver
7	1	Ryan Farquhar	2007 Kawasaki ZX6 600cc	Harker Racing	01 15 14.46	120.349	Silver
8	31	Steve Plater*	2007 Yamaha R6 600cc	AIM Racing	01 15 14.93	120.337	Silver
9	15	Chris Palmer	2005 Honda CBR 600cc	Solway Slate & Tile	01 15 15.20	120.330	Silver
10	7	Ian Lougher	2007 Honda CBR 600cc	Team Black Horse Racing	01 15 34.94	119.806	Silver
11	14	Dan Stewart	2006 Yamaha R6 600cc	Wilcock Consulting	01 15 41.99	119.620	Silver
12	28	Keith Amor*	2005 Honda RR 600cc	Wilson Craig/Uel Duncan Racing	01 15 45.03	119.540	Silver
13	9	Martin Finnegan	2007 Honda CBR 600cc	Alpha Boilers Racing	01 16 05.56	119.002	Silver
14	22	Ian Pattinson	2006 Honda CBR 600cc	Martin Bullock Raceteam	01 16 08.61	118.923	Silver
15	30	Jimmy Moore*	2007 Honda CBR 600cc	Team Black Horse Racing	01 16 22.98	118.550	Silver
16	21	Ian Armstrong	2006 Honda CBR 600cc	Padgetts Honda	01 16 23.94	118.525	Silver
17	44	Roy Richardson	2006 Yamaha R6 600cc	Ian Barnes Racing	01 16 34.44	118.254	Silver
18	26	Les Shand	2007 Yamaha R6 600cc	McKinstry Skip Hire	01 16 51.20	117.825	Silver
19	25	James McBride	2006 Yamaha R6 600cc		01 16 51.94	117.806	Silver
20	40	Paul Dobbs	2005 Triumph Daytona 675cc	Action Triumph	01 17 19.07	117.117	Bronze
21	18	Gary Carswell	2006 Honda CBR RR 600cc	Crossan Motorcycles	01 17 40.45	116.579	Bronze
22	37	Stephen Oates	2006 Suzuki GSXR 600cc	Hallett Aviation Racing	01 17 40.78	116.571	Bronze
23	33	Adrian McFarland	2006 Yamaha R6 600cc	Team Hardship Racing	01 17 53.39	116.256	Bronze
24	39	Mark Buckley	2006 Honda CBR 600cc	Crossan Motorcycles	01 17 55.99	116.192	Bronze
25	46	Tim Poole	2007 Triumph 675cc	Bill Smith Motorcycles	01 18 15.56	115.708	Bronze
26	35	Craig Atkinson	2006 Honda CBR 600cc	Martin Bullock Raceteam	01 18 16.52	115.684	Bronze
27	24	Paul Owen	2004 Honda CBR 600cc	Rapid Racing	01 18 32.00	115.304	Bronze
28	54	David Milling	2006 Honda 600cc	Dave Milling Motorcycles	01 18 34.42	115.245	Bronze
29	20	Davy Morgan	2007 Honda 600cc	Autotech	01 18 48.07	114.912	Bronze
30	48	Stefano Bonetti	Honda CBR 600cc		01 18 53.57	114.779	Bronze
31	71	Paul Shoesmith	2004 Yamaha R6 600cc	Speedfreak Racing	01 19 18.18	114.185	Bronze
32	53	Paul Duckett	2007 Triumph 675 RR 675cc	Investasure	01 19 32.21	113.849	Bronze
33	43	Mark Miller	Honda 600cc	Wolfman/Yoshiharu/Padgetts	01 19 33.88	113.809	Bronze
34	52	Dave Madsen-Mygdal	2007 Yamaha R6 600cc	CSC Racing	01 19 39.73	113.670	Bronze
35	76	David Coughlan	Honda RR 600cc	ATM Construction	01 19 45.08	113.543	Bronze
36	56	Chris McGahan	2007 Yamaha R6 600cc	Manx Glass and Glazing	01 19 53.68	113.339	Bronze
37	51	Alan Bennie	2005 Honda CBR 600cc		01 19 55.09	113.306	Bronze
38	45	Phil Harvey	2006 Yamaha YZF-R6 600cc	theFSD.com	01 20 02.69	113.127	Bronze
39	34	Manfred Vogl	2007 Yamaha R6 600cc		01 20 21.78	112.679	Bronze
40	50	Karsten Schmidt	2004 Ducati 750cc		01 20 22.18	112.669	Bronze
41	57	Mike Hose	2005 Honda CBR 600cc	RJP Racing	01 20 40.98	112.232	Bronze
42	67	Thomas Schoenfelder	Suzuki GSXR 600cc	ADAC Hessent-Thueringen	01 20 46.47	112.105	Bronze
43	60	Derran Slous	2005 Honda RR 600cc		01 20 48.81	112.051	Bronze
44	78	Stephen Harper	Honda 600cc		01 20 55.21	111.903	
45	65	John Crellin	Yamaha R6 600cc	J Richards	01 21 09.14	111.583	
46	81	Alan Connor	2006 Suzuki GSXR 600cc	Dunshaughlin RRSC	01 21 18.74	111.363	
47	70	Mike Crellin	Yamaha R6 600cc		01 21 29.06	111.128	
48	82	Ian Mackman*	Suzuki GSXR 600cc	Bill Smith Motorcycles	01 21 33.28	111.032	
49	74	Etienne Godart	Honda 600cc	Martin Bullock Raceteam	01 21 33.78	111.021	
50	89	Chris Petty	2005 Honda CBR 600cc	Dave Milling Motorcycles	01 22 00.16	110.426	
51	62	Alan Bud Jackson	2004 Yamaha R6 600cc	Oddfellows Arms	01 22 08.31	110.243	
52	63	Phil Gilmour	2004 Yamaha R6 600c	Austin Powered Racing	01 22 30.42	109.751	
53	79	Robert Barber*	2007 Triumph Daytona 675cc		01 22 32.53	109.704	
54	84	Angelo Conti*	2007 Triumph Daytona 675cc		01 22 41.58	109.504	
55	66	Kevin Murphy	2004 Triumph Daytona 600cc	C & C Ltd	01 24 23.19	107.306	
56	85	John Nisill*	2007 Honda CBR 600cc	Greenhey Engineering	01 24 51.92	106.701	
57	88	Wade Boyd	2005 Kawasaki ZX6 600cc	Hallett Aviation Racing	01 24 59.66	106.539	

RETIREMENTS

Time	No	Rider	Machine	Entrant	Location
11:02:25	27	William Dunlop	2006 Kawasaki 600cc	Lilley Racing	**Sulby Bridge** (19.90 miles)
11:04:01	32	Phil Stewart	2004 Honda 600RR 600cc		**Kirk Michael Village** (14.10 miles)
11:06:50	23	Chris Heath	Yamaha 600cc	Webtech Software	**Ballaugh Bridge** (17.00 miles)
11:10:01	12	Michael Rutter	2007 Kawasaki ZX6 R 600cc	MSS Discovery Kawasaki	**Crosby Hotel** (1) (4.51 miles)
11:13:34	29	John Burrows	2007 Honda RR 600cc	H.M. Sports Motorhomes	**Pits** (0.01 miles)
11:14:02	2	Adrian Archibald	2007 Suzuki GSXR 600cc	Relentless by TAS Racing	**Ballacraine** (7.50 miles)
11:22:50	42	Michael Dunlop	2006 Yamaha R6 600cc		**Parliament Square** (23.50 miles)
11:23:19	59	Frank Spenner	2006 Yamaha R6 600cc	ADAC Hessen-Thueringen	**Ballacraine** (7.50 miles)
11:27:33	47	Tim Maher	2007 Kawasaki ZX6R 600cc	Clarkes Hardware	**Parliament Square** (23.50 miles)
11:46:33	16	Mark Parrett	2007 Yamaha R1 600cc	Vixen Racing	**Quarterbridge** (1.25 miles)
12:03:22	41	Liam Quinn	2006 Yamaha R6 600cc	Team Racing	**Kirk Michael Village** (14.10 miles)

* Denotes newcomer riders

Bavaria Beer
SIDECAR TT

Moly double against all odds

HILTON
Arai
YAMAHA
MOTOR UK
Putoline
MOTORCYCLE OILS
metmachex
engineering
LOCKSIDE
racing.com
3
Haith
YOKOHAMA
micron
Andrassy
Wines
EXPRESS
TYRE
SERVICES
Stelling LTD
AUTO ELECTRICAL ENGINEERS
FACTORS TO THE TRADE
POLOS CAPS

AFTER A DRAMA-FILLED PRACTICE WEEK,
MOLYNEUX AND LONG – WITH A LITTLE HELP
FROM A DOG – REWROTE THE RECORD BOOKS
WITH THEIR TWO BAVARIA BEER SIDECAR
TT RACE WINS, EVEN IF THEY WEREN'T THE
FASTEST ON TRACK

By Dave Fern & Gary Pinchin

There was real surprise and delight for Dave Molyneux, as together with Rick Long he completed a winning Bavaria Beer Sidecar double – they were unexpected victories even for the all-time record winner in the 'chairs' as he made an emotional return to the Mountain Course.

Less than a year ago, the driver and sidecar constructor from Regaby, on the Island, had talked about hanging up his leathers. He had taken a battering in a big crash during practice for the 2006 event, but, with a little persuasion, not to mention financial input, he was back for more.

But his return was beset by mechanical problems. He had one engine blow up in testing at Jurby. During Monday practice he had a suspension problem at Crosby. On Tuesday the cam lobe sensor failed and shut down the system before he really got going. Then on Wednesday he went back to Jurby for more testing and finally things started to come together.

By contrast, fellow Manxman Nick Crowe, who had taken a winning double last year in the absence of the 'maestro', was flying and it was no surprise that, having set the pace in practice, he and Daniel Sayle should be packing the power in the first of the two races, run on Monday afternoon, given the weather problems of the rescheduled Bennetts Superbike TT Race.

Top: Allan Schofield and Peter Founds finished fifth in both races on their Suzuki GSX-R600-powered outfit.
© Double Red

Left: Lockside Yamaha's Steve Norbury and Scott Parnell were third in both races but had to fight back from sixth in the second race to claim a spot on the podium.
© Double Red

Right: The spirit of sidecar racing: newcomers Ekhard Rosinger and Peter Hoss came all the way from Trier in Germany and finished 36th and 27th in the two races.

© Jon Stroud

Bottom right: Never write off Moly! After all the despair of practice week, Dave Molyneux and Rick Long expected nothing from the races but came away as double winners.

© Double Red

SPOT THE DOG!

The unlikely hero for the Molyneux supporters was a dog that happened to go for an early-afternoon stroll. The pity was that the animal wandered on to the Course near the Glen Lough campsite.

There he was enjoying the sun, and all the fuss and attention as those kind men and women in orange overalls tried to tempt him back behind the fence lines, offering all sorts of tit-bits as bribes. But no, this was his moment, the chance to strut his stuff.

It's funny now to reflect on this incident, but it wasn't at the time. There were just 15secs left on the clock to the start of the second sidecar race when race control received the message that this miscreant mutt was on the loose and defying all attempts to bring him to heel.

There was only one solution: delay the start of the race and send in reinforcements to catch the poor chap, who by now was tiring of all of the commotion around him and was hoping his master, or mistress, would come and save him.

There was a happy ending to the story, not to mention the thanks of Dave Molyneux, who was able to make good use of the quarter-of-an-hour delay to fix an electronic problem that had threatened to rule him out of the race.

The rest is history. The local favourite powered to victory, and then admitted: "I hate dogs, but I'll have this one as a pet and I'll love it forever."

Not so charitable was Nick Crowe, one of Moly's rivals who reckoned the dog, had he caught it, would have been on the barbeque!

Crowe and Sayle forged away on the first lap of the Bavaria Beer Sidecar TT Race 'A', and by the time they reached Glen Helen they were running barely 50 metres down on Molyneux, who had been first away from the start. It was a fast, determined start, and one that put them 5secs up on John Holden and Andrew Winkle with Steve Norbury and Scott Parnell third, though by only a third of a second from Molyneux.

Former world champions Klaus Klaffenbock and Christian Parzer hadn't made it that far. They ground to a halt at Ballacraine with a gearbox problem, and it wasn't long before news came in that the leaders were also

running into trouble. They were reported as touring at Quarry Bends and pulled off at Sulby Crossroads, also with gearbox problems.

This meant that Holden/Winkle were heading the action at Ramsey by 6.55secs from Norbury/Parnell while Molyneux/Long were third, and only three quarters of a second down. On the dash over the mountain, the local favourite snatched second place, crossing the line some 9secs down on Holden, who had completed that opening lap at an average speed of 111.374mph.

Simon Neary and Stuart Bond stopped briefly to make minor adjustments, allowing Allan Schofield/Peter Founds

Molyneux had completed a lap at 111.713mph, strengthening his second place, giving him the chance of victory, also putting him 5secs ahead of Norbury with Schofield just ahead of Neary and Gary Horspole/Mark Cox. Molyneux was turning up the heat, running just 0.14sec down on Holden as they passed the Manx Radio commentary point at Glen Helen for the last time, while Norbury was 14.58secs down in third place.

By the time they reached Ballaugh Bridge, Molyneux was running out front, 2secs up on Holden, and he stretched that to 3secs at Ramsey. Again he picked up time over the Mountain, and his final lap in 20mins 04.83secs, an average speed of 112.738mph, gave him his 12th victory on his native Island, while for Long it was a seventh success.

John Holden/Andrew Winkle took second place ahead of Steve Norbury/Scott Parnell with Simon Neary/Stuart Bond holding onto fourth from Allan Schofield/Peter Founds, while Nigel Connole/Jamie Winn took sixth place.

"It's just really weird to be here," said Molyneux at the winner's media conference. "Nick [Crowe] had it in the bag, or so I thought – he has the talent and the speed, and I would have been happy to have been sixth. I rode my heart out."

That was the dramatic first instalment, but there was the stuff of Boy's Own to come even before Bavaria Beer Sidecar TT Race 'B' race started, on Wednesday, with Molyneux in a race against time even to make the start as an electronic problem threatened his participation. But then he was given a lifeline as race officials delayed the start when reports of a dog straying on to the track were received. This occurred with just 15secs to go to the start time, but officials called for a delay of a quarter of an hour and that gave Moly the vital time to make the necessary repairs.

"Every time I blipped the throttle, the engine cut out," Molyneux explained. "I could only think that the dashboard was the only thing that we hadn't changed, so I rushed

Opposite: Everyone, even winner Dave Molyneux, felt for Nick Crowe and Dan Sayle. They were quickest in practice and set the pace in both races – but broke down twice.
© Jon Stroud

Above: Former World Sidecar Champion Klaus Klaffenbock and Christian Parzer were sixth fastest in practice but never saw the chequered flag in either race due to technical problems.
© Double Red

to move up to fourth, though only for a few miles before the status quo was restored.

Holden had been given the hurry-up and he pulled out a further 2secs on the rest, led by Norbury/Parnell who had charged back in front of Molyneux/Long, the start of a real dice for second place that saw them swap places by the time they reached Ramsey for the second time.

It was exciting action, with Molyneux totally committed and Holden soon to realise just how much the Manxman wanted the race. The gap between them had been 12secs at Ramsey, but by the time they crossed the line to start the final lap, it was down to 2secs.

Right: Nigel Connole and Jamie Winn grabbed a pair of sixth places with their Eddy's Honda.
© Jon Stroud

Far right: Despite the lack of backing from Suzuki, John Holden and Andrew Winkle finished second in both races, hampered in the second by a dog-slow motor.
© Double Red

"THAT WAS THE HARDEST RACE OF MY CAREER. THE MOTOR WAS SO SLOW. WE HAD SWITCHABLE MAPS BUT IT DIDN'T MAKE ANY DIFFERENCE AT ALL."

JOHN HOLDEN

Bavaria Beer
SIDECAR TT

back to the truck in the paddock, grabbed some tools and a spare dash, and just managed to get it changed."

He and Long were up and running and lying fourth at Glen Helen on the opening lap as Crowe/Sayle, intent on showing what might have been earlier in the week, forged clear. Between these two outfits were Klaffenbock/Parzer and Holden/Winkle.

By the end of that first lap, Molyneux, who had borrowed the spare engine from Ian Hutchinson's Supersport bike, was running second, albeit 14.7secs down on Crowe, who was setting such a furious pace that on the second lap he raised the record to 116.667mph. Molyneux was a distant 38.69secs down, but holding second from Holden and Klaffenbock, while Allan Schofield/Peter Founds had moved into fifth place from Steve Norbury/ Scott Parnell.

Perhaps Crowe had been pushing too hard, for he ground to a halt with a blown engine at Ballahutchen, and then Klaffenbock was sidelined by machine problems at Union Mills. Molyneux was ahead and gunning for that magical 13th victory – one adrift of Mike Hailwood in the list of all-time winners.

"Unbelievable," said Molyneux after the race. "These

are the two most unexpected victories of my career. A week ago I didn't think it would happen. It was a case of plugging away and working hard. I'm not a defeatist – you enter and you want to do your best.

"I really feel for Nick [Crowe]. I know what it's like to be going so well, only to break down. But a week ago this wasn't going to happen. We were too slow and I'm still not as quick as I was. I was regaining confidence all the time but I'm probably not as fast in some places as I was before the crash last year."

John Holden and Andrew Winkle took second place on their LCR Suzuki, finishing 26secs down. Holden said: "That was the hardest race of my career. The motor was so slow. We had switchable maps but it didn't make any difference at all."

There was a further 63secs between them and third-placed Lockside Yamaha crew Steve Norbury/Scott Parnell. Simon Neary/Stuart Bond took fourth, ahead of Allan Schofield/Peter Founds, with Nigel Connole/Jamie Winn again sixth. Conrad Harrison/Kerry Williams headed off Glyn Jones/Chris Lake with Tony Elmer/Darren Marshall and Kenny Howles/Doug Jewell completing the top ten.

Below: Moly's 2006 TT had ended in a massive crash and he said he was finished with the event – but he bounced back to win both races this year in the unlikeliest of circumstances.
© Mac McDiarmid

"THESE ARE THE TWO MOST UNEXPECTED VICTORIES OF MY CAREER. A WEEK AGO I DIDN'T THINK IT WOULD HAPPEN."

DAVE MOLYNEUX

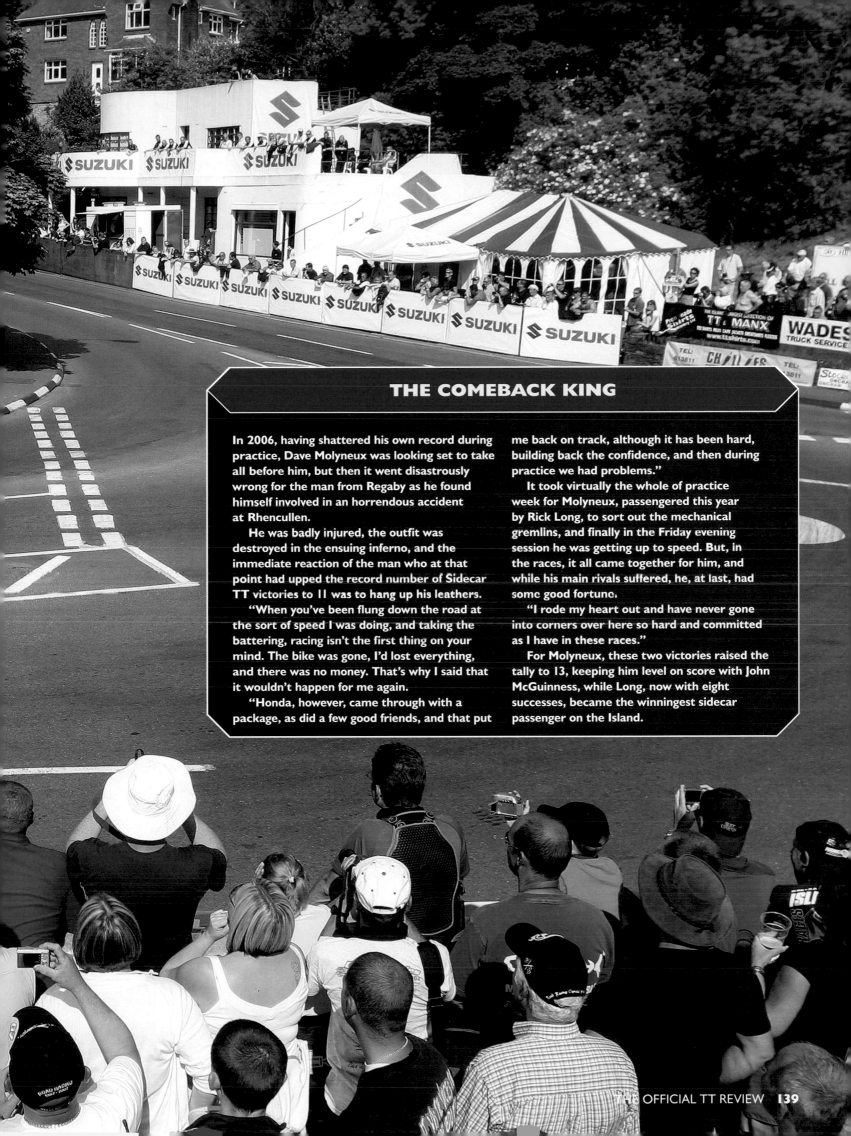

THE COMEBACK KING

In 2006, having shattered his own record during practice, Dave Molyneux was looking set to take all before him, but then it went disastrously wrong for the man from Regaby as he found himself involved in an horrendous accident at Rhencullen.

He was badly injured, the outfit was destroyed in the ensuing inferno, and the immediate reaction of the man who at that point had upped the record number of Sidecar TT victories to 11 was to hang up his leathers.

"When you've been flung down the road at the sort of speed I was doing, and taking the battering, racing isn't the first thing on your mind. The bike was gone, I'd lost everything, and there was no money. That's why I said that it wouldn't happen for me again.

"Honda, however, came through with a package, as did a few good friends, and that put me back on track, although it has been hard, building back the confidence, and then during practice we had problems."

It took virtually the whole of practice week for Molyneux, passengered this year by Rick Long, to sort out the mechanical gremlins, and finally in the Friday evening session he was getting up to speed. But, in the races, it all came together for him, and while his main rivals suffered, he, at last, had some good fortune.

"I rode my heart out and have never gone into corners over here so hard and committed as I have in these races."

For Molyneux, these two victories raised the tally to 13, keeping him level on score with John McGuinness, while Long, now with eight successes, became the winningest sidecar passenger on the Island.

RESULTS

Race A – Monday 4th June / Race B – Wednesday 6th June

RACE A – LAP ONE

Pos	Rider	Time	Speed
1	John Holden/Andrew Winkle	20 19.56	111.374
2	Dave Molyneux/Rick Long	20 28.37	110.576
3	Steve Norbury/Scott Parnell	20 29.61	110.464
4	Simon Neary/Stuart Bond	20 42.65	109.305
5	Allan Schofield/Peter Founds	20 45.07	109.092
6	Conrad Harrison/Kerry Williams	20 54.50	108.272
7	Gary Horspole/Mark Cox	21 00.70	107.741
8	Nigel Connole/Jamie Winn	21 00.86	107.726
9	Tony Elmer/Darren Marshall	21 10.24	106.931
10	Andy Laidlow/Patrick Farrance	21 11.74	106.805
11	Glyn Jones/Chris Lake	21 13.41	106.665
12	Gary Bryan/Ivan Murray	21 13.52	106.655
13	Phil Dongworth/Stuart Castles	21 22.25	105.929
14	Roy Hanks/Dave Wells	21 32.85	105.061
15	Steven Coombes/Darren Hope	21 39.95	104.487
16	Nev Jones/Joe Shardlow	21 41.88	104.332
17	Mark Halliday/Mark Holland	21 45.27	104.061
18	Brian Kelly/Dicky Gale	21 47.59	103.877
19	Tony Baker/Fiona Baker-Milligan	21 49.46	103.728
20	Roger Stockton/Pete Alton	21 50.75	103.626

RACE A – LAP TWO

Pos	Rider	Time	Speed
1	John Holden/Andrew Winkle	20 22.81	111.079
2	Dave Molyneux/Rick Long	20 15.87	111.713
3	Steve Norbury/Scott Parnell	20 27.66	110.639
4	Allan Schofield/Peter Founds	20 29.73	110.454
5	Simon Neary/Stuart Bond	20 33.29	110.135
6	Conrad Harrison/Kerry Williams	20 44.47	109.146
7	Nigel Connole/Jamie Winn	20 41.42	109.414
8	Gary Horspole/Mark Cox	20 47.88	108.847
9	Tony Elmer/Darren Marshall	20 48.33	108.808
10	Glyn Jones/Chris Lake	21 02.61	107.577
11	Andy Laidlow/Patrick Farrance	21 05.77	107.309
12	Gary Bryan/Ivan Murray	21 04.24	107.439
13	Phil Dongworth/Stuart Castles	21 08.02	107.118
14	Roy Hanks/Dave Wells	21 11.03	106.865
15	Douglas Wright/Dipash Chauhan	21 15.56	106.485
16	Nev Jones/Joe Shardlow	21 31.47	105.173
17	Brian Kelly/Dicky Gale	21 28.02	105.455
18	Mark Halliday/Mark Holland	21 30.99	105.212
19	Kenny Howles/Doug Jewell	21 23.76	105.805
20	Roger Stockton/Pete Alton	21 38.37	104.614

RACE A – LAP THREE

Pos	Rider	Time	Speed
1	Dave Molyneux/Rick Long	20 04.83	112.736
2	John Holden/Andrew Winkle	20 13.19	111.959
3	Steve Norbury/Scott Parnell	20 22.46	111.110
4	Simon Neary/Stuart Bond	20 27.18	110.683
5	Allan Schofield/Peter Founds	20 30.17	110.414
6	Nigel Connole/Jamie Winn	20 37.95	109.720
7	Conrad Harrison/Kerry Williams	20 53.57	108.353
8	Tony Elmer/Darren Marshall	20 50.92	108.582
9	Glyn Jones/Chris Lake	21 02.10	107.621
10	Andy Laidlow/Patrick Farrance	21 02.68	107.572
11	Gary Bryan/Ivan Murray	21 12.90	106.708
12	Roy Hanks/Dave Wells	21 04.70	107.400
13	Brian Kelly/Dicky Gale	21 19.54	106.154
14	Kenny Howles/Doug Jewell	21 21.13	106.022
15	Nev Jones/Joe Shardlow	21 31.40	105.179
16	Mark Halliday/Mark Holland	21 36.02	104.804
17	Douglas Wright/Dipash Chauhan	21 42.09	104.316
18	Roger Stockton/Pete Alton	21 37.48	104.686
19	Neil Kelly/Jason O'Connor	21 31.25	105.191
20	Howard Baker/Nigel Barlow	21 52.11	103.519

RACE B – LAP ONE

Pos	Rider	Time	Speed
1	Nick Crowe/Dan Sayle	19 42.84	114.833
2	Dave Molyneux/Rick Long	19 57.57	113.419
3	John Holden/Andrew Winkle	20 04.82	112.737
4	Klaus Klaffenbock/Christian Parzer	20 07.33	112.503
5	Steve Norbury/Scott Parnell	20 27.18	110.683
6	Allan Schofield/Peter Founds	20 28.05	110.605
7	Simon Neary/Stuart Bond	20 36.41	109.857
8	Nigel Connole/Jamie Winn	20 46.31	108.984
9	Conrad Harrison/Kerry Williams	20 46.63	108.956
10	Phil Dongworth/Stuart Castles	20 46.98	108.926
11	Gary Horspole/Mark Cox	20 53.44	108.365
12	Andy Laidlow/Patrick Farrance	20 55.67	108.172
13	Glyn Jones/Chris Lake	20 58.87	107.896
14	Gary Bryan/Ivan Murray	20 59.78	107.819
15	Tony Elmer/Darren Marshall	21 01.11	107.705
16	Kenny Howles/Doug Jewell	21 08.46	107.081
17	Roger Stockton/Pete Alton	21 20.51	106.074
18	Dave Wallis/Philip Iremonger	21 30.38	105.262
19	Mark Halliday/Mark Holland	21 33.03	105.047
20	Douglas Wright/Dipash Chauhan	21 45.56	104.039

RACE B – LAP TWO

Pos	Rider	Time	Speed
1	Nick Crowe/Dan Sayle	19 24.24	116.667
2	Dave Molyneux/Rick Long	19 48.19	114.315
3	John Holden/Andrew Winkle	19 52.82	113.872
4	Klaus Klaffenbock/Christian Parzer	20 08.12	112.430
5	Allan Schofield/Peter Founds	20 17.99	111.518
6	Steve Norbury/Scott Parnell	20 20.74	111.267
7	Simon Neary/Stuart Bond	20 25.92	110.796
8	Nigel Connole/Jamie Winn	20 28.55	110.560
9	Conrad Harrison/Kerry Williams	20 34.48	110.029
10	Gary Horspole/Mark Cox	20 34.88	109.993
11	Glyn Jones/Chris Lake	20 40.18	109.523
12	Tony Elmer/Darren Marshall	20 43.88	109.197
13	Andy Laidlow/Patrick Farrance	20 58.99	107.886
14	Gary Bryan/Ivan Murray	21 00.60	107.749
15	Kenny Howles/Doug Jewell	20 56.16	108.129
16	Roger Stockton/Pete Alton	21 09.61	106.984
17	Dave Wallis/Philip Iremonger	21 16.96	106.368
18	Douglas Wright/Dipash Chauhan	21 18.84	106.212
19	Bill Currie/Philip Bridge	21 32.22	105.112
20	Neil Kelly/Jason O'Connor	21 39.71	104.507

RACE B – LAP THREE

Pos	Rider	Time	Speed
1	Dave Molyneux/Rick Long	19 53.35	113.821
2	John Holden/Andrew Winkle	20 07.63	112.475
3	Steve Norbury/Scott Parnell	20 19.89	111.345
4	Simon Neary/Stuart Bond	20 19.37	111.392
5	Allan Schofield/Peter Founds	20 58.76	107.906
6	Nigel Connole/Jamie Winn	20 34.69	110.010
7	Conrad Harrison/Kerry Williams	20 40.70	109.477
8	Glyn Jones/Chris Lake	20 56.79	108.076
9	Tony Elmer/Darren Marshall	20 52.54	108.442
10	Kenny Howles/Doug Jewell	20 54.52	108.271
11	Gary Bryan/Ivan Murray	21 05.64	107.320
12	Andy Laidlow/Patrick Farrance	21 48.28	103.822
13	Roger Stockton/Pete Alton	21 17.11	106.355
14	Dave Wallis/Philip Iremonger	21 21.11	106.024
15	Douglas Wright/Dipash Chauhan	21 41.42	104.369
16	Bill Currie/Philip Bridge	21 32.92	105.055
17	Brian Kelly/Dicky Gale	21 37.61	104.675
18	Neil Kelly/Jason O'Connor	21 51.97	103.530
19	Tony Thirkell/Roy King	21 48.98	103.766
20	Mike Cookson/Diane Noakes	21 44.35	104.135

THE HIGHS

**DAVE MOLYNEUX
RICK LONG**

HM Plant Honda

The most successful pair in Sidecar TT action with the driver, 'Moly', taking his victory total to 13 with an unexpected winning double, while Long has now passengered eight winning rides.

**JOHN HOLDEN
ANDREW WINKLE**

LCR Suzuki

Made the running in the opening race, heading off Molyneux into the third lap before having to settle for second best and then next time out again running somewhat distantly behind the local hero.

**STEVE NORBURY
SCOTT PARNELL**

**Lockside Engineering
Sherbourne Yamaha**

Always in the hunt in the opening race and then worked hard next time out, clawing their way through from sixth place on the first lap to complete a double of third placings.

**SIMON NEARY
STUART BOND**

Neary Racing Baker Yamaha

With determined driving ran in the top five, coming through to claim fourth on the final lap of the opener, and then with a last charge down the mountain taking fourth in the second race.

**ALLAN SCHOFIELD
PETER FOUNDS**

Suzuki

Consistent performance across the two races, averaging 109.983mph as they claimed fifth place in the opener, all but mirroring that speed as they provided an action-replay finish.

THE LOWS

**NICK CROWE
DANIEL SAYLE**

A&J Groundworks LCR Honda

Broke down in Race 'A' with gearbox problems and Race 'B' with a blown engine – but some consolation was to receive the Jock Taylor Trophy for a super-fast 116.667mph lap in Race 'B'.

**KLAUS KLAFFENBOCK
CHRISTIAN PARZER**

Alpha Boilers LCR Honda

Retirement at Ballacraine on the opening lap of the first race, then more woe at two-thirds distance in the second race as engine problems halted them at Union Mills.

**ROY HANKS
DAVE WELLS**

Rose Hanks DMR Suzuki

Pulled in at Kirk Michael to make adjustments while running strongly in the second race, but unable to solve the problem fully and subsequently retired on the second lap.

**GARY HORSPOLE
MARK COX**

LCR Honda

Crashed at Ballaugh in the closing stages of the second race, having run in the top dozen. Horspole was airlifted to hospital suffering a shoulder injury; Cox was uninjured.

**PETER FARRELLY
JASON MILLER**

Ireson Yamaha

Stopped at Ramsey on the second lap of the second race to make adjustments. Out came the spanners, there was 4mins work around the carburettor, but they got going again, only to finish last.

RACE A – RESULTS

Pos	No	Rider	Machine	Entrant	Time	Speed	Replica
1	1	Dave Molyneux/Rick Long	2007 Honda CBR 600cc	HM Plant Honda Racing	01 00 49.06	111.668	Silver
2	7	John Holden/Andrew Winkle	2007 Suzuki K6 600cc		01 00 55.56	111.470	Silver
3	3	Steve Norbury/Scott Parnell	2007 Yamaha YZF R6 600cc	Lockside Engineering	01 01 19.73	110.737	Silver
4	5	Simon Neary/Stuart Bond	2005 Yamaha R6 600cc	Neary Racing	01 01 43.11	110.038	Silver
5	16	Allan Schofield/Peter Founds	2006 Suzuki K6 600cc		01 01 44.97	109.983	Silver
6	25	Nigel Connole/Jamie Winn	2005 Honda RR 600cc		01 02 20.23	108.946	Silver
7	24	Conrad Harrison/Kerry Williams	2003 Honda CBR RR 600cc	Printing Roller Services	01 02 32.54	108.589	Silver
8	14	Tony Elmer/Darren Marshall	2006 Yamaha R6 600cc	D.L. Elmer	01 02 49.49	108.101	Silver
9	19	Glyn Jones/Chris Lake	2006 Honda RR 600cc	DSC Racing	01 03 18.12	107.286	Silver
10	8	Andy Laidlow/Patrick Farrance	2006 Suzuki GSXR 600cc		01 03 20.19	107.227	Silver
11	10	Gary Bryan/Ivan Murray	2006 Yamaha R6 600cc		01 03 30.66	106.933	Silver
12	6	Roy Hanks/Dave Wells	Suzuki K6 600cc	Rose Hanks	01 03 48.57	106.432	Silver
13	29	Brian Kelly/Dicky Gale	2005 Honda DMR 600cc		01 04 35.14	105.153	Bronze
14	20	Kenny Howles/Doug Jewell	2007 Suzuki GSXR 600cc	Clive Price Racing	01 04 38.62	105.059	Bronze
15	34	Nev Jones/Joe Shardlow	2007 Suzuki GSXR 600cc		01 04 44.74	104.893	Bronze
16	36	Mark Halliday/Mark Holland	2004 Kawasaki ZX6RR 600cc	Hazel's Fashions of Tamworth	01 04 52.28	104.690	Bronze
17	46	Douglas Wright/Dipash Chauhan*	Honda 600cc	Dougie Wright & Eddy Wright Motorcycles	01 04 53.23	104.665	Bronze
18	15	Roger Stockton/Pete Alton	2007 Yamaha R6 600cc		01 05 06.60	104.307	Bronze
19	31	Neil Kelly/Jason O'Connor	1998 Honda CBR 600cc		01 05 16.00	104.056	Bronze
20	28	Howard Baker/Nigel Barlow	2005 Honda CBR 600cc	D & J Bikespares, Lincoln	01 05 35.77	103.534	Bronze
21	23	Tony Thirkell/Roy King	2005 Honda 600 RR 600cc	Merlin Race Paint	01 05 50.50	103.148	Bronze
22	18	Bill Currie/Philip Bridge	2007 Yamaha R6 600cc		01 06 00.87	102.878	Bronze
23	26	Mike Cookson/Diane Noakes	1998 Honda CBR 600cc		01 06 06.32	102.736	Bronze
24	39	Peter Farrelly/Jason Miller	2002 Yamaha R6 600cc		01 07 06.60	101.198	
25	52	Steven Coombes/Darren Hope	2006 Honda Ireson RR 600cc	Clive Price Racing	01 07 28.17	100.659	
26	38	Alan Langton/Christian Chaigneau	1997 Yamaha R6 600cc	Ray Sansbury	01 07 30.82	100.593	
27	27	Eddy Wright/Martin Hull	2006 Honda 600 RR 600cc		01 07 35.17	100.485	
28	60	Peter Allebone/Bob Dowty	2005 Kawasaki ZX6 600cc		01 07 35.19	100.485	
29	33	Bryan Pedder/Rod Steadman	2002 Yamaha Thundercat 600cc	Bill & Neil Coxon	01 08 20.98	99.363	
30	47	Geoff Smale/Karl McGrath	1999 Honda Ireson 600cc	Selfdrive Hire Ltd	01 08 33.87	99.051	
31	56	Keith Walters/James Hibberd	2006 Honda CBR 600cc		01 08 37.68	98.960	
32	48	Claude Montagnier/Laurent Seyeux	2007 Kawasaki ZXR 600cc		01 09 11.07	98.164	
33	50	Michael Thompson/Bruce Moore	2001 Yamaha Thundercat 600cc		01 09 16.70	98.031	
34	55	Dick Tapken/Willem Vandis	2001 Suzuki GSXR 600cc	Dialled In Racing	01 09 32.93	97.649	
35	45	Wayne Lockey/Stuart Stobbart	2000 Yamaha R6 600cc		01 09 45.96	97.345	
36	64	Eckhard Rossinger/Peter Hoss*	2003 Suzuki GSXR 600cc		01 09 59.66	97.028	
37	68	Robert Handcock/Mathew Buckley*	1998 Yamaha R6 600cc		01 10 19.14	96.580	
38	49	Brian Alflatt/Herve Chenu	2004 Honda CBR 600cc		01 10 28.40	96.368	
39	66	Masahito Watanabe/Hideyuki Yoshida*	2007 Honda PC47E 600cc	Rising Sun Racing	01 12 28.34	93.710	
40	30	Peter Nuttall/Neil Wheatley	2005 Honda RR 600cc		01 12 43.64	93.382	
41	70	Colin Smith/Tony Palacio	2003 Honda RR 600cc		01 14 00.21	91.771	
42	44	Dick Hawes/Tim Dixon	Suzuki 600cc	Dialled In Racing	01 14 35.76	91.042	
43	63	Jean-Louis Hergott/Christophe Darras	2005 Suzuki GSXR 600cc		01 18 55.98	86.040	

RACE B – RESULTS

Pos	No	Rider	Machine	Entrant	Time	Speed	Replica
1	1	Dave Molyneux/Rick Long	2007 Honda CBR 600cc	HM Plant Honda Racing	59 39.11	113.851	Silver
2	7	John Holden/Andrew Winkle	2007 Suzuki K6 600cc		01 00 05.26	113.025	Silver
3	3	Steve Norbury/Scott Parnell	2007 Yamaha YZF R6 600cc	Lockside Engineering	01 01 07.80	111.098	Silver
4	5	Simon Neary/Stuart Bond	2005 Yamaha R6 600cc	Neary Racing	01 01 21.70	110.678	Silver
5	16	Allan Schofield/Peter Founds	2006 Suzuki K6 600cc		01 01 44.80	109.988	Silver
6	25	Nigel Connole/Jamie Winn	2005 Honda RR 600cc		01 01 49.55	109.847	Silver
7	24	Conrad Harrison/Kerry Williams	2003 Honda CBR RR 600cc	Printing Roller Services	01 02 01.81	109.485	Silver
8	19	Glyn Jones/Chris Lake	2006 Honda RR 600cc	DSC Racing	01 02 35.84	108.493	Silver
9	14	Tony Elmer/Darren Marshall	2006 Yamaha R6 600cc	D.L. Elmer	01 02 37.52	108.445	Silver
10	20	Kenny Howles/Doug Jewell	2007 Suzuki GSXR 600cc	Clive Price Racing	01 02 59.14	107.825	Bronze
11	10	Gary Bryan/Ivan Murray	2006 Yamaha R6 600cc		01 03 06.02	107.629	Bronze
12	8	Andy Laidlow/Patrick Farrance	2006 Suzuki GSXR 600cc		01 03 42.95	106.589	Bronze
13	15	Roger Stockton/Pete Alton	2007 Yamaha R6 600cc		01 03 47.23	106.470	Bronze
14	21	Dave Wallis/Philip Iremonger	2000 Honda CBR RR 600cc	Compass	01 04 08.45	105.883	Bronze
15	46	Douglas Wright/Dipash Chauhan*	Honda 600cc	Dougie Wright & Eddy Wright Motorcycles	01 04 45.81	104.865	Bronze
16	18	Bill Currie/Philip Bridge	2007 Yamaha R6 600cc		01 04 55.30	104.609	Bronze
17	29	Brian Kelly/Dicky Gale	2005 Honda DMR 600cc		01 05 09.32	104.234	Bronze
18	31	Neil Kelly/Jason O'Connor	1998 Honda CBR 600cc		01 05 22.79	103.876	Bronze
19	23	Tony Thirkell/Roy King	2005 Honda 600 RR 600cc	Merlin Race Paint	01 05 25.88	103.794	Bronze
20	26	Mike Cookson/Diane Noakes	1998 Honda CBR 600cc		01 05 46.20	103.260	
21	37	Rod Bellas/Geoff Knight	2007 Honda 600cc		01 06 00.99	102.874	
22	27	Eddy Wright/Martin Hull	2006 Honda 600 RR 600cc		01 06 02.99	102.822	
23	53	Dylan Lynch/Aaron	2006 Honda R6 600cc		01 06 18.40	102.424	
24	30	Peter Nuttall/Neil Wheatley	2005 Honda RR 600cc		01 06 27.14	102.199	
25	41	Francois Leblond/Sylvie Leblond	2000 Honda CBR 600cc		01 06 34.20	102.019	
26	54	Mike Roscher/Michael Hildebrand*	1997 Yamaha Thundercat 600cc		01 07 23.73	100.769	
27	64	Eckhard Rossinger/Peter Hoss*	2003 Suzuki GSXR 600cc		01 07 45.14	100.239	
28	33	Bryan Pedder/Rod Steadman	2002 Yamaha Thundercat 600cc	Bill & Neil Coxon	01 07 50.68	100.102	
29	38	Alan Langton/Christian Chaigneau	1997 Yamaha R6 600cc	Ray Sansbury	01 08 02.72	99.807	
30	48	Claude Montagnier/Laurent Seyeux	2007 Kawasaki ZXR 600cc		01 08 09.09	99.651	
31	63	Jean-Louis Hergott/Christophe Darras	2005 Suzuki GSXR 600cc		01 08 15.95	99.485	
32	42	Wal Saunders/Eddy Kiff	2006 Yamaha R6 600cc	Dialled In Racing	01 08 28.42	99.183	
33	45	Wayne Lockey/Stuart Stobbart	2000 Yamaha R6 600cc		01 08 46.35	98.752	
34	40	Alan Warner/Bert Vloemans	2000 Kawasaki Ireson 600cc	Dialled In Racing	01 08 53.70	98.576	
35	55	Dick Tapken/Willem Vandis	2001 Suzuki GSXR 600cc	Dialled In Racing	01 09 35.04	97.600	
36	68	Robert Handcock/Mathew Buckley*	1998 Yamaha R6 600cc		01 09 40.12	97.481	
37	47	Geoff Smale/Karl McGrath	1999 Honda Ireson 600cc	Selfdrive Hire Ltd	01 10 42.02	96.059	
38	66	Masahito Watanabe/Hideyuki Yoshida*	2007 Honda PC47E 600cc	Rising Sun Racing	01 11 12.43	95.375	
39	67	Ian Salter/Deborah Salter	2006 Honda 600cc		01 11 30.33	94.977	
40	58	Ruth Laidlow/Mike Killingsworth	2007 Suzuki GSXR 600cc	Action Motorcycles	01 11 44.56	94.663	
41	70	Colin Smith/Tony Palacio	2003 Honda RR 600cc		01 12 33.98	93.589	
42	39	Peter Farrelly/Jason Miller	2002 Yamaha R6 600cc		01 12 43.01	93.395	

PokerStars
SENIOR TT

John McGuinness sets
new Superbike standards

130MPH LAP RECORD, RACE RECORD, SUPERBIKE RACE WIN DOUBLE – THE KING OF THE MOUNTAIN LIVED UP TO HIS NAME IN THE SENIOR TT

By Dave Fern & Gary Pinchin

The prestigious Senior TT. The PokerStars-sponsored finale to the Centenary Festival. The big race bore the same title as the one in that inaugural event a century earlier and now, as then, the riders lined up with machines that were at the cutting edge of technology.

The awesome power of the modern-day racers might make the pioneering 1907 Matchless and Norton machines seem pedestrian, but today's top machines – such as the Honda Fireblade in the hands of people like John McGuinness, Ian Hutchinson and Guy Martin, and the Suzuki GSX-R1000 of Bruce Anstey – still need riders with the special kind of skill suited to racing around this unique course on public roads.

While the media and spectators fed on the hype of the magical 130mph lap being broken and speeding the event into a new era, the riders were quietly ensuring that everything was right for this last intense challenge of the week. Ahead of them lay six laps of the 37.73-mile Mountain Course, and, vitally, conditions were just about perfect.

Michael Rutter – who would later admit publicly that he was riding with a broken scaphoid bone in his wrist – was the first away from the Glencrutchery Road start, the rasp of his Kawasaki breaking the silence and echoing away down Bray Hill as Adrian Archibald, hoping for an upturn in fortune was next away, followed by McGuinness, Martin

Finnegan, Anstey and Hutchinson. The latter two, like McGuinness, were aiming to add another victory to their earlier successes.

If anyone needed any convincing that McGuinness meant business, the evidence was clear to see. Over the first ten miles, from a standing start, he dashed through Quarterbridge and on to Glen Helen at an average speed of 132.76mph. The Lancastrian was on fire and already leading by a little over 2secs from his team-mate Hutchinson, with Guy Martin out-dragging Ian Lougher, Anstey and Rutter.

The big Honda, specially built for 2006 to suit McGuinness, had only been lightly refined for 2007 but was probably the best all-round package in the race in terms of power delivery and handling. But even so, the back end of the bike moved around as he attacked the course. He had pulled out a further second at Ballaugh Bridge and was leading on the road at Ramsey, by which stage he was running almost 4secs up on Martin, who was by now second on the road. Hutchinson was third on corrected time, even though he had clocked the fastest speed through Sulby at 191.20mph on the Leon Camier HRC-kitted BSB Blade.

There was no luck, however, for Ryan Farquhar, who was sidelined at The Hawthorne, and Anstey was slowing with handling problems. It would turn out to be a race of attrition with more than a third of the starters failing to make the finish. Finnegan was another rider in trouble early on and he pulled in at Ballig Bridge, unhappy with his Honda's handling; on the Friday before race week he'd solved his handling problems by fitting an Ohlins shock in a last-minute practice, and though he didn't get much chance

Below: John McGuinness sets off on what was to become a record-breaking Senior TT in every way.
© Double Red

Right: Guy Martin still couldn't find the last little bit to take the race to John McGuinness – but his time will come without a doubt.
© Stephen Davison

to prove its worth in Monday's Bennetts Superbike TT, he'd told the team he was confident the bike was more stable. But for whatever reason, come the Senior TT, he was unhappy with the handling again even though nothing had been changed.

McGuinness, though, was heading for a hat-trick of victories in this event, having won first for Yamaha and then for Honda. He later said the bike didn't miss a beat all through the TT fortnight and it certainly was on full song in the Senior. On the charge over Snaefell for the first time he pulled out his advantage to 6secs by the time he reached the Bungalow, and then powered into his second lap 9.69secs clear of Martin.

On that first lap McGuinness broke the record, in a time of 17mins 25.77secs, an average speed of 129.883mph. It was a pace that Martin was doing everything possible to match, and the Hydrex Honda rider clocked an impressive 128.690mph as he ran 2secs up on Hutchinson, while Lougher was a further 13secs down. Man of the moment for the Manx locals was Conor Cummins, who became the fastest-ever home rider as he recorded a lap of 125.612mph, running fifth ahead of Archibald, Rutter and the impressive Steve Plater.

Out front there was no relaxing. The pace was unrelenting. McGuinness knew what was expected of him, and he wanted to deliver. Mile by mile he was easing further ahead, but Martin decided something had to be done and pegged back a precious second or two on the leader on the dash into Ramsey. But any hopes he had were dispelled over the Mountain. McGuinness added to his lead again, and, incredibly, considering he had to slow

to enter the pits at the end of that lap, achieved a key milestone in the history of the TT. The commentator and the crowd went mad as they celebrated.

The lap time for McGuinness was confirmed as 17m 21.99secs, an average speed of 130.354mph. The magical marker had been broken – but the rider wasn't too concerned at the time. He and his pit crew were concentrating on preserving the momentum as they refuelled and changed the rear wheel. It was a typically slick and well-drilled operation. He was back out with minimal delay.

McGuinness had pitted with a lead of 14secs over Martin, whose second lap had been completed at 129.816mph, but he left with an added advantage of 6secs.

Hutchinson, running third, had to endure a lengthy stop of almost a minute as the chain stubbornly refused to drop into place at the first attempt as the rear wheel was slotted in. Lougher was fourth from Cummins, Archibald, Rutter and Plater.

The lead was up to 20secs at Glen Helen on the third lap, but Martin was fighting, riding hard, some would say throwing caution to the wind. He wanted the victory. As he had said pointedly earlier in the week: "To be anyone on the TT you have to win a six-lapper." That showed as he attacked. He upped the speed again, running 15mph faster than McGuinness on the dash to Ramsey and picking up 4secs.

While the duo up front were winning the adulation of the hordes of spectators packed in at the various favoured vantage points, others weren't so fortunate. By now Anstey had long since retired, as had Daniel Jansen, Nigel Beattie,

RECORD-BREAKING McGUINNESS

Speeds have always provided the talking points on the Island, but when Harry Collier clocked the fastest lap of the 1907 Senior race at 41.81mph aboard his Matchless and his brother Charlie won at an average speed of 38.22mph, never in their wildest dreams could they have imagined the pace of John McGuinness, who rewrote the record books a century later.

The 34-year-old Lancastrian's headline-grabbing second lap, when he beat the 130mph mark, excited the imagination. Whether or not that could be achieved had been a key part of the pre-event hype, and the main topic of conversation on the Island as the barriers were raised in the earlier races, all run at record pace.

McGuinness had always said it was achievable if the conditions were right, because there had been improvements to the Mountain Course, most noticeably at Brandish, which had been opened out and resurfaced. He also pointed to the continuing improvements in terms of the machines and the tyres.

Those thoughts were borne out on the opening lap as he powered his HM Plant Honda Fireblade to a record pace of 129.883mph, from a standing start, and then next time round upped his game into the unknown. Despite having to slow to enter the pits for refuelling and a tyre change, he completed the lap in 17mins 21.99secs, a record average speed of 130.354mph.

"That was fantastic, unbelievable, and that lap speed has really capped a great week for me," enthused McGuinness.

What made his day even more special was the pace he had run at throughout the six laps and 226.38 gruelling miles. His race-winning time of 1hr 46mins 44.23secs, an average speed of 127.25mph, sliced 54.61secs off the previous race record.

"That's something special and I'm proud to have done that," said McGuinness as he enjoyed his 13th victory in 11 years of racing on the Island, and gave Honda yet another success as they continued their long-standing relationship with the event that put them on the sporting map some four decades ago.

Left: One factor in McGuinness's TT success was having the right pit crew, people who wouldn't make time-consuming mistakes under pressure – and his pit stops were perfection throughout the TT.

© Double Red

Below: After a torrid time with handling problems, his bike catching fire and breaking down, Adrian Archibald's TT finally got off the ground in the Senior with a good fifth place.

© Mac McDiarmid

Bottom: Mark Miller finished 17th on the very standard 'factory' Aprilia; it was thought that the Italian manufacturer could be back for 2008 with true Superbike-spec machinery.

© Stephen Davison

Below: Third place in the
Senior went to Ian Hutchinson,
followed here by fifth-placed
Adrian Archibald.

© Double Red

Mark Parrett, Chris McGahan, Dan Stewart, Michael Dunlop and Keith Amor. They could only reflect on what might have been, while McGuinness was focussed on just one thing – maintaining the initiative, concentrating hard and responding to his signals. The leader was a comfortable 17secs ahead at the half-distance mark with Martin in turn 18secs in front of Hutchinson, who in turn had a 37secs advantage over Lougher with Archibald a further 17secs down.

Through the fourth lap McGuinness and Martin remained first and second on time – and on the road – with the Lancastrian maintaining his advantage, and such was their pace that they were pulling further ahead of third-placed Hutchinson while Lougher was feeling the heat and becoming an even more distant fourth, and adrift

of him Cummins was beginning to gain ground rapidly on Archibald. By the end of that fourth lap, McGuinness had extended his lead by 6secs, to 23.00secs, having put in a lap of 129.296mph compared with Martin's 128.566mph effort, with the Hydrex rider again losing out on the Mountain and undoing his speed into Ramsey.

The second round of pit-stops went without hitch for the leading pair, but Hutchinson lost time and Rutter's crew suffered a protracted effort to change his rear wheel. Archibald pitted with a slender lead of a third of a second over Cummins as news filtered through of more retirements, among them Paton-mounted Steve Linsdell on the only two-stroke in the race at Bishopscourt and John Burrows at Appledene.

Into the final third of the race, and at the first timing

Top: It was a shame Jimmy Moore's TT ended when his bike ran out of fuel – a disappointment for him in an otherwise great TT debut on a Black Horse Finance Honda.
© Double Red

Bottom left: Bruce Anstey said his Suzuki didn't handle but Relentless boss Phillip Neil went on record saying the team could find nothing wrong with it.
© Double Red

Bottom right: Mark Buckley finished 14th on the Lilley Racing Suzuki.
© Double Red

Bottom: After Michael Weynand smashed the other Bolliger Kawasaki to bits in practice, the Belgian team at least had something to celebrate when Gary Carswell finished 13th in the Senior.
© **Double Red**

Opposite: Good on Steve Linsdell for daring to do something different at this year's TT. He rode an ex-GP500 Paton two-stroke in the Senior but sadly failed to finish.
© **Double Red**

Opposite inset: Michael Rutter finally got a decent run on the MSS Kawasaki and finished eighth in the Senior. Straight after the race he revealed that he'd been riding all fortnight with a broken scaphoid.
© **Double Red**

point at Glen Helen, the computer screens in the press office flashed the news that McGuinness had a slightly diminished lead of 20.68secs over Martin with Hutchinson a further 40secs down. Again Martin bit back as they charged, momentarily airborne, through Ballaugh Bridge and the telling factor on speed was again at the Sulby speed trap – Martin 188.0mph, McGuinness 176.6mph.

No problem, though, for McGuinness. He was running to plan, riding his own race strategy. His advantage increased to 24.02secs by the end of the fifth lap, which he completed at an average speed of 122.867mph compared with Martin's 122.754mph. Hutchinson by now was 48secs down with Lougher a further 46secs adrift, but Archibald had reasserted himself over Cummins. Another retirement included TT veteran David Madsen Mygdal at the Gooseneck.

Nothing now was going to get in the way of a McGuinness victory. He was chasing win number 13 to match the earlier achievement of Sidecar maestro Dave Molyneux and as he powered through Glen Helen for the last time his lead over Martin was 24.28secs, the Hydrex

rider having more than a few anxieties as his Honda's chain was jumping off the sprocket – he could only hope that it would stay the distance. Just how much this problem was affecting Martin was revealed by the speed trap: he could manage only 168.60mph compared with McGuinness's ever-consistent 174.80mph and Hutchinson's 187.50mph. McGuinness just had to keep going and the race was his: at Ramsey for the final time his lead was 26.76secs, at the Bungalow it had grown to 28.81secs and at the finish line – which he crossed pulling an enormous wheelie – it had become 32.73secs, his speed for the last lap being 128.207mph. His race time was an incredible 54.61secs faster than the Senior race record, showing just how much McGuinness raised the bar again this year.

It had been a ride of sheer brilliance, raw speed and power, but as he pulled off his lid in the winner's enclosure he was overcome by the emotion of it all. "Unbelievable – brilliant, brilliant, brilliant," he enthused. "To get two wins in the week, take the 130mph lap and become the third most successful rider ever, all at the Centenary event, is absolutely fantastic and it's really something special.

"I'm so proud of what I've achieved. I tried really hard at the beginning of the race and felt very strong over the Mountain so I concentrated on hitting all my apexes and braking points – and to be the first man to break the 130mph barrier is unbelievable.

"The whole package has been brilliant and I've had the same people with me for the last two years – the bike has now won four TTs so maybe Honda will let me keep it for my collection! The track was in great condition and the weather was spot-on so I thoroughly enjoyed my afternoon's work.

"When I was an apprentice bricklayer I never even thought I could do this or win 13 races here. It's just incredible – unreal.

"I've got to say a big 'thank you' to the army of fans who were so appreciative, cheering all around the course, as well as all the marshals and organisers who helped make the show possible. I'm on a mega-high at the moment and the job's a dream!"

Second place went to a relieved Guy Martin, who had nursed his bike home: "I just cannot believe I got it home. "I've got to say a massive, massive thanks to the lads. They worked on the bike until 2am as we had a last-minute problem with the head gasket. I can't thank them enough and it paid off as we got on the podium – but I can't believe we got it on the podium. On the last three laps we had the chain jumping on the sprocket – which was no-one's fault, just one of those things. The TT is a hard race, six laps of 37.73 miles, and it's just mega-hard on a bike. I was pleased to get it home.

"I think before we come to the TT it's all written out. I'm a great believer in what goes around comes around and I think John...he's the man when it comes to the TT. I'm only 24 and I've got a lot to learn, and it's not my time and I think you've just got to be patient. If you try and rush these things you go out there like a bull in a china shop trying to make up a tenth here and there. You've got to realise when it's your time and make the most of it. It's just not my time yet."

Ian Hutchinson came in third, some 48secs down on Martin, and he reflected: "When I was sitting in the gravel trap at Oulton Park I wondered if any of this would be possible. The big bike was the hardest to ride because you need to be 100 per cent fit to do a good job, but I rode my heart out all week."

Ian Lougher was fourth, and complained about the handling of his Stobart Honda: "The bike was jumping a bit. One lap it would be great, next time round my legs would be off the pegs in the same place. It was just a difficult race."

If there was relief showing on Hutchinson's face, then there was even more delight for Adrian Archibald as he rounded off what had been a tough week with a hard, determined ride into fifth place: "I'm really happy to have finished the TT with a positive result and I have to say the GSX-R1000 Relentless Suzuki that I rode today is probably the best bike I've ever ridden round this place. Fifth is a positive result after the week I've had, and today's pace was very hot. I've also gone faster than ever before so I can go home a little happier, although I would have liked to have given Suzuki a podium – something they really deserved."

Conor Cummins received a terrific ovation as he came in sixth, the fastest Manx rider on the course, while

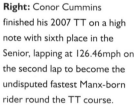

Right: Conor Cummins finished his 2007 TT on a high note with sixth place in the Senior, lapping at 126.46mph on the second lap to become the undisputed fastest Manx-born rider round the TT course.
© **Double Red**

Overleaf: Eighth in the Senior wrapped up an impressive first TT for Steve Plater on the AIM Yamaha.
© **Stephen Davison**

Below & opposite top:
Yyyyyyyes! Another Senior TT
win. 130mph lap record. 13th
TT victory. No wonder John
McGuinness punched the air for
joy as he crossed the line at the
end of the six-lap marathon.

© Stephen Davison & © Double Red

Opposite bottom: Marc
Ramsbotham lost his life
when he crashed at the 26th
Milestone towards the end of
the Senior TT.

© Double Red

newcomer Steve Plater rounded off a great week with
seventh: "That was a good race. I put in some good times
and got faster with each lap. I have had a really good TT
and my lap times from the first practice night to the final
race improved dramatically so I am happy with that.

"But it's not all down to me. I have a fantastic team
behind me and they all have vast experience at the TT and
that has helped me tremendously. I have to thank everyone
at the Optoma Loans AIM Yamaha team and team principal
Alistair Flanagan for giving me the opportunity to ride at
the TT this year. To pick up four silver replicas at my first
attempt is amazing."

Plater, like eighth-placed Michael Rutter, had slowed to
almost walking pace on the Mountain as they came across
a terrible last-lap incident at the 26th Milestone, where
the carnage was to cost the lives of three people (see
panel). At the time they didn't know what had happened
and finished the race, ahead of Ian Armstrong in ninth and
James McBride in tenth.

It had been a record-breaking event. Everyone cheered
the record lap at 130.354mph by McGuinness, and
acknowledged that his brilliant form all week really had
earned him the title of King of the Mountain. And, as he
had time to reflect on his achievements, the 34-year-old
from Morecambe pondered his future.

"It's not easy, never easy here," he said. "I've won
two races in the Centenary Festival. I might just hang my
leathers up now. I had the same feeling the previous year.
I don't know what else I have to prove now although I
enjoy riding here, but I've been doing it for 11 years. The
team has been brilliant, they've not put pressure on me this
week – I've done that myself. They've told me just to enjoy
myself and I've done that with four podiums. It's a big relief.
I'm thinking about not coming back, but we'll see."

Time will tell, but in everyone's eyes McGuinness is the
modern day 'Mountain Master', and that's taking nothing
away from the legendary Joey Dunlop whose record of 26
race wins is seemingly untouchable for all time.

Over the years tragedy and the Tourist Trophy have gone hand in hand and this Centenary Festival was no exception. As John McGuinness was receiving his trophy, having produced a marvellous winning ride in the prestigious Senior race, news of an horrific accident high on the Snaefell section was beginning to filter through.

While the Lancastrian's 13th TT victory and record 130mph lap will be part of Island legend for years to come, his achievements will also remain overshadowed by the tragedy that claimed the lives of three people and left two others seriously injured.

The accident occurred at the 26th Milestone, known as Joey's in tribute to the late, legendary Joey Dunlop, who amassed an unrepeatable 26 victories. After the leading riders had passed through on their last lap, 34-year-old Marc Ramsbotham, from Norfolk, lost control of his Suzuki for reasons unknown and crashed heavily. He died at the scene, victim number 224 in the history of the TT.

The death of a rider is one thing, but in the cold light of day, in a subdued paddock area, the thing that cut everyone to the quick was the news that two spectators had also perished.

Dean Adrian Jacob, 33, from Kidderminster, and Gregory John Kenzig, 52, from Queensland, Australia, had been watching an amazing performance by McGuinness, enjoying the warm sun on the heights of the Mountain, when tragedy struck. Two volunteer marshals, both residents on the Island, Hilary Beryl Musson and Janice Ann Phillips, were badly injured and airlifted promptly to Nobles Hospital in Douglas.

RESULTS

Friday 8th June

LAP ONE

Pos	Rider	Time	Speed
1	John McGuinness	17 25.77	129.883
2	Guy Martin	17 35.46	128.690
3	Ian Hutchinson	17 37.74	128.414
4	Ian Lougher	17 50.10	126.931
5	Conor Cummins	18 01.33	125.612
6	Adrian Archibald	18 05.32	125.150
7	Michael Rutter	18 08.13	124.827
8	Steve Plater	18 12.36	124.343
9	Keith Amor	18 17.80	123.728
10	Dan Stewart	18 17.92	123.714
11	Ian Armstrong	18 19.18	123.572
12	Chris Palmer	18 20.50	123.424
13	Nigel Beattie	18 20.94	123.374
14	Mark Parrett	18 23.64	123.073
15	James McBride	18 24.64	122.961
16	Mark Buckley	18 26.99	122.701
17	Ian Pattinson	18 30.10	122.357
18	Gary Carswell	18 33.22	122.014
19	Gary Johnson	18 34.87	121.833
20	Les Shand	18 46.00	120.629

LAP TWO

Pos	Rider	Time	Speed
1	John McGuinness	17 21.99	130.354
2	Guy Martin	17 26.32	129.816
3	Ian Hutchinson	17 37.40	128.455
4	Ian Lougher	17 53.74	126.500
5	Conor Cummins	17 54.03	126.466
6	Adrian Archibald	17 51.43	126.772
7	Michael Rutter	18 02.09	125.524
8	Steve Plater	18 03.86	125.319
9	Keith Amor	18 07.87	124.856
10	Ian Armstrong	18 12.95	124.277
11	James McBride	18 15.29	124.011
12	Chris Palmer	18 22.90	123.156
13	Nigel Beattie	18 34.18	121.909
14	Ian Pattinson	18 25.12	122.908
15	Mark Buckley	18 28.34	122.551
16	Gary Carswell	18 31.95	122.153
17	Gary Johnson	18 33.67	121.964
18	Les Shand	18 37.34	121.563
19	Stephen Oates	18 43.62	120.885
20	Phil Stewart	19 07.08	118.412

LAP THREE

Pos	Rider	Time	Speed
1	John McGuinness	18 21.02	123.365
2	Guy Martin	18 24.04	123.028
3	Ian Hutchinson	18 29.47	122.426
4	Ian Lougher	18 37.53	121.543
5	Adrian Archibald	18 41.22	121.143
6	Conor Cummins	18 47.89	120.427
7	Michael Rutter	19 08.55	118.261
8	Steve Plater	19 04.34	118.695
9	James McBride	19 22.81	116.811
10	Chris Palmer	19 22.69	116.823
11	Ian Armstrong	19 35.92	115.508
12	Mark Buckley	19 23.57	116.734
13	Ian Pattinson	19 26.65	116.426
14	Gary Carswell	19 19.09	117.185
15	Gary Johnson	19 33.00	115.795
16	Les Shand	19 32.75	115.820
17	Stephen Oates	19 46.37	114.491
18	Paul Dobbs	19 29.01	116.191
19	Mark Miller	19 39.45	115.163
20	Phil Stewart	19 43.30	114.787

LAP FOUR

Pos	Rider	Time	Speed
1	John McGuinness	17 30.52	129.296
2	Guy Martin	17 36.49	128.566
3	Ian Hutchinson	17 40.31	128.102
4	Ian Lougher	17 53.83	126.489
5	Adrian Archibald	18 01.50	125.592
6	Conor Cummins	17 56.60	126.164
7	Michael Rutter	17 58.26	125.970
8	Steve Plater	18 01.14	125.634
9	James McBride	18 18.65	123.631
10	Ian Armstrong	18 15.69	123.966
11	Chris Palmer	18 28.16	122.571
12	Ian Pattinson	18 27.67	122.625
13	Mark Buckley	18 34.20	121.906
14	Gary Carswell	18 31.04	122.253
15	Gary Johnson	18 52.43	119.944
16	Les Shand	18 38.02	121.490
17	Stephen Oates	18 43.30	120.919
18	Mark Miller	18 37.25	121.573
19	Paul Dobbs	18 46.20	120.608
20	Phil Stewart	18 46.56	120.569

LAP FIVE

Pos	Rider	Time	Speed
1	John McGuinness	18 25.49	122.867
2	Guy Martin	18 26.50	122.754
3	Ian Hutchinson	18 52.07	119.982
4	Ian Lougher	18 47.67	120.450
5	Adrian Archibald	18 44.17	120.825
6	Conor Cummins	19 05.92	118.532
7	Steve Plater	19 00.31	119.115
8	Michael Rutter	19 22.89	116.802
9	Ian Armstrong	19 13.15	117.789
10	James McBride	19 20.43	117.050
11	Chris Palmer	19 14.43	117.659
12	Ian Pattinson	19 19.06	117.188
13	Gary Carswell	19 22.49	116.842
14	Mark Buckley	19 33.66	115.730
15	Les Shand	19 31.51	115.943
16	Gary Johnson	19 50.36	114.106
17	Stephen Oates	19 40.82	115.029
18	Mark Miller	19 32.72	115.823
19	Paul Dobbs	19 29.73	116.119
20	Phil Stewart	19 28.33	116.258

LAP SIX

Pos	Rider	Time	Speed
1	John McGuinness	17 39.44	128.207
2	Guy Martin	17 48.15	127.162
3	Ian Hutchinson	17 47.61	127.226
4	Ian Lougher	18 05.25	125.159
5	Adrian Archibald	17 57.97	126.003
6	Conor Cummins	18 02.09	125.524
7	Steve Plater	17 59.64	125.808
8	Michael Rutter	18 02.30	125.500
9	Ian Armstrong	18 19.20	123.570
10	James McBride	18 17.32	123.781
11	Chris Palmer	18 21.56	123.305
12	Ian Pattinson	18 25.47	122.869
13	Gary Carswell	18 26.52	122.753
14	Mark Buckley	18 26.66	122.737
15	Les Shand	18 29.91	122.378
16	Gary Johnson	18 52.57	119.929
17	Mark Miller	18 35.58	121.756
18	Stephen Oates	18 48.35	120.378
19	Phil Stewart	18 38.52	121.435
20	Paul Dobbs	18 53.54	119.826

THE HIGHS

JOHN McGUINNESS
HM Plant Honda

Another faultless performance as he took all before him at relentless pace, smashing race and lap records as he won with ease. But he left everyone with a poser – was this his finale on the Island?

GUY MARTIN
Hydrex Honda

Gave it everything but, in defeat, he was magnanimous in his praise of the winner. Certainly a rider with big winning potential at the TT for the future, but left wondering what might have been but for his jumping chain.

IAN HUTCHINSON
HM Plant Honda

Big bike taxed his injured shoulder but he still gave everything to his race. Lost time in the second pit stop but still battled on to complete a heady week at the races.

CONOR CUMMINS
Team Millsport Yamaha

Fastest ever Manx rider around the Mountain Course, upping his first lap speed of 125.612mph to 126.466mph next time around to seal his highly successful TT year.

STEVE PLATER
AIM Yamaha

Top newcomer and impressed again; his speed of learning the intricacies of the course reflected in his continually improving lap times and positions – another Silver replica for his collection.

THE LOWS

IAN LOUGHER
Stobart Motorsport Honda

Expected better things than fourth place but struggled with inconsistent handling problems as the bike reacted differently at the same place each lap.

BRUCE ANSTEY
Relentless Suzuki by TAS

Began with high hopes of a podium place as a minimum, but by the time he reached Ballaugh Bridge on the opening lap he realised the dream was fading and at the end of the first lap pulled in with handling problems.

MARTIN FINNEGAN
Alpha Boilers Honda

Frustration as machine problems sidelined him on the opening lap at Ballig Bridge.

RYAN FARQUHAR
Mark Johns Motors Honda

Stopped on the opening lap at the The Hawthorne as mechanical gremlins took their toll, compounding the annoyance he had suffered earlier in the week when he ran out of fuel in the Superstock race.

KEITH AMOR
Robinson Concrete Honda

Newcomer who was deservedly elevated up the starting list to run ninth at the first pit stop but then encountered problems, stopping at the return road, and then retiring.

Pos	No	Rider	Machine	Entrant	Time	Speed	Replica
1	3	John McGuinness	2007 Honda Fireblade 1000cc	HM Plant Honda Racing	01 46 44.23	127.255	Silver
2	8	Guy Martin	2007 Honda 1000cc	Hydrex Honda	01 47 16.96	126.608	Silver
3	6	Ian Hutchinson	2007 Honda CBR 1000cc	HM Plant Honda Racing	01 48 04.60	125.677	Silver
4	7	Ian Lougher	2007 Honda CBR 1000cc	Stobart Motorsport	01 49 08.12	124.458	Silver
5	2	Adrian Archibald	2007 Suzuki GSXR 1000cc	Relentless by TAS Racing	01 49 21.61	124.202	Silver
6	10	Conor Cummins	2007 Yamaha YZF R1 1000cc	Team Millsport Racing	01 49 47.86	123.708	Silver
7	11	Steve Plater*	2007 Yamaha R1 1000cc	AIM Racing	01 50 21.67	123.076	Silver
8	1	Michael Rutter	2007 Kawasaki ZX10 R 1000cc	MSS Discovery Kawasaki	01 50 42.22	122.695	Silver
9	13	Ian Armstrong	2004 Yamaha R1 1000cc	Canteen Smithy	01 51 56.08	121.346	Silver
10	23	James McBride	2007 Yamaha R1 1000cc		01 51 59.14	121.290	Silver
11	25	Chris Palmer	2005 Yamaha R1 1000cc	Solway Slate & Tile	01 52 10.23	121.091	Bronze
12	27	Ian Pattinson	2006 Suzuki GSXR 1000cc	Martin Bullock Raceteam	01 52 34.07	120.663	Bronze
13	15	Gary Carswell	2007 Kawasaki ZX10R 1000cc	Bolliger Kawasaki/SK Support	01 52 44.30	120.481	Bronze
14	33	Mark Buckley	Suzuki GSXR 1000cc	Crossan Motorcycles	01 52 53.42	120.319	Bronze
15	26	Les Shand	2006 Honda CBR 1000cc	Barron Transport	01 53 35.52	119.575	Bronze
16	22	Gary Johnson*	2007 Yamaha R1 1000cc	Speedfreak Racing	01 54 16.91	118.854	Bronze
17	40	Mark Miller	Aprilia 1000cc	Wolfman/Yoshiharu/Padgetts	01 54 25.46	118.705	Bronze
18	28	Stephen Oates	2007 Suzuki GSXR 1000cc	Hallett Aviation Racing	01 54 33.81	118.561	Bronze
19	35	Phil Stewart	2007 Yamaha R1 1000cc		01 54 34.42	118.551	Bronze
20	52	Paul Dobbs	2003 Suzuki GSXR 1000cc	Dave East Engineering	01 54 44.70	118.374	Bronze
21	51	Stefano Bonetti	Suzuki GSXR 1000cc		01 55 13.49	117.881	Bronze
22	49	Craig Atkinson	2004 Suzuki GSXR 1000cc	Martin Bullock Raceteam	01 55 16.26	117.834	Bronze
23	55	Paul Shoesmith	2007 Yamaha R1 1000cc	Speedfreak Racing	01 55 30.03	117.600	Bronze
24	56	Roy Richardson	2006 Yamaha R6 600cc	Ian Barnes Racing	01 55 49.30	117.273	Bronze
25	53	George Spence	2006 Yamaha YZF R1 1000cc		01 56 07.52	116.967	Bronze
26	64	Adrian McFarland	2005 Yamaha R1 1000cc	Team Hardship Racing	01 56 23.25	116.703	Bronze
27	60	Ian Mackman*	2006 Suzuki GSXR 1000cc	Bill Smith Motorcycles	01 56 42.24	116.387	Bronze
28	47	Tim Poole	2007 Yamaha YZF R1 1000cc	Bill Smith Motorcycles	01 56 47.37	116.302	Bronze
29	46	Paul Duckett	2005 Kawasaki ZX10 RR 1000cc	Wilson & Collins	01 57 01.17	116.073	Bronze
30	62	Thomas Schoenfelder	2005 Suzuki GSXR 1000cc	ADAC Hessent-Thueringen	01 57 03.55	116.034	Bronze
31	34	James Edmeades	2007 Yamaha R1 1000cc	Speedfreak Racing	01 57 04.63	116.016	Bronze
32	66	John Crellin	2002 Suzuki GSX 1000cc	J Richards	01 57 14.73	115.849	Bronze
33	54	Stephen Harper	2006 Suzuki GSXR 1000cc		01 57 26.44	115.657	
34	43	William Dunlop	2006 Kawasaki 600cc	Lilley Racing	01 57 40.71	115.423	
35	61	David Paredes	Yamaha R1 1000cc	Bill Smith Motorcycles	01 58 03.03	115.059	
36	73	Fabrice Miguet	2006 Suzuki GSXR 1000cc		01 58 18.57	114.807	
37	58	Andrew Marsden	2004 Yamaha R1 1000cc	Austin Powered Racing	01 58 21.89	114.754	
38	79	Alan Connor	2006 Suzuki GSXR 1000cc	Dunshaughlin RRSC	01 58 30.85	114.609	
39	45	David Milling	2006 Honda 600cc	Dave Milling Motorcycles	01 58 44.42	114.391	
40	57	Alan Bud Jackson	2005 Suzuki GSXR 1000cc	BDS Fuels	01 59 52.35	113.310	
41	75	Chris Petty	2006 Suzuki GSXR 1000cc	York Suzuki Centre	02 00 03.16	113.140	
42	80	Derran Slous	2005 Suzuki GSXR 750cc		02 00 10.73	113.022	
43	67	Karsten Schmidt	2004 Ducati 750cc		02 00 34.72	112.647	
44	71	Robert Barber*	2007 Triumph Daytona 675cc		02 01 51.36	111.466	
45	74	David Hewson*	2006 Kawasaki ZX10 1000cc		02 02 20.01	111.031	
46	81	Etienne Godart	Honda 600cc	Martin Bullock Raceteam	02 03 13.79	110.223	
47	78	Sandor Bitter	2006 Suzuki GSXR 1000cc		02 03 44.00	109.834	

Time	No	Rider	Machine	Entrant	Location
10:53:14	4	Martin Finnegan	2007 Honda CBR 1000cc	Alpha Boilers Racing	Ballig Bridge (8.25 miles)
10:54:10	9	Ryan Farquhar	2007 Honda Fireblade 1000cc	Mark Johns Motors	Hawthorne Inn (6.75 miles)
11:03:56	63	Daniel Jansen	2005 Kawasaki ZX10 1000cc		Appledene Corner (6.00 miles)
11:06:35	70	Dirk Kaletsch	2004 Honda CBR 1000cc		Barregarrow Cross Roads (12.50 miles)
11:07:05	5	Bruce Anstey	2007 Suzuki GSXR 1000cc	Relentless by TAS Racing	Pits (0.01 miles)
11:07:57	16	Davy Morgan	2005 Honda 1000cc	Investasure	Pits (0.01 miles)
11:12:56	20	Mark Parrett	2007 Yamaha R1 1000cc	Ripley Land	Laurel Bank (Ebenezer Lane) (8.75 miles)
11:20:06	32	David Coughlan	2005 Yamaha R1 1000cc	Ridge Developments	Barregarrow Cross Roads (12.50 miles)
11:20:47	77	Alan Bennie	2005 Honda CBR 600cc		Pits (0.01 miles)
11:21:39	24	Dan Stewart	2006 Yamaha R1 1000cc		May Hill Cruickshanks Corner (24.00 miles)
11:23:05	82	John Nisill	2006 Yamaha R1 1000cc	PR Haulage/CJN Services	Pits (0.01 miles)
11:25:26	12	Keith Amor	2005 Honda CBR 1000cc	Robinson Concrete	Pits (0.01 miles)
11:30:54	37	Roger Maher	2006 Yamaha R1 1000cc		The Nook (37.00 miles)
11:35:19	42	Paul Owen	2004 Honda CBR 600cc	Back to Normal	Quarterbridge (1.25 miles)
11:37:56	68	Martin Hamberg	2006 Yamaha R1 1000cc	Hallett Aviation Racing	Pits (0.01 miles)
11:39:40	17	Nigel Beattie	2007 Yamaha R1 1000cc	CD Racing/Millsport Racing	Kirk Michael Douglas Road (14.00 miles)
11:41:29	69	Chris McGahan	2007 Yamaha R6 600cc		Pits (0.01 miles)
11:54:51	29	John Burrows	2006 Honda CBR 1000cc	H.M. Sports Motorhomes	Appledene Corner (6.00 miles)
12:05:29	38	Michael Dunlop	2004 Yamaha 1000cc		Ballaugh Bridge (17.00 miles)
12:09:19	31	Jimmy Moore	2007 Honda CBR 1000cc	Team Black Horse Racing	Signpost Corner (36.50 miles)
12:10:30	65	Steve Linsdell	2001 Paton PG500RC 500cc	Squadra Corse C.M.M.	Orrisdale Road North (15.80 miles)
12:13:05	50	Frank Spenner	2004 Yamaha R1 1000cc	ADAC Hessen-Thueringen	Pits (0.01 miles)
12:13:43	30	Liam Quinn	2006 Yamaha R1 1000cc	Team Racing	Pits (0.01 miles)
12:15:35	59	Christer Miinin	2006 Suzuki GSXE 1000cc	Martin Bullock Raceteam	Pits (0.01 miles)
12:22:33	83	Mike Hose	2005 Honda CBR 600cc		Pits (0.01 miles)
12:28:49	44	Dave Madsen-Mygdal	2007 Yamaha R1 1000cc	CSC Racing	Gooseneck (25.10 miles)
13:33:24	72	Marc Ramsbotham	2006 Suzuki K6 1000cc		Joey's (26.00 miles)

* Denotes newcomer riders

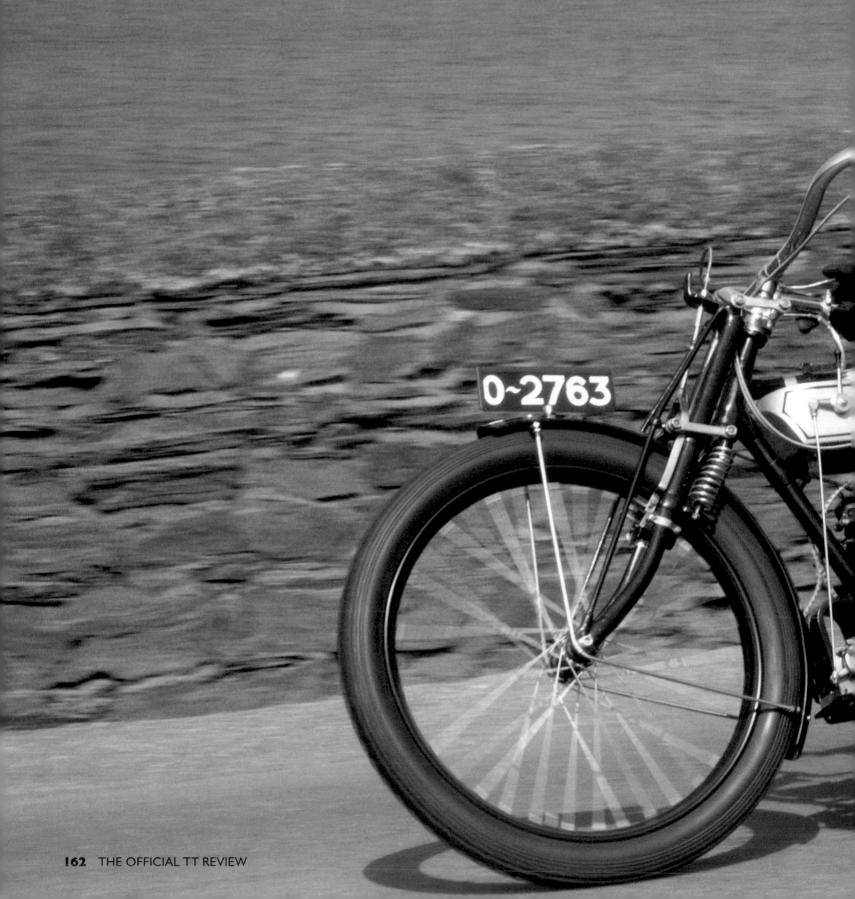

1907 TT
RE-ENACTMENT

0~2763

Rounding Devil's Elbow, on the coast road from Kirk Michael to Peel, George Cohen looks totally authentic aboard the Norton with which Rem Fowler won the twin-cylinder class in 1907.
© Ian Allen

1907 TT RE-ENACTMENT

A GLORIOUS TIME WARP SET THE SCENE PERFECTLY FOR THE CENTENARY CELEBRATIONS

By Mac McDiarmid

Top left: Geoff Duke OBE with the plaque he unveiled before the centenary re-enactment.
© Double Red

Top right: Paul Phillips, TT and Motorsport Development Manager, gets in period.
© Mac McDiarmid

While the cricket at Headingley endured the coldest weather in English test match history, just 7°C, huge Bank Holiday crowds delighted to a sunny re-enactment of the 1907 motorcycle TT – supported by Dunlop – over the original 15.8-mile St John's Course on 28 May.

But the day wasn't without difficulty. First we were informed that the Lieutenant Governor's car had broken down en route to St John's, then another vehicle had to be towed from the course before the re-enactment could begin, 50 minutes later than the exact anniversary. Earlier, the great Geoff Duke OBE, six times a TT winner and world champion, unveiled a plaque commemorating the centenary event.

One hundred years earlier, the first riders away were the Triumphs of Frank Hulbert and Jack Marshall in a field of just 25. For the re-enactment, almost 100 machines took part, pride of place going to the winner and runner-up in the 1907 twin-cylinder class.

Chris Read now owns the Vindec twin on which a 23-year-old Billy Wells placed second 100 years ago. The 69-year-old Cheltenham man beamed in undisguised pleasure at the chance to ride the TT course once more. Behind him was arrayed a mouth-watering feast of nostalgia:

David Plant on a 1908 Triumph similar to Jack Marshall's TT winner, Graham Rhodes on a factory 1905 Velo, Eric Alderson's 3.5hp Rex, Robert Lusk's 4.5hp Minerva, and many more.

Celebrity riders included seven-times TT winner Mick Grant on a '38 Speed Twin, 1993 F1 TT winner Nick Jefferies giving an outing to some seriously distressed ISDT waterproofs on a Scott twin, and the legendary Sammy Miller on a 1912 Humber V-twin. Even more colourful was current TT star Guy Martin, happily soaking in the atmosphere from the perch of a veteran Triumph. Bringing up the rear was Richard 'Milky' Quayle, Lightweight 400cc TT winner in 2002, on a light-hearted 'replica', the 'Shuttleworth Snap', on which George Formby had performed so heroically in the TT film *No Limit*.

Putting them all in the shade, however, was a winner from 1907, the same Peugeot-engined Norton on which Rem Fowler won the twin-cylinder class. Generously loaned by its owner, Roy Richards, patron of Birmingham's National Motorcycle Museum, this historic machine was badly damaged during the fire of 2003, but has been restored by the man privileged to ride it, George Cohen.

Thousands, many in period dress, lined the course as the parade began. Geoff Duke flagged them away, at his elbow the imposing St Mars silver trophy awarded to overall winner Charlie Collier in 1907, and still presented to the winner of the Senior TT to this day.

Off spluttered Cohen and Read in a cacophony of exposed valves as they fiddled to tune the throttles and air mixtures of their vintage machines. With its single speed, direct drive, primitive leather belt final drive and almost complete lack of brakes, the Norton was typical of the technology of its time. Ahead of it lay the daunting climb out of Glen Helen where, a century before, riders had pushed or pedalled 'fit to bust' before emerging gratefully on to Cronk-y-Voddy straight.

Opposite: The junction of Church Road and Albany Road in Peel, then and now.
© Mac McDiarmid (main image)
© FoTTofinder Bikesport Archives

Below: Chris Read with his Vindec twin, on which Billy Wells finished second in the 1907 twin-cylinder event.
© Double Red

"IT WAS AN HONOUR TO RIDE THAT MACHINE. THE CROWDS WERE SUPERB, WAVING EVERYWHERE. AT TIMES I ALMOST FELT LIKE REM FOWLER."

GEORGE COHEN

"It went up the hill perfectly," said a slightly surprised Cohen after the event. "By the end of Cronk-y-Voddy I'd managed to get the air and throttle levers set to optimum, and it was flying along."

Unlike in 1907, when after the first of ten laps the Norton led overall by a mere two seconds from the Vindec, Cohen now had a hard-charging Guy Martin for company. The pair paraded together for the rest of the lap, exchanging waves with the crowds, Cohen delighting himself by getting a foot down outside the chip shop where the bikes turn left into Peel's Church Street.

He was certainly grateful not to have as eventful a race as Fowler endured on the nail-strewn rough dirt roads of a century before. In all, Fowler suffered two crashes, a puncture and once rode through the flames of a competitor's burning machine. He lost eight minutes on lap two, caught back most of that by the time he set the fastest lap of the race – 42.91mph – on lap six, lost another eight

minutes on lap seven and briefly wandered away from his bike in despair before finally resuming the fray and claiming victory over Wells by 33 minutes.

Cohen's only problem, such was the untroubled speed of his lap, was that he and Guy Martin found themselves red-flagged as they approached St John's. Their progress had been so brisk that many riders had not yet begun their parade lap.

"It was the best thing I've ever done," Cohen said when he eventually crossed the finish line, arm in air, mouth in a wide grin. "It was an honour to ride that machine. The crowds were superb, waving everywhere. At times I almost felt like Rem Fowler."

Others echoed similar sentiments. "An amazing atmosphere," exclaimed Mick Grant. "Thousands of people, all round the course, hundreds in period dress, all waving madly. Just brilliant. They should do this every year."

Opposite top: Mick Grant enjoys the crowd's appreciation.
© Stephen Davison

Opposite bottom: George Cohen with the National Motorcycle Museum's 1907 Norton, which he restored.
© Stephen Davison

Below: To applause from John McGuinness, Richard 'Milky' Quayle's 'Shuttleworth Snap' takes the flag, which is being waved by Adrian Earnshaw, Minister of Tourism and Leisure.
© Stephen Davison

Dunlop TT Centenary
LAP OF HONOUR

THE LAP OF HONOUR, A REGULAR FIXTURE AT THE TT, WAS THE BIGGEST AND BEST EVER IN 2007

By Steve Burns

Previous page: Lined up at the start are Frank Perris (20), Tony Rutter (21), Con Law (25), Kel Carruthers (14), Ray Knight (23) and Nick Jefferies (17).
© Stephen Davison

Top: Streamliners together: Willi Marewski's Gilera 500 (8) and Klaus Held's NSU Sportmax 250.
© Stephen Davison

Opposite: Kel Carruthers, twice a TT winner, on a Yamaha TZ350 in evocative North American colours.
© Stephen Davison

Right: Johnny Rea on the Millar Racing Honda RC30 from 1992.
© Jon Stroud

Far right: Stuart Graham, though a works Suzuki rider in the 1960s, rode Honda Classic Racing team's RC174.
© Stephen Davison

It was difficult to know which way to look first. There were so many great bikes, so many heroes, so much noise. It was a truly awe-inspiring few moments as participants lined up along the Glencrutchery Road for the Dunlop TT Centenary Lap of Honour.

The Lap of Honour started in 1979, the year of the Isle of Man Government's Millennium, and has continued unabated ever since in various forms and guises with similar trends in quantity and quality. But this year's TT Centenary celebrations produced the biggest and best classic demonstration the Island has ever seen.

Both Honda and Yamaha classic collectors excelled in putting as many immortal motorcycles and riders out on the course to provoke a sense of times past at this, the oldest motorcycle event in history.

Jim Redman, a six-time TT winner and a regular participant in the TT Lap of Honour, was initially slated to ride a 1964 250cc Honda RC164, similar to the 48bhp, 15,000rpm, four-cylinder bike he rode to victory in that year's races, but unfortunately that never came off. At the last minute he had seemingly done a deal to ride one of the podium-placed Hondas from that morning's Superstock race, but the race organisers put the mockers on that and at the very last minute Padgetts stumped up a road-going Fireblade.

Despite all the trials and tribulations, Redman really enjoyed his lap. "You know it's just so good to come here

"IT IS VERY GOOD TO BE HERE AFTER SO LONG. I HAVE ENJOYED THIS EXPERIENCE VERY MUCH. YOU KNOW I WHEELIED AT THE START AND AT THE FINISH. FANTASTIC!"

PETER RUBATTO

again and enjoy myself," he said. "When I raced here there was always pressure for me to win at least two races. I certainly enjoy it more now.

"The TT was always an important race, perhaps not as important as the world championship, but it was one of the biggest Grands Prix in the season. It was a big thing to win a TT."

Redman headed a bunch of former factory Honda riders that included Luigi Taveri and Tommy Robb, and former 1960s Suzuki works rider Stuart Graham somehow ended up as an interloper for the Honda Classic Racing team aboard the 67bhp, 17,000rpm 297cc

RC174, the enlarged version of the 250cc six-cylinder bike (same 41mm bore but with a 37.5mm stroke instead of the 250's 31mm) with which Mike Hailwood had such a successful 1967 season.

Tommy Robb in particular really enjoyed his afternoon jaunt on a replica 1962 RC163. Now 72, the Irishman admitted that, following a career that included one win and 28 replicas, he still got as much of a buzz as ever about the prospects of a lap of the 37.73-mile circuit.

"I loved the place, and still do. Of course I was brought up on road circuits in much the same way as Irish riders are today," said Robb. "In fairness there were many challenging circuits in the Grand Prix schedule when I was a works Honda rider, but this was always the ultimate."

While Robb successfully completed his lap, his much-loved former team-mate Luigi Taveri had to pull off the track early on with the 1966-vintage 125cc RC149, the ear-shattering five-cylinder machine that revs to 21,500rpm and has an eight-speed transmission.

Ferry Brouwer's Yamaha Classic Racing team certainly matched their Japanese counterparts. But they chose to empower a string of riders (all resplendent in 1970s works team leathers) aboard the private machines that Yamaha provided in the late sixties and early seventies and that arguably kept the 250cc and 350cc classes in existence at that particular time. Michelle Duff, now a regular on the Classic Parade scene, was aboard a

1968 250cc RD05A from Japan, while Rod Gould was riding a YZ632 250cc machine – basically a replica of the semi-works TD2B on which Gould and Kent Andersson attempted to defend Yamaha's 250cc world championship that Gould had won in 1970. Also out in 'works' colours was none other than German Dieter Braun, who was attending his first TT in 37 years, having won his one and only TT (the 125cc for Suzuki) in 1970. The twice world champion admitted to making a mistake towards the end of his lap aboard a semi-works 1972 TD2B 250cc Yamaha: "It was at the right-hander towards the end [Signpost] and I didn't realise that it turned right so suddenly and I went straight on. This is my first visit since 1970 and I have found it quite strange."

Another Yamaha legend to appear, albeit one from the spannering side, was American-domiciled Australian Kel Carruthers. Although he won a 250cc world title for Benelli in 1969, he was aboard one of the first water-cooled TZ 350cc (1973) machines. The bike was resplendent in faintly replica North American Yamaha colours, which Carruthers ran when he finished second to his team-mate, Finn Jarno Saarinen, in the 1973 Daytona 200 on a Yamaha 350 twin.

Kel did have problems getting off the line this time though. "Aaagggh that was my fault," said the two-time TT winner. "As I peddled to the line I couldn't find a neutral [gear] and I probably tried to chug away in second. After

that she went round very well indeed and I thoroughly enjoyed it.

"Apart from a brief visit seven years ago, this is my first proper visit for 37 years and it's been great. The TT was always special to me even though my first priority was always the world championship."

Bernard Murray lined up aboard Boet van Dulmen's 1981 square-four 500cc Yamaha. This was also the bike on which Charlie Williams dominated the 1982 Senior TT only for it to pack up at Ballaugh on the penultimate lap. Murray, however, was a little unnerved by his experience at lap's end.

"It was extremely enjoyable," said Murray. "But I was wary about riding a two-stroke, and having to remember to keep my left hand hovering over the clutch [two-strokes of the time were prone to seizing in the mixed Manx weather conditions], but I kept waving to the crowd anyhow."

Another classic Yamaha in evidence was Charlie Williams' 1981 Maxton-framed TZ-G, although it was Tony Rutter who actually took the bike out on the course. Rutter was busy on Tuesday morning, thoroughly enjoying fettling the ex-factory two-stroke.

"The 1970s were always my favourite times at the TT," said Rutter. "Of course I won two Junior races on 350cc Yamahas but my favourite bike was the 750cc TZ – that was fantastic."

"THE BIKE WAS STEERING A BIT TIGHT, BUT PERHAPS THAT WAS ME NOT LEANING OVER AS FAR AS I SHOULD. BUT APART FROM THAT THE OLD THING WAS JUST AS I'D REMEMBERED IT. MY ONLY COMPLAINT IS MY LEFT HAND IS NOW VERY TIRED AFTER ALL THAT WAVING."

NICK JEFFERIES

While there was plenty of exotic machinery on view, there was even more interest in the array of riders who had travelled from the four corners of the globe to be present and 'compete' in this centenary event.

South African Paddy Driver was a top-rank privateer on the world scene in the 1960s and was present on the Island for the first time in years. His mount – a 1958 Manx Norton – was in keeping with his independent status, but unfortunately the machine didn't go the distance.

Also representing British machinery was the Matchless G50, which was raced so successfully by Barry Sheene in classic events in recent years. Tom Dickie was aboard the famed machine for the Lap of Honour.

Not content with a lap in the TT re-enactment at St John's the previous week, seven-time TT winner Mick Grant was back on the Mountain Course on more recent machinery. Grantie rode his 1984 Suzuki RGB that he took to third place in that year's Senior race. Unfortunately for Mick the RG wasn't as reliable on this occasion as he failed to complete the lap.

In between checks on the Yamaha, Tony Rutter kept a close eye on his 1983 Formula II Ducati Pantah 600 that he was saving for Friday's Parade of Champions, and said of the bike: "This has been completely rebuilt by John Hackett and it's had only about three minutes of running time, which is a pity because we could do with more. I had a lot of success on the 600 [Ducati] but it wasn't my favourite bike because it was quite difficult to ride."

Con Law had finished second in the Senior Classic aboard an RG500 Mk IV Suzuki in 1983 and was back on a similar machine for this lap. He was beaming from ear to ear in pitlane after the experience. "That was brilliant – it made me feel very young again," said the two-time Junior TT winner.

Fellow Irishman Johnny Rea, another former Junior TT winner, took over the headlines from his BSB starlet son for a day by turning out on an early 1990s Millar Racing Honda RC30. He was somewhat taciturn in pitlane afterwards: "I'd forgotten how quick these things go."

Nick Jefferies completed an emotional lap aboard his 1993 Formula One Castrol Honda RC30. "The bike was steering a bit tight," said Jefferies, "but perhaps that was me not leaning over as far as I should. But apart from that the old thing was just as I'd remembered it. My only complaint is my left hand is now very tired after all that waving."

Racing journalist Mat Oxley was raving about his lap aboard the 1998 Honda RC45, which Michael Rutter took to second place in that year's Formula One race behind Ian Simpson. Oxley, an *MCN* reporter when he won the 1985 Production 250cc race, said: "It was fantastic. I sort of behaved myself on it but I had to give it a bit of a buzz where the crowds were big, just so they could hear the scream of the V4 engine. The bikes round here are so quiet now, so it was nice to generate a bit of noise."

Barry Woodland won three 400cc Production races in the mid-1980s, and was out on a Flitwick Yamaha in his first Island visit for 16 years. "It really is nice to be back," he said. "It's a bit depressing though because I'd rather be competing than tooling round. I'm impressed with the circuit layout now, and I can see why the times are so fast these days. I also impressed myself in that I remembered where everything goes."

From the immediate post-war era there was a host of 125cc and 250cc NSU Sportmax machines that were ridden so successfully at the TT between 1953 and 1955, a period when NSU was the biggest motorcycle manufacturer in the marketplace. Werner Haas and Rupert Hollaus, both TT winners and world champions, reflected this on the track.

Former German champion Ernst Hiller made a first-ever TT visit and demonstrated a 1954 BMW as raced by Walter Zeller. The machine, although not supercharged,

Opposite: Nick Jefferies with the Castrol Honda RC30 on which he won the Formula One TT in 1993.
© Stephen Davison

Above: Trevor Nation was proud to be aboard a very precious motorcycle – the Ducati on which Mike Hailwood won the 1978 Formula One TT.
© Jon Stroud

Left: Ronald Mullin's Petty Manx 350 at Gooseneck.
© Jon Stroud

still had all the aesthetic qualities of Georg Meier's 1939 Senior TT-winning machine.

German Peter Rubatto was aboard a replica of his 1987 Formula One Bimota and was another making a welcome return to the Isle of Man after a prolonged absence, the Hein Gericke rider not having returned since managing Baldassarre Monti's tragic visit in 1994. He was in a jovial mood as he photographed everyone and everything: "It is very good to be here after so long. I have enjoyed this experience very much. You know I wheelied at the start and at the finish. Fantastic!"

A two-time Production TT winner in the 1980s, former works Norton rider Trevor Nation was in an emotional state after his lap aboard Mike Hailwood's 1978 Formula One-winning Sports Motorcycle Ducati that was being looked after at the TT by Steve Wynne – the same engineer who worked with Hailwood all those years ago.

"I had to be so careful with such a historic bike," Nation explained. "It was such a privilege to ride this. To have the Sports Motorcycle people here helping us was great too. I really enjoyed being out there again after so long [1995 was Trevor's last racing year]. You know the TT was what got me interested in racing and I have such a passion for the place. I just wish that some of my results

could have reflected what the event means to me."

In the sidecar category, two-time TT winner Dick Greasley was having his first ride of any kind for 20 years. Armed with a Bruce Ford-Dunn built 750cc Yamaha of 1982 vintage, Greasley had restored his famous yellow and black North American Yamaha colours and was very excited before departing.

"I'm really looking forward to this," said Greasley. "I've not been aboard a sidecar since my last TT here in 1987. We actually tried to get my old Busch outfit [a 1978 winner] for this, which would have been nice, but it wasn't to be.

"I've so much to be grateful to the TT for. In only my second year here in 1975 we were numbered 39 in both races yet finished with a second and a third. I particularly remember the 500 race because we'd never ridden a 500 Yamaha before and we were learning about it as we raced, but we got a great result and because that race was then a Grand Prix it actually set us up to get into the world championships. I suppose most people remember me for getting the first 100mph lap, but that race in 1975 really kickstarted my career."

Greasley's last comment sums up so much of what the TT has been about these past 100 years – an inspiration!

Opposite: Former works Honda rider and three-time TT winner Luigi Taveri on the Honda Classic Racing 125cc RC149.

© Dave Purves

Below: Racing journalist Mat Oxley, who won a TT race in 1985, returned to the Island to ride a 1998 Honda RC45; alongside him is Heinz Rosner's MZ-RE.

© Stephen Davison

MCN

PARADE OF CHAMPIONS

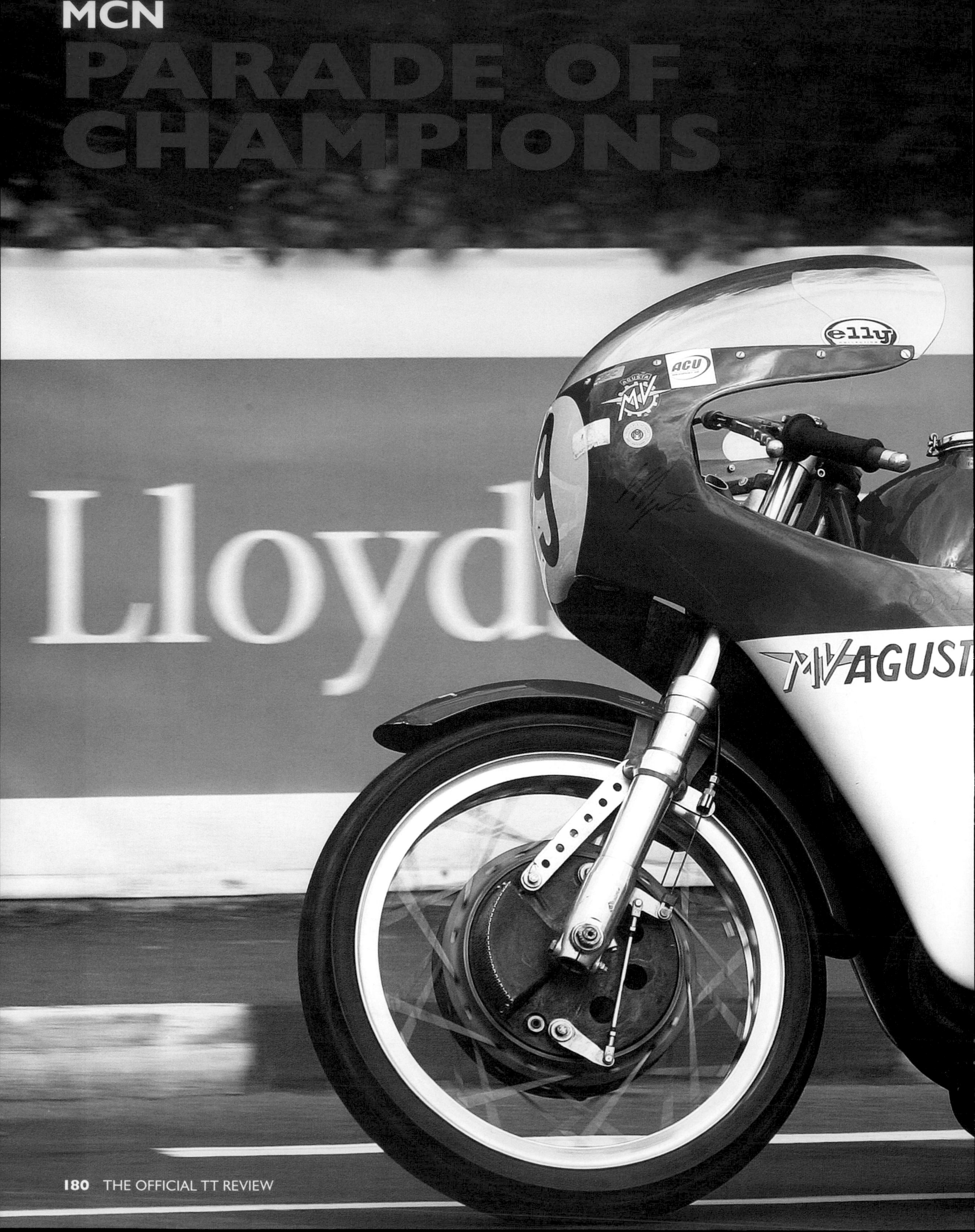

Below: Giacomo Agostini, 10-times TT winner and 15-times world champion, waves to the crowds at Quarterbridge from his 500cc MV Agusta.
© **Double Red**

THERE HAD NEVER BEEN SUCH A GATHERING OF TT LEGENDS – AND IT WAS AWESOME

By Steve Burns

Below: Six-time TT winner John Surtees, like Ago, lapped on an MV Agusta.

© Dave Purves

Opposite top: Charlie Williams' Mitsui Yamaha TZ on which he won the Junior TT in 1980.

© Double Red

Opposite bottom: Phil Read rode this Gilera to third place in the 1963 Senior TT.

© Double Red

The final dose of nostalgia of the Centenary TT celebrations was the *MCN* TT Centenary Parade of Champions, run after Friday's Senior TT.

It was an apt title for the show. True, there were some interlopers with no TT pedigree, such as Noriyuki Haga and Neil Hodgson, but in fairness to them their presence didn't detract from the otherwise gloriously retro character of the event. And the fact that Giacomo Agostini and John Surtees, with 22 world titles between them, were both out on contemporary and authentic 500cc MV Agustas meant that the Parade certainly had historic credence fitting to the event.

Agostini, who has been a regular visitor to the Island in recent years and is a willing participant in any historical reminisce, looked resplendent aboard the same 500cc three-cylinder MV on which he won his last TT in 1972. "There is always a lot of emotion to come back here," said Ago. "I won the TT ten times and it was always a very important Grand Prix for me." For a full interview with Ago, turn to page 193.

Likewise John Surtees seemed to turn back time as he belied his 73 years. The seven-time TT winner was also aboard a 1970s 500cc MV Agusta and, despite fighting a cold, he was incredibly fast – and keen to sum up his TT experiences afterwards.

"I have fond memories of the TT," said Surtees. "The pressure to do well here was great in my time – it was all about getting those eight points [the score for a Grand Prix winner at the time]. It was always a difficult place to learn, and we certainly didn't have the time to flit over pre-season or in the weeks leading up to the event to recce the course because of our racing commitments.

"It was always a challenge to ride here. Everywhere else

"I HAVE FOND MEMORIES OF THE TT. THE PRESSURE TO DO WELL HERE WAS GREAT IN MY TIME – IT WAS ALL ABOUT GETTING THOSE EIGHT POINTS."

JOHN SURTEES

"THE TT HAS BEEN IMPORTANT TO ME SINCE I WAS A KID, BECAUSE I USED TO COME WITH MY DAD WHEN HE RACED HERE. I ALWAYS WANTED TO RACE HERE, WIN HERE AND BE THE FASTEST MAN HERE."

CARL FOGARTY

we were scratching at 102 per cent, but here it was always about getting in a rhythm."

Four-time World Superbike Champion Carl Fogarty spoke with real emotion about his feelings for the TT during the previous day's Day of Champions get-together.

"The TT has been important to me since I was a kid," said Foggy, "because I used to come with my Dad [George] when he raced here. I was brought up on the place and I always wanted to race here, win here and be the fastest man here. I was very fortunate that I achieved all those things and, in many ways, that means more to me than anything I achieved in World Superbike."

The next day the three-time TT winner had the privilege of leading off the Parade of Champions aboard the MV Agusta F4 on which Martin Finnegan had finished fourth in the PokerStars Superstock race.

Despite some trepidation about remembering the way the course went, Foggy showed that old habits die hard and hounded the travelling marshal who was supposed to lead the 'parade' round for the entire lap. Any of Foggy's misapprehensions relating to his memory of the course had obviously quickly dissipated.

"I was itching to get past him [the marshal]," said Foggy. "But he said to me beforehand that if I passed him he'd have the lap red-flagged, and that would have annoyed a lot of people.

"It was such a great experience and it made me feel like making a comeback, but that would probably cost me a divorce."

Through his Radio TT broadcasts, eight-time winner Charlie Williams is as immersed in the TT in the 21st century as he was during his racing days. He was really looking forward to his lap aboard the Mitsui Yamaha TZ, on which he won the Junior in 1980 – and was even fettling his own bike in the paddock during the week.

"I bought the bike off Mitsui at the end of that season," said Williams, "but then sold it on. It's now in the hands of Phillip Morris and he's brought it here for me to ride. It's nice to have it back." Williams' cheery pre-lap mood didn't last, however, as the TZ gave up the ghost at Glen Helen.

Tony Rutter had more luck with another of Charlie's TZs, as the 1981 TZ-G did complete the lap. Although Rutter had had to abandon plans to ride his 1983/84 Formula Two-winning Ducati Pantah, he was quite pleased to take the 250cc Yamaha out again. As he had previously admitted before Tuesday's lap, the Duke had never been one of his favourite motorcycles.

Ferry Brouwer's Yamaha Classic Racing Team was out in force again in the Parade, Dieter Braun continuing his 'strange' TT experience by leading the factory-liveried machines once again.

Rod Gould had been very disappointed on Tuesday when his 250cc YZ635 Yamaha packed up and he couldn't complete the lap. But the former 250cc World Champion was in better fortune this time as he finally completed a tour of the Mountain Course.

Chas Mortimer, eight-time winner on the Isle of Man, joined the Brouwer squad for the Parade of Champions.

Opposite: Three-time TT winner Carl Fogarty had the privilege of leading off the *MCN* TT Centenary Parade of Champions.
© Stephen Davison

Above: Complete with period Arai helmet, eight-time TT winner Chas Mortimer smokes off the line on the Yamaha Classic Racing Team RD05A.
© Stephen Davison

The 57-year-old was in fine form and, like all Brouwer's boys, resplendent not only in Yamaha works colours of the 1970s but also a fantastic period Arai helmet. No doubt the helmets were courtesy of the boss – Brouwer is CEO of Arai Europe.

"The TT was always important to me," recalled Mortimer, one the leading GP privateers in the early 1970s. "Obviously there was big motivation because of the world championship points at stake, but I always enjoyed the challenge of the place."

Dennis Ireland was visiting the TT for the first time in eight years and loving every moment. However, the 1982 Classic race winner's mood was a little despondent when the RG500 he rode that day wouldn't fire up and the Kiwi was forced to revert to a lap on a road-going machine.

"The track is very similar, although a few of the bends have been ironed out – especially Brandish," said Ireland. "The speeds the boys are doing now are exceptional, and the modern-day road bikes have some poke. It's a phenomenal landmark for the TT to reach 100 years. It's survived all the knockers."

James Whitham – a works Suzuki star in his time at the TT – turned up to ride an ex-David Jefferies production

bike. He was really enjoying his return to the TT, during which he doubled up tourist duties along with being a pit attendant for his friend Paul Shoesmith in that morning's Senior.

"I was more nervous working in the pits for 'Shoey' than riding back out there," said Whit. "It's fantastic the speeds the boys achieve round here these days, and it's brilliant to see so many people over here enjoying themselves. I've brought over some friends who have never been before and they have been totally gobsmacked."

Whitham's fellow Tyke, Mick Grant, was another who turned out in his old racing leathers and really looked as if he was in a time warp. He looked terrific aboard the 1978 Kawasaki KR750 two-stroke triple on which he won that year's Classic race and broke his own outright lap record.

Before the lap Grant was adamant that there was to be no hooliganism from him while out on the track.

"I just want to go round nice and steady, and let everyone see the bike," said Grantie. Reports from trackside stated that this promise went out of the window once the Green Meanie reached the top of Bray Hill...

There were plenty of other 1980s and 1990s stars in

Opposite: Tony Rutter at Ago's Leap on an ex-Charlie Williams 1981 Yamaha TZ-G.
© Jon Stroud

Below: Mick Grant rode the Kawasaki KR750 two-stroke triple on which he won the 1978 Classic TT.
© Double Red

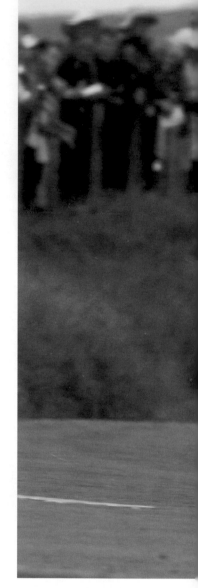

Left: Mitsuo Itoh, the only Japanese rider to have won a TT, rode Suzuki's impeccably restored 50cc RK67 from 1967.
© Double Red

Below: A unique gathering of TT legends. Back row, standing (from left): Stuart Graham, Tony Rutter, Jim Redman, Frank Perris, John Surtees, Giacomo Agostini, Phil Read, Bill Smith, Phil McCallen, Michelle Duff, John Reynolds, Nick Jefferies, Heinz Rosner, Ralph Bryans, Graeme Crosby, Iain Duffus, Brian Reid, Carl Fogarty (James Whitham behind his left shoulder) and Brian Morrison. Front row, squatting (from left): Noriyuki Haga, Barry Smith, Michael Wynn, Tommy Robb, Ralph Bryans, Kel Carruthers, Sammy Miller, Rob Fisher, Kenny Arthur, Dave Molyneux and Mick Boddice.
© Stephen Davison

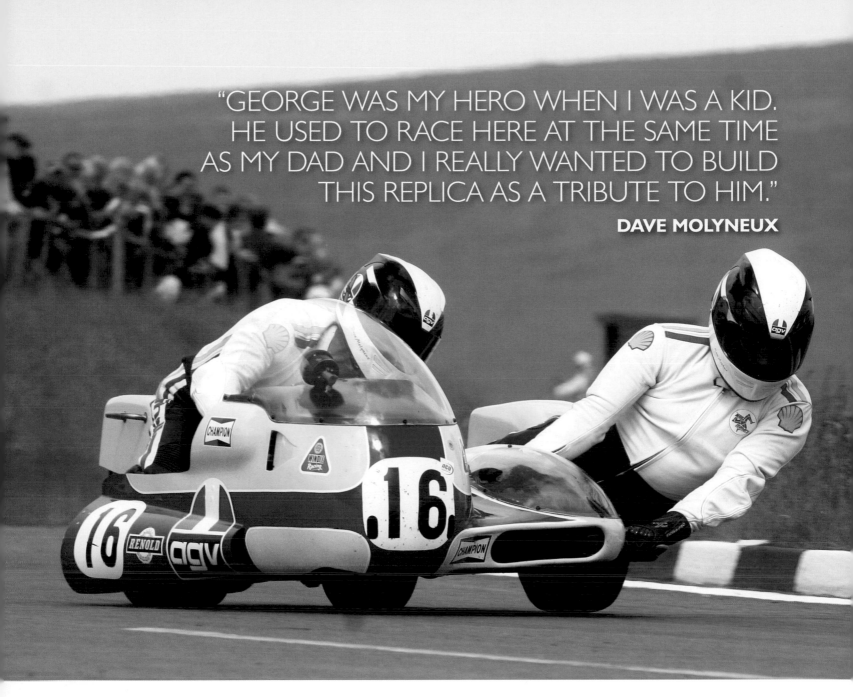

"GEORGE WAS MY HERO WHEN I WAS A KID.
HE USED TO RACE HERE AT THE SAME TIME
AS MY DAD AND I REALLY WANTED TO BUILD
THIS REPLICA AS A TRIBUTE TO HIM."

DAVE MOLYNEUX

attendance. Quiet Ulsterman and five-time TT winner Brian Reid was out on his Loctite TZ250cc of 1991 vintage, owned by John McGuinness, while three-time winner Dave Leach took his OW01 Yamaha for a spin – he finished third on the bike in the 1990 Senior.

"I've got so many good memories of this place, and this bike too," said Leach. "It's been a great week to be here."

Phillip McCallen, the winner of 11 TTs, was mobbed wherever he went in the paddock Friday morning, but loved it all and could hardly contain himself in preparing to go out on his 1997 F1-winning Honda RC45.

"The TT was the be-all-and-end-all for me," said the Ulsterman. "I'm really proud of what I achieved here, and I am honoured to be asked to do this lap."

To complement the majority of post-1960s machines, there was a smattering of ancient nostalgia too. Sammy Miller was on a Gilera 500-4 streamlined replica. "It's such an easy bike to ride, lots of torque," said the veteran Irishman.

Phil Read was aboard the Gilera he rode to third place in the 1963 Senior. The seven-time world champion was enjoying the centenary celebrations of an event he ironically condemned in the early 1970s. Still a winner all these years on, Read obliged one of the many

photographers with a shot before he went out on the Italian four-cylinder, but only after he called for a number one to be put on the bike's plate!

Suzuki brought a magnificently restored 1967 RK67 50cc machine to be ridden by Mitsuo Itoh, the only Japanese rider to have won a TT. An incredible jewel of a machine, it has a 14-speed transmission and a parallel twin-cylinder two-stroke engine that revs to 17,500rpm – and it reaches a top speed of over 100mph! Owing to the delicacy of the machine, Itoh only rode the bike from Creg-ny-Baa back to the finish line.

The little Suzuki was being looked after by leading 1970s works Suzuki mechanic Martin Ogbourne, who was enjoying talking about bikes and the TT. He spannered for most of the Heron Suzuki TT stars of the 1970s and 1980s, but his eyes lit up when mentions were made of Pat Hennen's debut in 1977 and Mike Hailwood's ride in 1979, on works RG500s.

"It used to be quite nervous for a mechanic here, never mind the riders," Ogbourne quipped. "We built Mike's bike in the factory, you know, and barely touched it here. In those days you had to build the suspension and forks especially for the event. We were under so much pressure with Mike in '79 to make sure the bike lasted the race."

Above: Dave Molyneux's wonderful replica of his childhood hero George O'Dell's 1977 double TT-winning Windle-Yamaha, complete with the 1977 world champion's passenger, Kenny Arthur, alongside him.

© **Mac McDiarmid**

Strangely there were only three sidecars in the Parade, and only one of vintage looks. Multi-winners rode them all. Mick Boddice drove a contemporary Ireson-Honda, while 11-time winner Rob Fisher was aboard a ex-Dave Saville 1993 Windle Yamaha. It was left to the winningest sidecar TT rider in history, Dave Molyneux, to provide the nostalgia. Molyneux has lovingly built a replica of his childhood hero George O'Dell's 1977 double TT-winning Windle-Yamaha, and for good measure he had the 1977 world champion's passenger, Kenny Arthur, in the chair for him.

"George was my hero when I was a kid," said Moly. "He used to race here at the same time as my Dad and I really wanted to build this replica as a tribute to him. The icing on the cake is that Ken took up my offer to be in the chair for me."

And so the curtain came down on the 100th TT races. History passed before our eyes in that last hour of the 2007 event, this finale providing a fitting tribute to all the men, women and machines that have competed on the most famous circuit of them all. Ironically, it was left to a more contemporary icon, a man who has never raced in a TT or even witnessed the event prior to this year, to sum it all up.

"Hats off to the TT. It's amazing that something like this can last 100 years. It deserves all the congratulations it gets." The legendary figure making the comment? None other than Kevin Schwantz, the 1993 500cc World Champion.

Above: Another Yamaha Classic Racing Team entry, this time the 125cc RA97 of Michelle Duff.
© Double Red

Right: Phillip McCallen, the winner of 11 TTs, at Braddan Bridge on his 1997 F1-winning Honda RC45.
© Double Red

"ON THIS CIRCUIT YOU HAVE EVERYTHING. IT IS UP AND DOWN, FAST STRAIGHTS, IT IS A VERY SPECIAL PLACE."

Right: Giacomo Agostini – the Valentino Rossi of his era.
© Stephen Davison

Giacomo Agostini returned to the Mountain Course, naturally enough aboard a 500cc MV Agusta, for the *MCN* Parade of Champions.

It was a time of mixed emotions for the legendary Italian race ace as he recalled the great TT triumphs that he enjoyed, although there was also the memory of the close friend who didn't return home after being involved in an accident at the event. The man who was even more than the Valentino Rossi of his era, the crowd puller who provided the magic when he raced and charmed the ladies, was back and enjoying every minute of his time on the Island, including the lavish black-tie dinner on Thursday evening where he spoke eloquently to the assembled gathering.

Agostini enjoyed a glittering career as the dominant force of the 1960s and 1970s. He won 122 Grands Prix, collecting 15 world titles along the way, and chalked up ten TT victories. His epic TT battles with Mike Hailwood are legend in this round-the-island high-speed dash, taking in the rigours of riding public roads, dashing through towns, villages and open countryside, and over the heights of Snaefell.

However, he had a rude awakening the first time he ventured on to the course. "It was so different, challenging, a very hard circuit to learn. There were so many things, parts where you thought maybe 20mph was fast, others where you were going at over 150mph.

"It was very difficult, but on this circuit you have everything. It is up and down, fast straights, it is a very special place. Soon I thought to myself, if you can win on the Isle of Man then it is like winning a world championship."

In his time on the Island, the races counted to the world championship, and he rode MV Agustas. He rode 350cc bikes in the Junior races (then for machines up to 350cc) and 500cc bikes in the Senior events, and in each he tasted the winner's champagne five times, the first of those successes coming in the 1966 Junior TT.

"That was a very good feeling, one that I enjoyed, but the actual race, I cannot remember too much. There have been so many. But the Senior in 1967 I do have memories of. It was a big battle with Hailwood, and I was ahead of him, leading the race until the very last lap."

During that race, Agostini regained his outright lap record and looked all set to win the Senior race for the first time, but mechanical gremlins ruled him out with only a handful of miles remaining. "I was well ahead, but then the chain broke on my bike, and that was it. I was very upset, but Mike was a real gent.

"After winning the race, he picked me up, and said, 'you were the real winner of that, come with me and we'll have a party'. He was one of the best, a nice person on and off the track."

Agostini has plenty of good TT memories but there are also painful ones that he prefers not to talk about. His friend Gilberto Parlotti succumbed to injuries sustained during the 1972 125 TT and Agostini, along with several other leading riders, said he wouldn't return to race in the event in future years. However, that didn't stop him honouring his commitments to race later that fateful day and win the Senior TT. At the time he was reported as saying, "The worst feeling in the world is having breakfast with a friend and never seeing them again."

That was not something to dwell on before he rode an MV Agusta for his lap of honour in 2007: "The memories will come flooding back as I make that special lap in this Centenary week – I will think back to when I was much younger and riding much faster. I would like to go fast again on this lap, but now it is for pleasure and I must take care.

"It will be a special time, many people are coming and it will be very nice," he added, before explaining what the TT had done for him. "It made people appreciate me, to win was something special. If you beat Mike Hailwood, then you really were somebody and he was the one man everyone tried to beat on the Island.

"The TT races made people take me seriously. The races were very hard, and they still are. If you forget safety, then the racing is the best in the world, but you are on normal roads, and that is dangerous."

They are mixed messages, but then the TT has always been, and still is, a mix of mind-numbing speeds in one of the toughest sporting environments, once likened by one race winner as being the motorcycle racing equivalent of climbing Mount Everest.

Dave Fern

Left: Past and present Titans of the TT, with a total of 23 victories between them...
© Stephen Davison

Blackford Pre-TT Classic
BILLOWN

CLASSIC RACES WITNESS A WINNING VISIT FROM ONE OF THE CURRENT TT STARS

Words and photos by John Watterson

Road racers by nature tend to be quite eccentric characters, but the mould was certainly thrown away when Guy Martin came along. He lives and breathes racing, and even builds sit-on specials fitted with potent motorcycle motors to participate in lawnmower races.

Guy's also an exceptional engine tuner and a brilliant road racer, but the talented Lincolnshire ace does have one small chink in his armour. When it comes to getting out of his day job to sneak in an extra bit of racing, he's

not averse to telling the odd fib or two to get his way!

Over the May Bank Holiday weekend he convinced his Hydrex Honda team bosses that he was nipping down to Billown to do a couple of parade laps on a friend's old banger, when in fact he was racing a works replica Triumph Trident in the Blackford Pre-TT Classic on the eve of the first timed practice for the most important TT of the millennium.

"It was mint, I really enjoyed that, I could have ridden round there all day," he spurted out at sixty-to-the-dozen. He spoke almost as quickly as he rode the Trident Racing triple to victory in the 850cc Classic race over nine laps of a road course lined with walls and trees, and made all the more hazardous by liberal deposits of leaked sump

OIL ON CIRCUIT

ALL AROUND

Opposite: Guy Martin on his way to victory on the 750 Triumph Trident.

Top: Racing between the hedges – early doors in the Post-Classic/850cc Classic event, with 350 Yamaha-mounted Jamie O'Brien (80) leading Guy Martin (0), Chris Palmer (5) and Peter Rubatto (93).

Left: Warning board – every picture tells a story.

oil on roads that were already damp and greasy.

With cement dust and oil marking the racing line virtually the whole of the way round the 4.25-mile course on the outskirts of the Island's ancient capital Castletown, the roads were indeed very treacherous.

It was a resident of the former garrison town, Chris Palmer, who led the early part of the race on Fred Walmsley's venerable Manx Norton, but once Martin had weighed up the conditions he blasted the 750 Triumph past to take a never-to-be-relinquished lead. Palmer tried valiantly to stay in touch for a couple of laps, but the single-cylinder Norton didn't have the legs of the triple on the long, fast straights.

"I didn't expect to stay with him," conceded Palmer

later. "I held on for a lap or two but always knew he had the extra power in the Triumph, so it was only a matter of time before he cleared off."

Alan Oversby was third in class on his Craven Manx Norton, fourth finisher on the road behind Germany's Peter Rubatto, a former TT regular who was later excluded as his Bimota Yamaha 750 was found to be 10 years younger than the minimum cut-off. "A slight misunderstanding between Peter and myself," explained the Southern 100 Racing Club's hard-working entries secretary George Peach.

With Rubatto out of the equation, the winner of the Post-Historic class was Dave Spencer, who came out on top of an intriguing four-way TZ350 Yamaha scrap with Bill

"I DIDN'T EXPECT TO STAY WITH HIM. I HELD ON FOR A LAP OR TWO BUT ALWAYS KNEW HE HAD THE EXTRA POWER IN THE TRIUMPH, SO IT WAS ONLY A MATTER OF TIME BEFORE HE CLEARED OFF."

CHRIS PALMER

Wark, Jamie O'Brien and Roger Hurst, the former Team Green Kawasaki star.

O'Brien's bid went awry on lap seven when he was lucky to escape crashing after running wide on to the pavement and skimming the straw bales on the exit to Ballakeighan Corner, only to slip off at the first-gear right-hand hairpin in Ballabeg seconds later.

Earlier in the programme, Palmer had tasted success in the Senior race on the same 500cc Norton, beating the Honda twin of Roy Richardson by more than 5secs, with Oversby again occupying the final spot on the podium.

Richardson, on the day his beloved Blackpool football team won the play-off for the vacant spot in the English Championship League, had double reason to celebrate when he took a smaller Honda from the same Martin

Bullock stable to victory in the 350cc Junior race ahead of Derek Whalley and Paul Coward on the Fenna Aermacchi. The conditions were arguably at their worst in this race, with Whalley reporting fourth-gear slides on spilt oil at Williams' Corner on the undulating back section of the course.

Rich Hawkins, who pulled out of the same race when well-placed for a top-six finish, was another unhappy at the conditions, which had been just about perfect when he won the first race of the meeting 24 hours earlier. The Singles races were held after the last of the solo practices and Hawkins proved formidable on his 350cc Ducati MkIII, beating the slower AJS of Chris Palmer by 7.6secs.

Mervyn Stratford won the 250cc class for the third time in four years on his loyal Greeves Silverstone.

Returning to the main race day, Geoff McMullan made light work of the Lightweight 250cc class on the same Suzuki Super-Six with which he won the Classic MGP the previous August. There were support class wins for John Jones and Keith McKay, riding Matchless and Laverda respectively.

The sidecar race didn't enjoy the best of conditions and speeds were the slowest for nine years. Nick Houghton piloted his 900cc Nourish Windle to a comfortable maiden victory over the course, partnered by Paul Thomas, who scored back-to-back-wins with Stuart Digby in 2004 and '05. Runners-up were 2006 winners Ralf Engelhardt and Winnfried Viecenz on the mighty 980cc Busch BMW flat-twin, from local residents Dick Hawes and Tim Dixon on the smaller 750 version.

Opposite & above: Roy Richardson's Honda on the way to victory in the Junior 350cc race, which was run in damp conditions.

Left: The Post-Classic/ 850cc Classic pack heads towards the Iron Gate.

Post-TT Steam Packet Races
BILLOWN

CONOR CUMMINS COMPLETES A BRILLIANT FORTNIGHT WITH A WIN AND A SECOND PLACE

Words and photos by John Watterson

At the end of a fortnight in which he firmly established himself alongside some of the biggest names in road racing, Conor Cummins grabbed a first and a second in the Post-TT Steam Packet-sponsored national meeting at Billown. Twenty-four hours after finishing a magnificent sixth in the Senior TT sponsored by PokerStars, the 21-year-old Manxman showed why he's already being tipped for ultimate stardom.

Riding for Ballymoney-based JMF Millsport Racing, the quietly spoken 6ft 4in rider from Ramsey looked every bit the consummate professional as he followed home seasoned campaigner Ian Lougher in the red-flag-interrupted 600cc race. One hour later he capped off a memorable week with a win in the 1000cc event on a Yamaha R1 from the same Millsport stable, leaving Lougher

et al in his wake. Such is Cummins' maturity and undoubted ability, it's hard to believe he's still only in his second season of pure road racing.

Watched by massive crowds in idyllic conditions, Lougher led the opening event on the programme from start to finish, using the short, three-race programme as early practice for July's full Southern 100 meeting over the same 4.25-mile course on the outskirts of Castletown.

The 43-year-old Welshman had already built up a 2sec lead when the original race was halted for an accident involving one competitor, his out-of-control machine and several spectators at the Cross Four Ways junction on lap two. The restart, over a reduced six-lap distance, saw Lougher resume his advantage – initially over Blackpool's Roy Richardson and then Cummins.

Well-signalled, Lougher controlled the race from the front on his Black Horse Finance Honda, but Cummins was always there waiting in the wings if he overshot any of the three first-gear corners that are as much a feature of the course as the long, fast straights and bumpy, twisty sections.

Below: Mark Parrett (46) with Conor Cummins in the 600cc race, followed by Tim Poole.

"IT'S A FANTASTIC RESULT FOR ME. I KNEW I HAD THE BEST BIKE OUT THERE SO I PUT THE HAMMER DOWN AND WENT FOR IT EARLY ON…"

CONOR CUMMINS

Adrian McFarland came good in the latter stages, producing the race's fastest lap on the penultimate circuit when he briefly showed the front wheel of his Yamaha R6 alongside the similar machine of Cummins, who promptly upped his pace on the final lap to secure second place by 0.34sec. Lougher, crossing the line 3.7secs to the good, reported a welcome trouble-free run after a week of indifferent form and fortunes on the Mountain Course.

William Dunlop, the elder of Robert Dunlop's two talented sons, had more than his share of Irish luck to thank for his success in the concurrently run 250cc class. When the battery of his twin-cylinder Flynn Honda went flat in the initial race, just as the red flags came out to halt it, he rolled his machine to a standstill at Castletown Corner and ran back to the paddock – more than half a mile away – to grab a spare battery. Having returned to the bike and fitted the fully charged battery, he fired up the machine just in time to make the restart, going on to win by the narrow margin of one second from respected course expert Chris Palmer, who had endured his own problems with a seized motor in practice.

Palmer, the former British champion and double TT winner who lives within earshot of the Billown Course, had no such problems in the 125cc race, leading it from start to finish from William's father Robert Dunlop and race one victor Lougher.

New Zealander Paul Dobbs won the 400cc event for the second year in succession on his Yamaha, repelling a late charge from Mark Parrett, with the TT's most prolific finisher Dave Madsen-Mygdal a lonely third.

Cummins was not prepared to accept second best in the final race of the evening, the nine-lap 1000cc race.

Pushed hard by Lougher over the opening lap, when just 0.29sec divided the pair, he really piled on the coals over the next couple of laps to stretch his lead to 2.5secs. Riding his superstock machine, Lougher was fully aware of

the limitations of his Honda and eventually succumbed to pressure from friend and rival Chris Palmer (R1 Yamaha) on lap five. By then, Cummins was well away and chalked up his maiden Billown success by a clear margin of 12.5secs over Palmer, with a fastest lap of 108.786mph. Paul Cranston, a course regular, finished fourth on the P&J Honda from Tim Poole and the Manxman Stephen Oates, like Cummins a relative newcomer to pure road courses.

"It's a fantastic result for me," admitted Cummins after becoming the fifth different winner of the 1000cc Steam Packet race in its 11-year history. "I knew I had the best bike out there so I put the hammer down and went for it early on. Once I had built up a lead I simply watched my pit boards and didn't go for lap times."

A new star was definitely born at the Post-TT meeting.

Top left: 250cc race winner William Dunlop (86) leads John Burrows.

Top right: Atmospheric view of 600 start from Castletown Bypass.

Below: Ian Lougher leading Roy Richardson out of Castletown Corner in the restarted 600 race.

2007
GALLERY

The TT is never just about racing.
It's so much more than that…

1

2

© Stephen Davison

© Jon Stroud

© Jon Stroud

© Double Red

© Jon Stroud

© Jon Stroud

© Double Red

© Stephen Davison

© Mac McDiarmid

© Double Red

© Jon Stroud

© Jon Stroud

© Stephen Davison

© Jon Stroud

© Double Red

© Jon Stroud

© Phil Masters

© Double Red

© Stephen Davison

© Jon Stroud